D1522576

# The Alliance for Progress

# The Alliance for Progress

## A RETROSPECTIVE

Edited by L. Ronald Scheman

With Forewords by Edward M. Kennedy
and Dante B. Fascell

PRAEGER

New York
Westport, Connecticut
London

Library of Congress Cataloging-in-Publication Data

The Alliance for Progress.

    Bibliography: p.
    Includes index.
    1. Alliance for progress—Congresses. 2. Economic
assistance, American—Latin America—Congresses.
3. Technical assistance, American—Latin America—
Congresses. I. Scheman, L. Ronald.
HC125.A42    1988    338.91′73′08    88-6035
ISBN 0-275-92763-6 (alk. paper)

Library of Congress Catalog Card Number: 88-6035

ISBN: 0-275-92763-6

First published in 1988

Praeger Publishers, One Madison Avenue, New York, NY 10010
A division of Greenwood Press, Inc.

Printed in the United States of America

The paper used in this book complies with the
Permanent Paper Standard issued by the National
Information Standards Organization (Z39.48-1984).

10  9  8  7  6  5  4  3  2  1

*To Raúl Prebisch, whose constant stimulation, probing, and inspiration moved an entire generation of Americans to a new vision of its potential*

# Contents

# Tables

# *Acronyms*

| | |
|---|---|
| AID | Agency for International Development |
| ALADI | Latin American Integration Association |
| BID | Inter-American Development Bank (English: IDB) |
| CACM | Central American Common Market |
| CECLA | Special Coordinating Committee for Latin America |
| CIAP | Inter-American Committee on the Alliance for Progress |
| CIDA | Inter-American Committee on Agricultural Development |
| CIECC | Inter-American Council for Education, Science and Culture |
| CIES | Inter-American Economic and Social Council of the OAS |
| CEPAL | United Nations Economic Commission for Latin America (English: ECLA) |
| ECLA | United Nations Economic Commission for Latin America |
| FAO | Food and Agriculture Organization |
| GATT | General Agreement on Tariffs and Trade |
| GSP | General System of Trade Preferences |
| IAAG | Inter-Agency Advisory Group; under CIAP |
| IBRD | International Bank for Reconstruction and Development (World Bank) |
| IDB | Inter-American Development Bank |
| IICA | Inter-American Institute for Agricultural Cooperation |
| ILO | International Labor Organization |
| ILPES | Latin American Institute for Economic and Social Planning |
| LAFTA | Latin American Free Trade Association |
| OAS | Organization of American States |
| OECD | Organization for Economic Cooperation and Development |

| | |
|---|---|
| PAHO | Pan-American Health Organization |
| PRI | Partido Revolucionario Institucional |
| SELA | Latin American Economic System |
| UNCTAD | United Nations Conference on Trade and Development |

# Foreword by Senator Edward M. Kennedy

Twenty-five years ago, President Kennedy summoned the peoples of this hemisphere to join in an Alliance for Progress. In his speech, President Kennedy freely acknowledged "the failures and the misunderstandings of the past," but he also called upon the people of the Americas to work together to build a better future—"to demonstrate to the entire world that man's unsatisfied aspiration for economic progress and social justice can best be achieved by free men and women working within a framework of democratic institutions." This was our hope then—economic development, social justice, and political democracy—and this remains our dream today.

The first goal of the Declaration of Punta del Este was "to improve and strengthen democratic institutions through application of the principle of self-determination by the people." Today, 94 percent of the people of the Americas live under democratic rule, more than at any other time in our history. And so it is proper that we celebrate the triumph of democracy in our hemisphere and honor those great leaders who have so bravely guided their countries out of dictatorship and military rule. The names on this list will live in the history of this hemisphere: Alfonsín of Argentina, Neves and Sarney of Brazil, Sanguinetti of Uruguay, García of Peru, Duarte of El Salvador, Cerezo of Guatemala.

In January of 1985, I traveled to Latin America to show my support for democracy and to learn how the United States can best assist the nations of Latin America in dealing with the crisis of the external debt. On that trip, I learned that the ideals of the Alliance for Progress have not dimmed or faded with the passage of time. The spirit of John F. Kennedy lives on, and the flame that he kindled in the hearts of millions of Americans throughout this hemisphere still burns brightly.

If anyone should doubt that democracy is still the most powerful political idea in the world today, let them go where I have been: to Brazil, where the people are now engaged in lively debate about the structure of their new constitution; to Uruguay, where hopes are high and the people revel in their freedom; to Argentina, where new leaders and new ideas excite the people in even the most distant provincial capitals; and to Peru, where a young and charismatic leader summons his people to meet the staggering challenge of poverty and unemployment.

And let them also go to Chile. Today the struggle for democracy and human dignity goes on in that proud and beautiful country, proving anew that the fire of freedom cannot be extinguished, that even when the darkness descends, when dictators rule and law is lost, the flame still warms and moves millions of individual and indomitable hearts.

Those who gathered at Punta del Este to give life to the Alliance believed that political freedom walked hand in hand with social justice and economic development. And, at its heart, the Alliance for Progress was a plan and a commitment to attack poverty and underdevelopment. The focus was on economic growth and increased incomes, on improved housing and land reform, on fair wages and satisfactory working conditions, on wiping out illiteracy and building schools, on eradicating disease and improving public health. The call was for more of everything by everybody—more investment by both private and public sectors, greater economic integration among the nations, expansion of trade, and more effective regulation of commodity markets. And during that decade of the 1960s, much was accomplished.

But if the framers of the Punta del Este Declaration and Charter were right, if progress through economic growth and national development is essential to the success of democracy, then the democracies of this hemisphere are in deep and worsening trouble. For today, 15 years after that great decade of development came to an end, the menacing shadow of international debt has fallen over all the nations of the Americas. This crisis has come as part—and in the midst—of Latin America's worst depression since the 1930s. Two full decades of growth have been wiped out, and efforts to restore that growth are now being choked off by the need to export capital to the North to service their debts.

Now, the three largest democracies in Latin America—and the three biggest debtors—have been forced to impose regimes of harsh austerity at precisely the time when economic growth is most important to them. How long will their people accept ever-rising unemployment and ever-declining standards of living? But unless there is some relief, continued stagnation lies ahead.

The stakes have never been higher. The Baker proposals were an important first step, but the United States can surely do more. The President must be personally involved. We need strong and resolute political leadership to solve this crisis, and without that leadership today we may be paying the bill for generations to come.

The health and well-being of the democracies in this hemisphere are of enormous consequence to the people of the United States, but the future of Latin America should also be of concern to those who live beyond the borders of our two continents. Part of the solution to the debt crisis will surely lie with the good will and support of the European community and Japan. I would therefore propose that the Cartagena Consensus, led by Argentina, Brazil, and Mexico, should invite the finance ministers of the other industrialized nations of the world to join with them for discussions about how to resolve the debt crisis and restore growth to the nations of Latin America. Since 1961, our world has become more interdependent, and any new effort at new solutions must include many who were not part of the old Alliance.

There is yet another crisis which threatens peace and stability in Latin America. With no realistic hope of success, with no estimate of how much the war will cost or how long it will last, with thousands already dead and no end in sight, this Administration persists in pursuing a failing and flawed policy in Nicaragua. The contras' war against the government of Nicaragua has only made a bad situation worse.

But beyond the tragedy of Nicaragua, this policy sends a troubling message to the people of this hemisphere. Despite the heroic efforts of the Contadora nations to negotiate an end to the killing, despite the entreaties of the nations in the Contadora Support Group to stop funding the contras, the United States continues its unilateral effort to impose unilateral solutions in Nicaragua. Our unwillingness to let the democratic leaders of Latin and Central America achieve their own solution to the violence implies that the "Yankee-knows-best" approach to the problems of this hemisphere still exists in Washington, D.C. That approach is perhaps the inevitable result of viewing the world through an ideological prism that casts every problem into a Cold War context.

And so, sadly, we see that the founding principle of the Alliance—which called upon the nations of the Americas to work together as equals and as partners—has not always prevailed. Today we must work to restore that sense of shared purpose and common destiny.

When the final measure of those early years is taken, we will see that, although much still remains to be done, we have come a great distance. There has in fact been progress. The challenges are still great, but the promise and the hopes are even greater.

Let us pledge to remain true to the common dream that has guided all our peoples since the first pioneers set foot upon our shores. They understood, as we do today, that our greatest problems are made by man and therefore can be solved by man. Together I am confident that our own efforts will bring us closer to the great goals of liberty, prosperity, and justice for all the people of our hemisphere.

# Foreword by Congressman Dante B. Fascell

Much has been written about the Alliance for Progress' alleged lack of "progress," but its failure was only in not attaining its too lofty goals and promises. I was "present at the creation"—as a junior congressman—and I shared in the excitement that was generated by the founders of the Alliance for Progress. Their achievements serve today as a special reminder of the importance of a sense of promise and confidence that the future offers hope. The list of contributors and participants in the Alliance is too long to recount here, but a few names do stand out:

President Juscelino Kubitschek of Brazil, whose call for Operation Pan-America in 1959 became the clarion call for what was to become the Alliance for Progress;

President Alberto Lleras of Colombia, who played a critical role in developing the concept of the Alliance and attracting other Latin leaders;

The father of Latin American economic thought, Raul Prebisch;

Dr. Milton Eisenhower, whose fact finding trips to the region were so influential, and his brother, President Dwight Eisenhower, both for his support of Kubitschek's appeal and for the creation of the Inter-American Development Bank, which was one of the pillars of the Alliance and has been the one constant actor over the past 25 years that has tried to bring economic and social development to Latin America;

Undersecretary of State and Secretary of the Treasury Douglas Dillon, who was directly involved in the implementation of Alliance policy;

Ted Moscoso, first director of the Alliance for Progress, whose Operation Bootstrap in Puerto Rico was the precursor for the Alliance as a grassroots, self-help, socioeconomic approach to development; and

President John F. Kennedy, who took up the challenge of economic and social progress in Latin America and instilled the Alliance in its early days with a spirit of enthusiasm, dedication, and determination both in the United States and throughout the hemisphere.

The Alliance for Progress was the precursor of many of the development policies that we follow today. First, the Alliance was not an attempt to impose development from the outside; it was a cooperative effort in which all participants were peers. It was basically a Latin plan to be developed, implemented, and funded by the Latin nations themselves. The development experience of the last two decades has proven the validity of this approach, for development can only occur indigenously; it cannot be imposed from without.

Second, the Alliance for Progress was, above all else, about people. If 80 percent of the people are outside the mainstream—politically, economically, and socially—then the best-laid plans will be for naught. Development means human development, and what the Alliance sought to do was develop human resources and involve the people in the development process.

In fact, the New Directions adopted by Congress in 1973 as the basis and focus of U.S. bilateral development assistance evolved directly from the Alliance for Progress' principle that "people count." That is, the development process must ensure that its benefits are distributed to those in society who are normally left out if a broad basis for progress is to be established and equitable development is to take place. The importance that was placed by the Alliance on human resource development is evidenced by the fact that between 1960 and 1975 some 250,000 foreign nationals were trained in the United States, one-third of them from Latin America—an unprecedented effort to train an entire generation of government and business leaders. The decline in this effort during the late 1970s was reversed when both Congress and the Administration realized in the early 1980s that providing greater training opportunities for foreign nationals was vital both to indigenous development objectives and to U.S. foreign policy interests.

Third, the four pillars of the Reagan Administration's development policy were all elements of the Alliance—policy dialogue, emphasis on the private sector, the concept of technology transfer, and institution building. This last element, institution building, may be one of the most enduring outgrowths of the Alliance. The Alliance generated numerous indigenous institutions throughout the region aimed at bringing the fruits of development—education, health, housing, clean water—to those at the lower rungs of society. These institutions have not only survived, but grown multifold over the years. Their vitality and diversity have added to the pluralistic nature of society in Latin American and clearly have played an important role in the revival of democratic institutions over the past several years—a living legacy of the Alliance.

This is the challenge that we must not allow to lapse. Except for the advanced sectors of the economy in Brazil, Argentina, Venezuela, Mexico, and a few other countries, Latin America's social and economic problems remain very much the same as they were when the Alliance was founded in 1960. There is much greater indigenous capability to deal with the development task today, but that task is made even more difficult by two fundamental roadblocks that must be removed before we can recommence the development process that was interrupted by the second oil crunch in the late 1970s. Those two barriers are the external debt overhang in Latin America and the civil strife in Central America and, to a lesser extent, in several other countries.

To draw on a well-known quote, the torch has now been passed to a new generation of leaders, and what this new generation must do is devise a way around these two obstacles so that the development process may be rejoined – probably not with the great enthusiasm that accompanied the early days of the Alliance, but maybe with greater pragmatism and realism as to what is feasible. And, given the budgetary climate in the United States and in other donor countries, the evaporation of new commercial credit, and current world economic conditions, this task must be confronted without the expectation of massive inflows of external resources or of rapid world economic growth to pull developing countries out of their current economic malaise. So, with limited resources, we must find a way out of the current holding pattern that is stymieing development. We can hope that this volume, which reviews the mechanisms and accomplishments of the Alliance for Progress, can assist in this process.

The Alliance for Progress aimed higher than any other peaceful multilateral enterprise in history. If its greatest failing was in promising too much, the progress that was made was due in part to the promise and enthusiasm that accompanied the Alliance. It attracted the best minds and talent of the day because it offered, for the first time, a nonviolent path to change. The achievements of the Alliance can be traced to the unprecedented cooperative effort undertaken by the nations of the region and to the support and generosity of the American people. The principles that spelled success for the Alliance – peaceful international cooperation and the sharing of burdens by those most able to bear them – are still valid today and could serve as the basis for guiding us past the current obstacles of debt and war and for returning the hemisphere to the path of development.

# *Preface*

The problem, wrote George Santayana, is not that we do not know but that we do not remember. That observation sums up, as of 1987, one of the principal dilemmas in United States–Latin American relations. How many "new approaches" to inter-American relations are really new? Many of those currently offered to help Latin America out of the financial morass in which it finds itself today are unsettlingly reminiscent of efforts made 25 years ago at the time of the Alliance for Progress. Very likely, the Alliance was reminiscent in its day of ideas that circulated 25 years earlier under FDR's "good neighbor" policy. Yet how rarely do policymakers look at the travails of their predecessors. How rarely, in the pressure of day to day events, do we seek to examine what succeeded and what failed in our previous experience and why.

In the hope of contributing to a better perception of what we know, the Center for Advanced Studies of the Americas, together with the Georgetown University School of Foreign Service and Tufts University's Fletcher School of Law and Diplomacy, jointly sponsored a conference on March 13–14, 1986, to take a retrospective look at the Alliance for Progress. This meeting occurred exactly 25 years after President Kennedy delivered his speech announcing U.S. support for the Alliance.

The importance of reviewing the accomplishments of the Alliance for Progress, and of bringing together the principal actors in the drama to focus attention once again on their effort, was impressed upon me in a class in which I participated at George Washington University. During a discussion of Latin American policy, one student asked, "What was that?" upon hearing of the Alliance for Progress. None of the students could respond. It was evident that discussion of the effort had almost disappeared from the textbooks. These students, who had not even been born at the time of the Alliance, were not alone in their ignorance of its history. Abe Lowenthal, in his comments at the meeting, noted that far more of his students were familiar with the Bay of Pigs than with the Alliance.

The goal of the conference was not to determine whether the Alliance was a success or failure, but what lessons could be learned from the experience. There were at least seven years in which large amounts of money, unprecedented for that time, were channeled to Latin America for development purposes. The men and women (although there were few women in policy positions in those days—another important indicator of change) who determined the policies of the Alliance were the leaders of their day. They were the vanguard of the new wave in Latin American development studies and among the foremost experts on hemispheric affairs from the United States. They devoted considerable energy in the prime years of their lives to make this unique and unprecedented experiment work. Fortunately, many of them are still with us, but the opportunity to get them together to analyze their efforts will not recur easily. It seemed important, on this twenty-fifth anniversary of the launching of the Alliance for Progress, to provide such a forum.

The question posed to these leaders was how they felt about their efforts in the light of 25 years of history. Were they pleased about the results? Did they have regrets? What did they think the Alliance did right? What would they do differently if they had another opportunity?

Intention and motivation are the stuff of which results are made—and one of the important criteria by which their effects on history must be measured. In that regard, considering the stature and dedication of the people who ran the Alliance, both from Latin America and the U.S., it seemed important for the benefit of future generations that these men, assembled for perhaps the last time, voice their own expressions of satisfaction or regret.

One final word on perspective. While analyzing the numbers for the first chapter in the volume, I came across a 1962 study of the OAS that examined the withdrawal of capital from the region by large multinational corporations. It noted with dismay that one company had expatriated $32 million more than it had invested in a country. The trend, it noted, was ominous. While the trend was indeed ominous, the numbers give pause. They are a vivid indication of what has happened to the world in the last quarter century. In 1986, $32 million would hardly merit a dot on a chart. Is this a reflection of how much Latin America has grown—or of how much inflation has distorted our perception of numbers? This question should be kept in mind in analyzing the data of Latin America in the 1980s—especially when we try to compare today's conditions to those that confronted the Alliance planners in 1961.

This book is not intended to duplicate the fine volumes that have been written about the Alliance by William D. Rogers, Jerome Levinson and Juan de Onís, Tad Szulc, John Dreier, Harvey Perloff, and others, to mention only some of the U.S. commentators. Some idea of the extensive literature will be found in the footnotes to some of the essays in this volume.

Thanks are due to all of the persons who collaborated in making this volume possible, and especially to those who contributed their time to make the conference a success. Special thanks go to JoAnne de la Riva, the tireless director of administration of CASA, who made the conference happen and who organized everything so that the production of this volume was relatively easy. David Lessard, an able conference manager, Alison Rafael, who put in long hours editing this volume, and John Chazal, who helped in the research and organization stages, were also indispensable. My thanks to all.

# I
## *The Origins and the Concept*

*1*

# The Alliance for Progress:
## Concept and Creativity

*L. Ronald Scheman*

Twenty-five years have passed since President Kennedy summoned the Latin American diplomatic corps to the White House, on March 13, 1961, to announce that the United States was prepared to support a hemisphere-wide development program he called the Alliance for Progress. In those 25 years, the Alliance has become an almost forgotten chapter in history, an aberration in the long history of U.S. indifference and neglect of its neighbors. It was always controversial in its origins, execution, and even in its demise. Because of that controversy, it is important to take a closer look at what actually happened during those years, the Alliance years, of the 1960s. The essays in this volume, written by the participants in the Alliance from both the U.S. and Latin America, propose to do that.

In its time, the Alliance for Progress was applauded as a new era in inter-American cooperation. It had been praised as an example of the best in U.S. policy toward Latin America, merging strategic and security interests with economic and social measures considered vital for sustained, democratic growth. It was also condemned as another exercise in hegemony and denigrated as the imposition by the U.S. of its own social and political criteria upon different cultures. One former ambassador, Ellis Briggs, called it "a North American blueprint for upheaval throughout Latin America," while others criticized it as being "on a scale too small and a pace too slow." The date of the Alliance's demise was equally controversial; some identify it with President Kennedy's assassination, charging that President Johnson's more pragmatic focus on economic performance undermined the vital political and social reform aspects of the Alliance. Others give it a quieter burial in the "low profile" or "benign neglect" days of President Nixon.

President John F. Kennedy approached the concept of the Alliance with trepidation. He knew the underlying problems would not yield easily to solutions. He was convinced, however, that economic development in Latin America depended upon establishing the base for a more participatory economic and political system. It would have been easy to go through the motions of helping Latin America using the old patterns, throwing money at the problems in the conviction that an upturn in the economies would hide the disagreeable from view, at least "on his watch." But Kennedy's vision was far broader. He decided that if it was worth doing at all, an effort had to be made to help the Latin American nations escape from their cyclical pattern of poverty and dictatorships. It was essential to take the risk to try to establish an institutional base that would favor the growth of democratic societies. He understood that the enormity of the task required compelling inspirations and prodigious visions, even mythology, in order to break the inertia of centuries of tradition. If fundamental transformations in political and social institutions were needed to move Latin America on the path to modernization and development, then timid steps dwelling on obstacles and difficulties would doom the enterprise from the beginning.

As difficult as we perceive our problems today, Latin America of 1961 was a vastly different world from 1986. As Walt W. Rostow points out in Chapter 24, the late 1950s were marked by a sharp deterioration in the terms of trade for Latin America in the world economy, contributing to a significant loss of momentum in the Latin economies. A burgeoning population growth—among the fastest in the world at over 3 percent per annum—threatened to inundate the ill-prepared societies. It was a young continent in which over half the population was under the age of 20 and was rapidly approaching a job market in economies that were proving unable to generate employment. Mass migration to the cities was transforming the countryside, as it was throughout the western world, resulting in dismal urban sprawl and slum conditions. Forty million people were expected to migrate to the cities during the 1960s while job creation was proceeding at a pace that would produce only 5 million new jobs. Illiteracy abounded. Agriculture lagged behind population growth, forcing increased food imports, while commodity prices for Latin America's exports, particularly coffee and sugar, were continually falling. The continent's role in world trade was stagnating since most of the economies remained largely dependent on single products for foreign exchange. About 62 percent of Brazil's export earnings in 1959 were from coffee, 71 percent of Chile's were from copper, 58 percent of Bolivia's were from tin, while Colombia earned 78 percent of its foreign exchange from coffee and Honduras depended on bananas for 57 percent of its hard currency earnings. Efforts to diversify were stymied by a lack of capital and domestic savings. The brunt of the diminishing per capita production rates fell on families in the lower income brackets as a result of inequitable taxation and land tenure systems and unremitting inflation: These phenomena were creating a widening gap between rich and poor.

Into that bubbling caldron came the sudden threat of "alien ideologies" that fed on the underlying problems. Fidel Castro's ascent to power in Cuba was the seminal event of the period, marked by the admonition in his address of July 26,

1960, that the Andes would become the Sierra Maestra of South America. The threat was not taken lightly in Washington and was reinforced by the obviously strong inroads of Marxist doctrine in Latin America's educational system and economic thinking. However, while these negative political factors were conditioning U.S. public opinion to support the initiatives of the Alliance, they were not the predominant motives of the policymakers. The people who shaped the Alliance were primarily troubled about the underlying inequities that were distorting the political evolution of the Latin American nations. As Lincoln Gordon emphasizes in Chapter 4, populism and unrealistic national policies were perceived as a greater immediate threat than communism.

The precarious condition of Latin America had by no means been ignored by the leading thinkers of the region. The Alliance was not, as is widely perceived, invented in the U.S. nor conceived in the Kennedy Administration. Its origins were firmly rooted in the widespread frustration and new currents of thought that were beginning to sweep Latin America at the time. Influenced by the innovative thinking emanating from the United Nations Economic Commission for Latin America (ECLA), under the leadership of the Argentine economist Raúl Prebisch, new Social Democratic and Christian Democratic political forces were beginning to adopt development-oriented reformist policies. Venezuela's new democratic government, under Romulo Betancourt, had already begun to implement a program in education, housing, health, and land reform when Fidel Castro was still in the mountains. The essays of Douglas Dillon, Lincoln Gordon, Arthur Schlesinger, and Felipe Herrera in this volume about the origins of the Alliance make this abundantly clear.

The catalytic force came in 1958 from Juscelino Kubitschek, the dynamic president of Brazil, with his proposal for an "Operation Pan-America" to revive the hemisphere. Douglas Dillon describes in Chapter 2 how impressed he was by the arguments of the Latin Americans of that time and how they served to catalyze the thinking of the Eisenhower Administration, leading to the creation of the Committee of Presidential Representatives (Committee of Twenty-One) in 1958. The Act of Bogota, which followed shortly thereafter in 1959, gave birth to the Inter-American Development Bank and led President Eisenhower to recommend to the U.S. Congress the establishment of a fund for social development, which later became the Social Progress Trust Fund. It also led the United States to begin consideration of the first major commodity agreement, the International Coffee Agreement. Indeed, the program of the Alliance for Progress was laid out in its major components in Milton Eisenhower's "Report to the President on United States–Latin American Relations" in December 1958, a remarkably prescient report that contained the basic elements repeated in almost every report since produced on inter-American relations.

The Alliance for Progress, as finally articulated by President Kennedy, went far beyond anything that had ever been proposed or undertaken by the United States and Latin America, as Lincoln Gordon and Arthur Schlesinger point out. It sought to address the underlying relationships of a society as they interacted in the social, economic, and political institutions of the nations. That is why it is today difficult to speak of the success or failure of the Alliance in terms of GNP growth or quantities of financial assistance. Even at that time, the real issues were clouded by a certain amount of impatience to demonstrate tangible results. The late Harvey Perloff, a member of the Alliance's "Nine Wise Men," once commented that "the Alliance functioned as though it was ready to go out of business any moment" with high visibility projects and short term goals predominating, partially to satisfy the insatiable Congressional appropriations hearings.[1] Unlike the Marshall Plan of the previous decade, which had as its basic mission the provision of capital for developed but devastated economies, the Alliance was rooted in ideas. It gave substance to the concept of an entirely new future for Latin America. It addressed issues of social equity and institutional reform that required the careful building of institutions and infrastructure. While the simultaneous pursuit of such diverse goals as social justice, economic growth, political stability, and private sector investment may seem naive in retrospect, the major objective of the Alliance for Progress was in affecting attitudes and building institutions capable of changing the direction of Latin America.

In one sense, the answer to the question of whether the Alliance was successful could be a resounding "yes," as a new generation of leaders educated during the days of the Alliance takes its place in the 1980s with a firm dedication to democratic principles and sophistication in regard to global economic issues. On the economic side, the positive achievements relate to the new institutions that are now maturing in the nations of the Americas. These are only now providing new instruments and flexibility in the social and economic structure. They have established a whole new entrepreneurial class with diverse interests in everything from industry to mortgage banking. In one sense, the greatest success of the Alliance may be said to be the confidence it generated that Latin America could absorb massive amounts of capital, leading to the unprecedented influx of over $200 billion in loans from commercial banks in the succeeding decade of the 1970s.

On the other hand, a number of participants in the policymaking at the time questioned the Alliance's tangible accomplishments.[2] These were clearly disappointing, especially when the specific economic advances were juxtaposed with the devastating population growth rates which left increased unemployment, housing shortages, illiteracy, and landless peasants in spite of the Alliance efforts. William D. Rogers, the U.S. head of the Alliance programs in the mid-1960s commented that "the stark fact was that the lives of most people had changed remarkably little during the Alliance period."[3] Another negative impact was the enormous amount of flight capital of the time, which is attributed to the uncertainties resulting from the unstable period of change.[4] Continuing capital flight, combined with the unprecedented binge of foreign borrowing and corruption which ensued in the 1970s, drained the resources of the countries and hobbled Latin America's development for decades to come.

On the Latin American side, there were sharply conflicting perceptions. Many statesmen agreed with the views articulated by former Colombian President

Alberto Lleras Camargo who saw the Alliance for Progress as a major turning point in the attitudes of the United States toward Latin America. Others expressed an underlying mistrust of the motives of the United States, ranging from cynical appraisals of the Alliance's links to U.S. security interests, because of the advent of Fidel Castro, to more serious opposition from vested interest groups that were affected by the various "reform" proposals. The essays that follow explore many of these arguments. Perhaps one of the most interesting appraisals of the Alliance in the light of history comes from four Latin American economists who reviewed the condition of Latin America in the 1980s as it confronted the debt crisis. They state:

The starting point for Latin America is much better than is frequently realized. Savings rates, despite recent declines, are quite high. Governments are effective providers of social services . . . which, despite wide country variations, are comparable to those of other developing countries at similar income levels. The same thing, however, cannot be said about their effectiveness as producers and regulators. Economic infrastructure has been established in the advanced countries of the region. Export expansion has been impressive in several cases: Brazil now sells aircraft to the United States, and Argentina sells turbines for electricity plants in the international market. The successes of the 1960s and 1970s inevitably left positive results, along with the buildup of imbalances and inefficiencies that brought them to a halt.[5]

Perhaps the most important point missed by those debating the merits of the Alliance was that the effort unleashed enormous forces of creativity in the hemisphere. The energies of men such as Juscelino Kubitschek of Brazil, Carlos Lleras Restrepo of Colombia, Eduardo Frei of Chile, Raúl Prebisch of Argentina, José Figueres of Costa Rica, and Romulo Betancourt of Venezuela, to mention a few, were galvanized and focused on development. Albert O. Hirschman, writing toward the latter part of the Alliance in 1967, spoke of this creativity when he said that we learned a great deal, but what we learned is not what we expected to learn.[6] Referring to the inherent creativity that always exists in any human venture, always underestimated in the developing countries by both bureaucrats and scholars, he cited the innovative abilities of the Latin American leaders in taking on tasks unparalleled in the region's history. It is always difficult to gauge the wide range of forces set in motion when engaging in the internal political systems of other nations. This was especially true of the myriad of forces—political, institutional, and social—that were set in motion by the Alliance for Progress.

It is important to reflect on the criteria for evaluation of the long-term reforms targeted by the Alliance planners. These cannot, by definition, be derived from cold annual economic data. Decades—sometimes generations—are the proper measure. President Ortiz Mena of the Inter-American Development Bank, who was Finance Minister of Mexico during the Alliance's early days, expresses doubt in Chapter 9 that the wide-ranging changes and momentum that took place in the decade would have been possible without a central focus such as the Alliance for Progress. In Chapter 21, former Panamanian President Nicolas Ardito Barletta, one of the young economists during the early Alliance days, states that new development issues were inscribed on the political agenda, new professions gained respectability, and the forces for peaceful revolution gained a legitimacy that they had been rapidly losing in the turmoil of the day.

Equally underestimated was the powerful individualism and instinct for freedom that resides in Latin America. Arthur Schlesinger points out that, in retrospect, nationalism, not class revolution, is the "most potent political emotion in Latin America, then and now." Throughout the Alliance years, and in the preceding decade, fears were continually expressed that it was "one minute to midnight" and that the people of Latin America were prepared to trade their freedoms for the undefined lures of communism. Given the emergence of Fidel Castro and the aggressive policies of the communist nations to influence education, it was feared that the minds of youth would be indelibly influenced and the light of freedom extinguished in the countries of the hemisphere. Both history and recent experience show a different outcome. In Soviet bloc countries, as well as those temporarily under the sway of Marxist regimes, no form of education has been devised that can wipe out the indomitable instinct for individual expression and freedom. Military force can repress it, as was the case in Latin America in the succeeding decade. A generation may be intimidated into docility. But no philosophy can eradicate liberty from the human mind, certainly not in the fiercely independent minds of the people of Latin America.

Indeed, the experience of Latin America in the years following the Alliance for Progress is a case in point. Howard Wiarda, in his trenchant chapter in this book, asks why, given the profound hopes and ideals of the Alliance, Latin America entered one of the darkest and most repressive periods in its history during the decade following the Alliance. Leaving the answer to that question aside for the moment, one can only be buoyed by the resurgence of democracy throughout the hemisphere during the last few years. Perhaps, as the skeptics assert, it is because the treasuries were empty, leaving the military with no incentive to remain in power. Perhaps it is due to the fact that the military finally perceived their inability to manage a modern state, as the general public quickly learned. But it is also possible that the ideals and ideas sowed by the Alliance fell on fertile ground, and that the traditional Latin American culture, marked by strong components of individualism and independence, could not be repressed indefinitely—especially after the momentum provided by the Alliance years. It is no coincidence that the young people who grew up during the Alliance years are those who are moving into positions of power in their countries as the resurgence of democracy grows. Whether this too is just another turn in a perpetual cycle, future generations will have to judge.

The financial aspects of the Alliance and its aftermath contain equally intriguing lessons. There was much talk during the planning of the Alliance of the importance of external resources and investment. The daring ambitions of the Alliance were to channel to the region $20 billion in foreign assistance in a decade, with $10 billion coming from official sources and $10 billion from private sources.

That amounted to $2 billion a year, a target that was just barely met (see Table 1.1). The attention given to the external component, however, overlooked the fact that the major investment in production came from internal sources as a result of continually increasing rates of domestic savings. All of the capital needed to reproduce the previous years' production, plus most of the increment, came from domestic investment. The role of foreign capital was marginal, as the data demonstrate. By 1970, the Inter-American Development Bank was able to report that the region was mobilizing considerable domestic resources with increased internal investment. The bank reported that in the 1966–69 period, domestic savings accounted for 91 percent of total investment instead of the 80 percent forecast at Punta del Este.[7] Domestic savings coefficients of over 20 percent were reached in Argentina, Brazil, and Mexico. On the institutional side, the impact of the establishment of the Inter-American Development Bank is only just beginning to be felt. When one compares the $2 billion annual target for external finance during the Alliance years to the situation today when the IDB alone appropriates almost $4 billion annually to the region (which could soon be $6 billion if agreement is reached on the proposed replenishment), the long-term impact of institutional changes becomes apparent. To that should be added the World Bank allocations for Latin America, which currently amount to over $3 billion. This means that from these two institutions alone the region will be shortly receiving $10 billion annually in external resources. In the context of history, this trend is only just beginning. Even discounted for inflation, the numbers are impressive. The full impact of these institutions is yet to be felt.

Indeed, the real legacy of the Alliance, frequently overlooked, is the enormous confidence it helped to generate at that time in the financial community. This confidence was ultimately the Alliance's undoing. By the end of the decade, growth rates of the GNP were reaching a steady 3 percent per capita, exceeding the Alliance targets. This far exceeded the boldest projections or wildest imagination of any planners or politicians, and it took place before the enormous inflow of external resources that occurred in the 1970s. Compared to the 1960s target of $20 billion in carefully measured doses for specific programs, in the 1970s $200 billion flowed to Latin America, as the current debt load will attest, without any planning or program. While it was part of a premeditated effort to rechannel some of the capital extracted from the developing countries by the oil-rich nations of the Middle East in the mid-1970s, its effects on the Alliance were at first electric and ultimately devastating. It totally diverted the focus of the region from the need for international cooperation. The elaborate infrastructure for national planning and cooperation established as part of the Alliance was no longer necessary. No one had to go to any inter-American conferences or meetings. No inter-American agencies, integration of markets, or national plans were required. All the astute minister of finance had to do was go to his neighborhood bank and sign a loan. It literally rained money in Latin America in the 1970s. In short, with the influx of commercial loans in the 1970s, the inter-American infrastructure of the Alliance went down the drain, not because of its failures, but because it became

Table 1.1
Latin America: Authorizations for Official External Financing, 1961–1970
(Millions of US $ Authorizations by Agency and Calendar Year)

| | 1961 | 1962 | 1963 | 1964 | 1965 | 1966 | 1967 | 1968 | 1969 | 1970 | Annual Average 1961–70 |
|---|---|---|---|---|---|---|---|---|---|---|---|
| 1. United States, Bilateral | 1 403.1 | 838.8 | 897.0 | 1 450.5 | 950.5 | 1,072.3 | 1 140.8 | 1 114.6 | 693.2 | 687.1 | 1 024.8 |
| AID | 451.2 | 517.5 | 603.5 | 1 006.9 | 533.5 | 744.9 | 556.0 | 645.3 | 503.1 | 455.2 | 601.7 |
| Loans^a | 270.8 | 305.6 | 326.3 | 616.9 | 343.7 | 509.9 | 394.9 | 328.5 | 277.7 | 217.0 | 359.2 |
| Grants^b | 35.0 | 83.8 | 112.1 | 93.5 | 88.7 | 88.5 | 95.1 | 88.7 | 88.4 | 85.6 | 85.9 |
| Food for Peace^c | 145.4 | 128.1 | 165.1 | 296.5 | 101.1 | 146.5 | 66.0 | 228.1 | 137.0 | 152.6 | 156.6 |
| EXIMBANK^d | 803.0 | 186.1 | 214.3 | 314.4 | 313.5 | 277.0 | 478.6 | 433.3 | 164.1 | 203.5 | 338.8 |
| Treasury^e | 147.0 | 125.0 | 60.0 | 96.3 | 69.8 | 12.5 | 75.0 | 4.8 | 0 | 0 | 59.0 |
| Others^f | 1.9 | 10.2 | 19.2 | 32.9 | 33.7 | 37.9 | 31.2 | 31.2 | 26.0 | 28.4 | 25.3 |
| 2. International Financial Institutions | 1 025.6 | 898.9 | 733.6 | 577.4 | 1 017.6 | 1 067.6 | 978.7 | 1 433.4 | 1 215.3 | 1 508.8 | 1 045.7 |
| IDB | 292.9 | 328.8 | 260.1 | 299.3 | 375.6 | 394.00 | 495.8 | 430.9 | 637.1 | 644.2 | 415.2 |
| Ordinary Capital | 129.2 | 83.7 | 179.4 | 164.0 | 123.6 | 98.8 | 170.3 | 193.6 | 214.5 | 194.5 | 155.1 |
| Fund for Special Operations | 48.1 | 40.2 | 33.6 | 49.4 | 196.6 | 291.3 | 313.1 | 210.1 | 412.5 | 443.0 | 203.1 |
| Social Progress Trust Fund^g | 115.6 | 204.9 | 47.1 | 85.9 | 51.2 | 0 | 0 | 0 | 0 | 0 | 50.5 |
| Other funds^h | 0 | 0 | 0 | 0 | 4.2 | 3.9 | 12.4 | 27.2 | 10.1 | 6.7 | 6.5 |
| Other Financial Institutions | | | | | | | | | | | |
| IBRD | 206.8 | 328.0 | 303.7 | 103.3 | 371.1 | 322.6 | 156.8 | 551.4 | 344.3 | 609.6 | 330.5 |
| IFC | 10.7 | 9.4 | 0 | 9.1 | 9.4 | 12.0 | 7.7 | 18.0 | 2.8 | 20.5 | 9.9 |

| | | | | | | | | | | | |
|---|---|---|---|---|---|---|---|---|---|---|---|
| IDA | 59.0 | 11.4 | 3.6 | 23.0 | 3.5 | 7.5 | 2.0 | 9.1 | 11.7 | 21.0 | 15.2 |
| IMF | 456.2 | 221.3 | 166.2 | 142.7 | 258.0 | 331.5 | 316.4 | . 424.0 | 219.4 | 213.5 | 274.9 |
| Subtotal (1+2) | 2 428.7 | 1 737.7 | 1 630.6 | 2 027.9 | 1 968.1 | 2 139.9 | 2 119.5 | 2 548.0 | 1 908.5 | 2 195.9 | 2 070.5 |
| 3. Bilateral OECD[i] | 85.9 | 151.9 | 197.2 | 180.4 | 208.0 | 176.7 | 157.6 | 157.6 | 81.2 | 192.8 | 159.0 |
| ANNUAL TOTAL | 2 514.6 | 1 889.6 | 1 827.8 | 2 208.7 | 2 176.1 | 2 316.6 | 2 277.1 | 2 705.6 | 1 989.7 | 2 388.7 | 2 229.5 |
| ACCUMULATED TOTAL | 4 404.2 | 6 232.0 | 8 440.7 | 10 616.8 | 12 933.4 | 15 210.5 | 17 916.1 | 19 905.8 | 22 294.5 | | |

a. Loans appearing in IID. Status of Loan Agreements as of December 31, 1970. Office of the Controller.
b. Grants for the Alliance for Progress, mainly for technical assistance. Data are for fiscal years.
   SOURCE: Unpublished AID data.
c. Includes loans and grants. Data are for fiscal years. Also includes funds from other countries that are not members of the OAS, which amount to an estimated 2.5 percent of the total.
   SOURCE: US Overseas Loans and Grants as of 1970. AID.
d. The principal function of EXIMBANK is to promote United States exports, but those loans also provide financing for development. Data include loans from EXIMBANK but not guaranteed investment funds.
   SOURCE: EXIMBANK. Statement of Loans and Authorized Credits 1961-70.
e. Short-term loans for stabilization of balance of payments.
   SOURCE: US Treasury Department. Treasury Bulletin 1961-70.
f. Includes Peace Corps and Pan American Highway. Data are for fiscal years.
   SOURCE: Unpublished AID data.
g. United States fund administered by the IDB.
h. English, Swedish, Canadian, Argentine and Vatican funds administered by the IDB.
i. Disbursements.

SOURCE: Organization of American States. Inter-American Economic and Social Council. (OAS-CIES) Latin America's Development and the Alliance for Progress. OAS/Ser. H/X. 19. CIES/1636. Rev. 2. Corr., January 1973. Hereinafter cited as OAS-CIES.

irrelevant. Even though their effect was skewed, and they barely replaced the drain of the local economies from the outflow of resources in the form of increased oil prices and higher interest rates, the petrodollars nonetheless took care of local demand.

By the mid-1970s, hardly a word was heard about the Alliance for Progress.

## THE NUMBERS

The real impact of any effort involving social change and institution building cannot be measured in numbers. Inestimable intangible benefits are rooted in changes of attitudes and motivation that weigh far more heavily on the future than can be expressed as dollars transferred or houses built. The people who receive an education and new perceptions of their destiny, the officials who acquire new tools for managing society's needs, and the institutions that facilitate new patterns of behavior are the elements that make the difference. The numbers may give a hint of the factories built or tractors used. But their one-dimensional view is universally misleading. This is especially true of the Alliance for Progress, given the nature of social "invention" that was involved.

Having said this, however, it still must be acknowledged that one cannot evaluate the Alliance without looking carefully at the numbers. This is because the Alliance, in one sense, demanded it. It declared its own criteria for success, with precise objectives, as no intergovernmental program ever attempted before. In one sense, it was the most elaborate catalogue of the components for development ever set forth in a public document. Its agenda ranged from the designation of specific levels of education to the administrative machinery in ministries of health, from specific targets for internal savings to the role of cooperatives. It was a *tour de force* of social and economic engineering.

Nonetheless, President Kennedy set the cautionary tone in his initial message when he emphasized that the goals were nothing more than a beginning. "If we are successful, if our effort is bold enough and determined enough," he affirmed, "then the close of this decade will mark the beginning of a new era in the American experience." Not the achievement of these goals, but a beginning. Not the completed edifice, but the building of a foundation that would enable societies to begin to evolve in a more balanced fashion. The major goal was to get the basic institutional elements in place so that there would be a more coherent framework for the eventual realization of true democracy and human freedom. It is in this context that the numbers that follow should be appraised.

The Charter of Punta del Este, signed on August 17, 1961, set forth 94 specific objectives toward national economic and social goals, according to the Organization of American States.[8] They covered almost every aspect of social and economic activity. They ranged from the major objective of achieving sustained economic growth by raising per capita income not less than 2.5 percent per year, to more general goals of social justice and more equitable income distribution. In a number of areas specific targets were set forth, such as reform of tax and agrarian structures, provision of low-income housing and health services, strengthening of labor organizations, and the achievement of economic integration. In spite of the tone of President Kennedy's initial address, many of the goals were extraordinarily specific, such as the improvement of life expectancy in the decade by "a minimum of five years," the provision of potable water to "not less than 70 percent of the urban and 50 percent of the rural population, and a 50 percent reduction in infant mortality." No area of national activity was sacrosanct from the ambitions of the Alliance planners. It was truly a remarkable undertaking if not the most blatant example of hubris seen in modern life.

## Economic Growth

While per capita economic growth was impressive, with rates reaching 3.5 percent annually in the closing years of the Alliance (1968–69) compared to an average of 2 percent for the 1950s and the early 1960s, there were great variations in individual countries (see Tables 1.2 and 1.3). This was to be expected in a

Table 1.2
Latin America: Annual Growth Rates of Gross Domestic Product (Percentages)

| Country | 1961–65 | 1966–69 | 1966 | 1967 | 1968 | 1969 |
|---|---|---|---|---|---|---|
| Argentina | 2.9 | 4.5 | 0.2 | 2.3 | 4.7 | 6.6 |
| Barbados | 3.5 | 5.5 | 4.0 | 7.8 | 6.5 | 2.3 |
| Bolivia | 5.9 | 6.1 | 7.0 | 6.3 | 7.2 | 4.8 |
| Brazil | 3.1 | 7.4 | 5.1 | 4.8 | 8.4 | 9.0 |
| Chile | 4.7 | 2.9 | 7.0 | 2.3 | 2.7 | 3.5 |
| Colombia | 4.6 | 5.2 | 5.4 | 4.2 | 5.5 | 5.8 |
| Costa Rica | 5.7 | 6.8 | 7.3 | 7.1 | 5.8 | 7.6 |
| Dominican Rep. | 2.3 | 4.5 | 12.4 | 3.3 | 3.1 | 7.0 |
| Ecuador | 4.8 | 5.5 | 4.6 | 6.5 | 5.2 | 4.9 |
| El Salvador | 7.7 | 2.8 | 7.2 | 5.4 | -1.2 | 4.2 |
| Guatemala | 5.5 | 5.2 | 5.5 | 4.1 | 5.7 | 5.6 |
| Haiti | 1.3 | 1.9 | 1.9 | 1.4 | 2.0 | 2.5 |
| Honduras | 4.9 | 5.5 | 7.6 | 6.5 | 7.0 | 3.1 |
| Jamaica | 5.3 | 4.4 | 3.8 | 2.9 | 6.1 | 4.1 |
| Mexico | 7.7 | 7.2 | 6.9 | 6.3 | 8.1 | 7.3 |
| Nicaragua | 9.6 | 4.8 | 3.1 | 5.3 | 4.7 | 4.4 |
| Panama | 7.6 | 7.3 | 7.6 | 8.6 | 7.0 | 6.5 |
| Paraguay | 4.7 | 5.2 | 1.3 | 6.7 | 4.8 | 4.2 |
| Peru | 6.1 | 2.5 | 5.7 | 4.6 | 1.4 | 1.7 |
| Trinidad & Tobago | 3.3 | 3.2 | 3.7 | 5.7 | 3.3 | 1.0 |
| Uruguay | 0.3 | -0.1 | 3.3 | -6.6 | 1.2 | 5.5 |
| Venezuela | 7.9 | 4.3 | 2.3 | 4.0 | 5.3 | 3.5 |
| Latin America | 4.9 | 5.7 | 4.5 | 4.4 | 6.3 | 6.5 |

Source: Inter-American Development Bank, Socio-Economic Progress in Latin America; Social Progress Trust Fund Annual Report, 1970.

Table 1.3
Latin America: Variation in Per Capita Product (Percentages)

| Country | 1961-65 | 1966-69 | 1966 | 1967 | 1968 | 1969 |
|---|---|---|---|---|---|---|
| Argentina | 1.3 | 2.9 | -1.4 | 0.7 | 3.1 | 5.0 |
| Barbados | 2.3 | 4.5 | 2.8 | 6.9 | 4.8 | 1.9 |
| Bolivia | 3.3 | 3.4 | 4.3 | 3.6 | 4.5 | 2.1 |
| Brazil | 0.1 | 4.3 | 2.1 | 1.7 | 5.3 | 5.8 |
| Chile | 2.2 | 0.5 | 4.5 | -0.1 | 0.4 | 1.2 |
| Colombia | 1.4 | 1.9 | 2.1 | 1.0 | 2.1 | 2.5 |
| Costa Rica | 2.1 | 3.3 | 3.7 | 3.8 | 2.1 | 4.0 |
| Dominican Rep. | -1.2 | 0.8 | 8.5 | -0.3 | -0.5 | 3.3 |
| Ecuador | 1.3 | 2.1 | 1.1 | 3.0 | 1.7 | 1.5 |
| El Salvador | 3.8 | -0.9 | 3.3 | 1.6 | -4.6 | 0.4 |
| Guatemala | 2.3 | 2.0 | 2.4 | 1.0 | 2.6 | 2.5 |
| Haiti | -0.7 | -0.1 | -0.1 | -0.7 | -0.1 | 0.4 |
| Honduras | 1.5 | 2.0 | 4.0 | 3.0 | 3.4 | -0.3 |
| Jamaica | 3.1 | 2.3 | 1.1 | 0.9 | 4.1 | 2.0 |
| Mexico | 4.1 | 3.6 | 3.4 | 2.7 | 4.5 | 3.6 |
| Nicaragua | 6.1 | 1.1 | -0.8 | 1.6 | 1.4 | 0.4 |
| Panama | 4.1 | 3.9 | 4.2 | 5.1 | 3.6 | 3.1 |
| Paraguay | 1.6 | 1.9 | -1.8 | 3.4 | 1.5 | 0.9 |
| Peru | 2.9 | -0.6 | 2.5 | 1.4 | -1.7 | -1.4 |
| Trinidad & Tobago | 0.3 | 1.8 | 1.5 | 4.1 | 2.2 | -0.9 |
| Uruguay | -1.0 | -1.3 | 2.0 | -7.7 | 0.0 | 4.3 |
| Venezuela | 4.3 | 0.7 | -1.2 | 0.5 | 1.7 | -0.1 |
| Latin America | 1.9 | 2.7 | 1.6 | 1.4 | 3.2 | 3.5 |

Population growth rates during the period considered were 1 per cent in the industrialized countries, 1.4 per cent in Southern Europe, 2.4 per cent in Africa, 2.5 per cent in Southern Asia and 2.7 per cent in the Middle East and Eastern Asia. These compare with an average rate of 2.9 per cent for Latin America.

Source:    Inter-American Development Bank, <u>Socio-Economic Progress in Latin America; Social Progress Trust Fund Annual Report</u>, 1970.

sprawling hemisphere with enormous differences in standards of living, political systems, and levels of productivity. While the accelerating pace of Argentina, Brazil, and Mexico at the end of the decade served as the region's engines of growth, the OAS study noted that only seven countries had actually reached the appointed target of 2.5 percent per capita annual growth. Twelve nations fell short of the goal. In two countries, Uruguay and Haiti, per capita income actually declined during the decade. In comparison, during the 1950s, without any Alliance to blaze the way, six of the countries, including Brazil, Mexico and Venezuela, achieved a per capita growth rate of 2.5 percent (see Table 1.4).

Latin America's economic performance became truly impressive. In the 1970s, prior to the impact of the 1973 oil shock, annual growth rates for the region were climbing to a composite average of almost 7 percent, or almost 4 percent per capita, the highest in its modern history (see Table 1.5). It should be borne in mind that these were the years before the influx of commercial capital from the recycling of petrodollars. The only external stimulus to Latin America in those years was the increasing momentum of the Alliance efforts and an expansive world economy. Measured by economic growth rates, the impact of the Alliance speaks for itself.

### Industrialization

The industrial sector was clearly the most dynamic during the period. The impact of industrialization of the economies of the region, as reflected in the figures, however, was ambiguous. The overall percentage of economic activity

Table 1.4
**Latin America: Average Annual Growth Rates of Per Capita GDP at Factor Cost, 1951–1970 (Percentages)**

| Country | 1951-55 | 1956-60 | 1961-65 | 1966-70 | 1951-60 | 1961-70 |
|---|---|---|---|---|---|---|
| Group I (countries that grew at an average per capita rate of more than 2.5 percent between 1961 and 1970) | | | | | | |
| Panama | 1.0 | 2.8 | 4.7 | 4.6 | 1.9 | 4.6 |
| Nicaragua | 5.0 | -0.5 | 5.7 | 2.2 | 2.2 | 3.9 |
| Mexico | 2.8 | 2.6 | 3.6 | 3.6 | 2.7 | 3.6 |
| Bolivia | -0.5 | -2.7 | 2.8 | 3.7 | -1.7 | 3.2 |
| Brazil | 3.7 | 3.7 | 1.6 | 4.3 | 3.7 | 2.9 |
| Costa Rica | 4.5 | 2.1 | 1.8 | 3.3 | 3.3 | 2.6 |
| El Salvador | 1.6 | 2.1 | 3.7 | 1.6 | 1.8 | 2.6 |
| Group II (countries that grew at a rate below 2.5 percent between 1961 and 1970) | | | | | | |
| Guatemala | -1.5 | 3.1 | 2.1 | 2.4 | 0.8 | 2.3 |
| Argentina | 0.9 | 1.2 | 2.1 | 2.1 | 1.0 | 2.1 |
| Peru | 4.0 | 1.8 | 3.4 | 1.0 | 2.9 | 2.1 |
| Chile | 1.3 | 0.8 | 2.4 | 1.3 | 1.1 | 1.9 |
| Colombia | 2.0 | 0.7 | 1.3 | 2.3 | 1.4 | 1.7 |
| Ecuador | 2.1 | 1.4 | 1.1 | 2.3 | 1.8 | 1.7 |
| Honduras | -0.6 | 1.4 | 1.9 | 1.5 | 0.4 | 1.7 |
| Venezuela | 4.8 | 2.5 | 1.6 | 0.9 | 3.6 | 1.3 |
| Paraguay | -0.1 | 0.3 | 1.5 | 0.7 | -0.2 | 1.0 |
| Dominican Rep. | 3.0 | 2.1 | -2.2 | 2.8 | 2.6 | 0.3 |
| Group III (countries whose GDP growth rate declined in 1971-70) | | | | | | |
| Uruguay | 2.7 | -3.3 | -0.4 | 0.3 | 0.6 | -0.1 |
| Haiti | -0.4 | 0.2 | -1.2 | -0.2 | -0.1 | -0.7 |
| Latin America | 2.2 | 2.0 | 2.1 | 2.7 | 2.1 | 2.4 |

Sources: Data taken from ECLA figures, national accounts of the countries and the OAS Secretariat, OAS-CIES.

Table 1.5

Latin America: Annual Variations in Gross Domestic Product by Countries, 1961–1980 (Percentages)[1]

| Country | 1961–70 | 1971–75 | 1976–80 |
|---|---|---|---|
| Argentina | 4.4 | 2.8 | 1.6 |
| Bahamas | n.a. | n.a. | 6.2 |
| Barbados | 8.3 | — | 2.0 |
| Bolivia | 5.0 | 5.7 | 3.2 |
| Brazil | 6.1 | 10.9 | 6.8 |
| Chile | 4.5 | −0.9 | 7.3 |
| Colombia | 5.2 | 6.1 | 5.5 |
| Costa Rica | 6.0 | 6.1 | 5.2 |
| Dominican Republic | 5.4 | 9.1 | 4.9 |
| Ecuador | 5.5 | 8.9 | 5.7 |
| El Salvador | 5.7 | 5.5 | 3.7 |
| Guatemala | 5.5 | 5.6 | 5.7 |
| Guyana | 3.7 | 3.4 | −0.1 |
| Haiti | 0.3 | 3.7 | 4.1 |
| Honduras | 5.2 | 2.1 | 6.6 |
| Jamaica | 5.4 | 1.7 | −2.9 |
| Mexico | 7.0 | 5.7 | 5.6 |
| Nicaragua | 7.0 | 5.6 | −1.3 |
| Panama | 8.0 | 5.0 | 3.4 |
| Paraguay | 4.5 | 6.7 | 10.3 |
| Peru | 5.1 | 4.6 | 1.6 |
| Trinidad & Tobago | 4.0 | 2.9 | 6.1 |
| Uruguay | 1.6 | 1.4 | 5.1 |
| Venezuela | 6.1 | 4.9 | 3.5 |
| **Latin America** | **5.7** | **6.6** | **5.2** |

*Preliminary estimates.

n.a. Not available.

[1] At constant market prices with reference to the base year used by each country. For Latin America, the figures were calculated by converting national values into dollars of 1980 purchasing power. In this connection, see Methodological Note in the Statistical Appendix.

Source:   Inter-American Development Bank (IDB), *Economic and Social Progress in Latin America*,
            1980–81

involved in industry and mining in 1969 stood substantially higher than in 1950, with corresponding declines in the agriculture, forestry and fishing sectors (see Table 1.6). The data indicate that the progress was an extension of trends already apparent and accelerating in the previous decade. In several countries the industrial sector did not grow as fast as it did during the 1950s. By the end of the decade, however, value added growth rates in the manufacturing sector were increasing at record rates in almost all countries, with overall growth for the region at 8.6 percent led by Argentina, Brazil, and Mexico, where growth averaged over 9 percent per year (see Table 1.7).

Other data were not as comforting. In the area of trade, Latin America's growth, although positive in real terms, lagged substantially behind the overall growth in world trade, reducing Latin America's percentage of global economic trade.[9] Already signs abounded that the protectionist policies adopted by the Latin American nations, contributing to rapid domestic growth, were creating an industrial plant that was virtually isolated from the outside world. The impact of the increasing industrialization on employment was an even greater concern. While outpacing the rest of the economy in value added growth, it did not result in substantially higher employment. Industrial employment grew at an average rate of 2.6 percent during the Alliance years, virtually the same as during the previous decade when it achieved a rate of 2.5 percent (see Table 1.8). Taking population

Table 1.6

**Latin America: Changes in National Economic Structures—1950, 1960, and 1969 (Selected sectors as percentages of overall GDP, at 1960 prices)**

| Countries grouped according to percentage of GDP accounted for by the agricultural sector (in 1960) | Agriculture Forestry, and Fishing | | | Manufacturing Industry, Mines and Quarries | | | Business and Finance | | |
|---|---|---|---|---|---|---|---|---|---|
| | 1950 | 1960 | 1969 | 1950 | 1960 | 1969 | 1950 | 1960 | 1969 |
| **More than 30%** | | | | | | | | | |
| Bolivia | 31.9 | 30.6 | 24.8 | 29.7 | 22.3 | 26.0 | 10.0 | 10.9 | 11.5 |
| Colombia | 39.4 | 34.1 | 30.5 | 18.1 | 21.2 | 21.6 | 15.1 | 15.7 | 16.8 |
| Dominican Rep. | 31.8 | 31.6 | 25.8 | 12.1 | 15.7 | 14.2 | 17.4 | 16.6 | n.a. |
| Ecuador | 39.6 | 36.8 | 31.7 | 18.0 | 18.0 | 19.2 | 11.4 | 14.1 | n.a. |
| El Salvador | 37.6 | 32.4 | 25.5 | 13.7 | 13.7 | 18.3 | 19.3 | 21.4 | 24.2 |
| Guatemala | 33.0 | 30.3 | 27.2 | 10.1 | 10.9 | 13.5 | 30.3 | 30.2 | 33.1 |
| Haiti | 51.7 | 48.5 | 46.1 | 12.9a | 14.7a | 13.6b | 12.1 | 12.2 | n.a. |
| Honduras | 50.1 | 44.3 | 38.5 | 9.2 | 13.1 | 17.8 | 13.1 | 14.5 | 15.6 |
| Nicaragua | 41.7 | 34.2 | 29.9 | 10.3 | 11.6 | 14.9 | 17.2 | 19.0 | 19.0 |
| Paraguay | 40.7 | 38.9 | 34.4 | 17.6 | 16.7 | 18.7 | 18.7 | 18.3 | 18.2 |
| **From 20 to 30%** | | | | | | | | | |
| Brazil | 27.8 | 22.1 | 19.8 | 18.6 | 23.3 | 25.0 | 15.6c | 14.3c | 13.6c |
| Costa Rica | 34.9 | 27.0 | 24.0 | 14.9 | 16.2 | 19.2 | 11.5c | 15.1 | 15.6 |
| Panama | 30.9 | 24.9 | 21.0 | 9.1 | 13.2 | 18.2 | 10.7 | 11.9 | 12.9 |
| Peru | 24.9 | 24.1 | 18.4 | 14.7 | 17.9 | 22.2 | na.a | 14.3 | n.a. |
| **Less than 20%** | | | | | | | | | |
| Argentina | 19.1 | 17.4 | 15.5 | 30.0 | 33.3 | 36.9 | 19.0 | 19.1 | 18.9 |
| Chile | n.a. | 12.1 | 10.1 | n.a. | 33.2 | 35.6 | n.a. | 17.8 | 17.6 |
| Mexico | 18.8 | 16.6 | 12.8 | 23.3 | 24.1 | 26.5 | 29.6 | 30.7 | 30.3 |
| Uruguay | 23.4 | 19.3 | 20.9 | 17.4 | 21.2 | 22.1 | n.a. | 17.2c | 23.0c |
| Venezuela | 7.9 | 7.2 | 7.8 | 33.1d | 37.9d | 35.9d | 11.0 | 12.6 | 14.0 |

a. Includes construction.
b. Excludes mines and quarries.
c. Excludes finances.
d. Includes all petroleum activities.
n.a. Not available.

Source: OAS-CIES

Table 1.7
Latin America: Manufacturing Value Added

| | Annual Values in Millions of 1963 U.S. Dollars | | | | | | | Rates of Growth of Value Added | |
|---|---|---|---|---|---|---|---|---|---|
| Country | 1961 | 1962 | 1963 | 1964 | 1965 | 1966 | 1967 | 1968 | 1961-1968 | 1968 |
| Argentina | 4,592 | 4,352 | 4,112 | 4,476 | 5,218 | 5,134 | 5,044 | 5,471 | 2.5% | 8.5% |
| Barbados* | 7 | 8 | 8 | 8 | 8 | 8 | 9 | 10ᵉ | 5.2 | 10.0ᵉ |
| Bolivia | 48 | 54 | 58 | 61 | 66 | 73 | 76 | 87 | 8.9 | 14.5 |
| Brazil | 4,359 | 4,487 | 4,966 | 4,900 | 4,775 | 5,587 | 5,711 | 6,385 | 5.6 | 11.2 |
| Chile | 575 | 633 | 684 | 750 | 761 | 789 | 850 | 863 | 6.0 | 1.3 |
| Colombia | 744 | 826 | 905 | 961 | 943 | 973 | 983 | 1,048 | 5.0 | 6.6 |
| Costa Rica* | 75 | 83 | 91 | 95 | 102 | 114 | 127 | 136 | 8.9 | 7.1 |
| Dominican Rep. | 135 | 164 | 169 | 172 | 126 | 166 | 174 | 170 | 3.3 | -2.3 |
| Ecuador | 135 | 141 | 153 | 179 | 181 | 190 | 201 | 208 | 6.4 | 3.5 |
| El Salvador | 90 | 98 | 107 | 121 | 138 | 157 | 168 | 179 | 10.3 | 6.5 |
| Guatemala | 139 | 140 | 159 | 179 | 191 | 201 | 213 | 224 | 7.1 | 5.2 |
| Haiti | 39 | 41 | 42 | 44 | 45 | 46 | 48 | 49 | 3.3 | 2.1 |
| Honduras | 51 | 54 | 55 | 64 | 69 | 77 | 83 | 90 | 8.5 | 8.4 |
| Mexico | 2,712 | 2,829 | 3,054 | 3,416 | 3,687 | 4,018 | 4,331 | 4,724 | 8.3 | 9.1 |
| Nicaragua | 48 | 55 | 63 | 71 | 75 | 88 | 94 | 103 | 11.5 | 9.6 |
| Panama | 64 | 79 | 89 | 94 | 101 | 111 | 123 | 131 | 10.8 | 6.5 |
| Paraguay | 60 | 59 | 60 | 63 | 65 | 67 | 72 | 71 | 2.4 | -1.4 |
| Peru | 487 | 549 | 582 | 619 | 625 | 685 | 721 | 777 | 6.9 | 7.8 |
| Trinidad-Tobago | 76 | 84 | 90 | 105 | 105 | 113 | 119 | 136 | 8.7 | 14.3 |
| Uruguay* | 336 | 338 | 334 | 356 | 357 | 363 | 341 | 347 | 0.5 | 1.8 |
| Venezuela | 816 | 887 | 947 | 1,066 | 1,159 | 1,166 | 1,233 | 1,304 | 6.9 | 5.8 |
| Latin America | 15,588 | 15,961 | 16,728 | 17,800 | 18,797 | 20,126 | 20,721 | 22,513 | 5.4 | 8.6 |

*Includes mining, which in these countries contributes a very small proportion to gross domestic product.
ᵉIDB estimates.

SOURCE: IDB, Socio-Economic Progress in Latin America, 1969

growth into account, Table 1.8 indicates that a lower proportion of the working population was employed in industry in 1968 than in 1950. Given the parallel objectives of creating jobs and fostering a more equitable distribution of income, the impact of industrialization had mixed results. This affords some indication of the massive problems that face a hemisphere for which 50 percent of the population is under the age of 18.

### Agriculture

The agricultural sector was the problem child of the Alliance. The great transformation of rural populations, as a diminishing agricultural work force is required to meet the demands of food production, has affected Latin America as it

Table 1.8
Latin America: Industrial Employment Indicators in Selected Countries:[a]
1950, 1955, 1960, 1968 (In thousands of persons and in percentages)

| Country | 1950 | | | 1955 | | | 1960 | | | 1968 | | |
|---|---|---|---|---|---|---|---|---|---|---|---|---|
| | Economically active population | Employment in the industrial sector | Percentage of active population employed in industrial sector | Economically active population | Employment in the industrial sector | Percentage of active population employed in industrial sector | Economically active population | Employment in the industrial sector | Percentage of active population employed in industrial sector | Economically active population | Employment in the industrial sector | Percentage of active population employed in industrial sector |
| Argentina | 6 946 | 1 575 | 22.7 | 7 397 | 1 606 | 21.7 | 7 811 | 1 660 | 21.0 | 8 905 | 1 971 | 22.1 |
| Brazil | 17 125 | 2 191 | 12.8 | 19 645 | 2 495 | 12.7 | 22 848 | 2 850 | 12.5 | 28 702 | 3 444 | 12.0 |
| Chile | 2 219 | 383 | 17.3 | 2 356 | 423 | 18.0 | 2 494 | 447 | 17.9 | 3 028 | 538 | 17.8 |
| Colombia | 3 872 | 570 | 14.7 | 4 322 | 640 | 14.8 | 4 794 | 748 | 15.6 | 6 131 | 868 | 14.2 |
| Guatemala | 977 | 80 | 8.2 | 1 078 | 92 | 8.5 | 1 225 | 105 | 8.6 | 1 524 | 109 | 7.2 |
| Mexico | 8 515 | 973 | 11.4 | 9 784 | 1 210 | 12.4 | 11 409 | 1 556 | 13.6 | 14 930 | 2 071 | 13.9 |
| Panama | 265 | 18 | 6.8 | 299 | 22 | 7.4 | 339 | 26 | 7.7 | 424 | 51 | 12.0 |
| Peru | 2 577 | 450 | 17.5 | 2 803 | 487 | 17.4 | 3 145 | 536 | 17.0 | 4 025 | 680 | 16.9 |
| Uruguay | 855 | 180 | 21.1 | 916 | 201 | 21.9 | 987 | 205 | 20.8 | 1 089 | 219 | 20.1 |
| Venezuela | 1 806 | 172 | 9.5 | 2 113 | 234 | 11.1 | 2 458 | 295 | 12.0 | 3 157 | 394 | 12.5 |
| TOTAL | 45 157 | 6 592 | 14.6 | 50 713 | 7 410 | 14.6 | 57 510 | 8 428 | 14.7 | 71 915 | 10 345 | 14.4 |

a. Countries for which information is available on industrial employment in 1968. This group of countries accounted for 87 percent of the economically active population in Latin America in 1968, and for 90 percent of industrial employment in the region in 1960. In both cases the figures do not include Barbados, Cuba, Jamaica or Trinidad and Tobago.

Source:   OAS-CIES

has all countries during the twentieth century. The Latin American equation, however, contained another ingredient – a dispossessed and impoverished landless peasantry – which injected a political element far more volatile than in other Western nations. Promoting equity and social justice was as important to the Alliance programs in rural areas as was the goal of improving food production. The two did not easily mix.

Agriculture had the poorest showing of all sectors during the 1960s. Despite the rhetoric and attention to the development of infrastructure in agricultural education, extension, and credit facilities, the region was unable to alter what Rostow refers to as its "perverse agricultural policies." The average per capita growth in the agricultural sector during the Alliance years was 2.6 percent annually, compared to an average of 3.9 percent in the previous decade.[10] The major impact here too was institutional, establishing a basis for better understanding of the underlying factors involved in improving agricultural production. Considerable growth was registered in agricultural education facilities; average enrollment increased in intermediary and advanced facilities from approximately 30,000 per year in 1960 to 115,000 per year in 1970 (see Table 1.9). While mechanization of agriculture also posted impressive gains, with rapidly expanding numbers of tractors in use,[11] there was significant shortfall in other essential elements of an effective agricultural sector such as the improvement of storage facilities, transportation and distribution.

More important in terms of Alliance goals was the objective of agrarian reform. Housing, work, and land (*techo, trabajo y tierra*) were the touchstones of President Kennedy's March 13 address, and the concept of agrarian reform was among the most specific of the Charter of Punta del Este, which reserved its strongest words for "the transformation . . . of unjust structures and systems of land tenure . . . as a guarantee of freedom and dignity."

The emphasis on land reform was the major element that the U.S. pressed on Latin American nations in the early years of the Alliance and the one that contributed most to the image of the Alliance as a U.S. program. It was not an element foreign to U.S. policy. Since the early days of the Republic, U.S. political thinking placed an extraordinarily high value on the importance of land ownership as a basis for political stability. It was reflected in environments as diverse as Puerto Rico at the turn of the century and Japan under General MacArthur's occupation administration. Land reform, however, is an uniquely domestic concern, interplaying with a wide range of national economic and political forces. In Latin America, it rapidly became one of the most contentious and controversial issues of the Alliance. While the OAS was able to report early in the Alliance that "virtually all of the countries of the region have passed laws to promote agrarian reform or have started some type of program to transform or change the systems of land tenure and use," little real progress was recorded.[12]

Two things became apparent in the area of land reform in most of the countries. First, traditional resistance in the societies was far more potent than contemplated, even though considerable resistance was clearly foreseen. The major landowners'

Table 1.9
Latin America: Enrollment in Agricultural Schools at Intermediate
and Advanced Levels, 1960 and 1969

|  | 1960 | | 1969 | |
| --- | --- | --- | --- | --- |
| Country | Inter. | Adv. | Inter. | Adv. |
| Argentina | 2,903 | 3,319 | 6,500 | 8,200 |
| Bolivia | n.a. | 197 | n.a. | n.a. |
| Brazil | 6,663 | 2,757 | 19,643 | (10,035) [a] |
| Chile | 2,523 | 718 | 6,000 | 1,150 |
| Colombia | 2,845 | 1,508 | 8,890 | 4,720 |
| Costa Rica | 94 | 67 | 2,400 | 400 |
| Dominican Republic | 123 | n.a. | 990 | 610 |
| Ecuador | 348 | 482 | 792 | 1,465 |
| El Salvador | 115 | n.a. | 245 | 173 |
| Guatemala | 102 | 220 | 308 | 706 |
| Honduras | 104 | 167 | 143 | 320 |
| Mexico | 0 | 1,367 | 2,955 | 2,412 |
| Nicaragua | 30 | 120 | 683 | 129 |
| Panama | 90 | 70 | 190 | 150 |
| Peru | 3,194 | 743 | 15,000 | 5,321 |
| Uruguay | 566 | 251 | 802 | 1,200 |
| Venezuela | 980 | 1,121 | 3,500 | 3,800 |
| SUBTOTALS | 20,902 | 13,311 | 69,291 | 45,746 |
| TOTAL | 34,213 | | 115,037 | |

a.   1967 figure; not included in totals
n.a.   not available.

Source:   OAS-CIES

expected defense of their interests ran true to form. The issues, however, were fraught with social and political implications affecting the balance of power in the society. Broad and deeply rooted cultural perceptions and prejudices inhibited land reform from becoming a major part of the agenda. Not only the landed interests but the middle classes felt themselves vulnerable to an awakened peasantry. Second, far less meaningful activity went on than the rhetoric suggests. While statistics are not readily available, if there had been serious reform, someone would have been making more noise about it.

The real impact of land reform remains elusive. Data on land redistribution were always scarce. A 1969 Report to the U.S. Congress noted that 400,000 families were resettled and received titles to their land.[13] The Inter-American Development Bank as recently as 1986 reports that more than 3 million families have benefitted over the quarter of a century since the beginning of the effort, but that 90 percent of those are in the three countries of Mexico, Bolivia, and Peru (see Table 1.10).

Equally important, the concept of agrarian reform was always recognized as encompassing vastly more than the mere redistribution of land. It was viewed as an integral process to improve the economic capacity of the farmer, his ability to farm and get his products to market. This meant credit facilities, fertilizer, machinery, extension services and education. All of these, including rural and community development projects, water, and health were given careful attention in the planning process. According to the OAS, however, few of the countries provided the necessary resources for these complementary services.[14] It is true that much had to be done on such preliminaries as the legal definition of parameters and cadastral surveys. In this, much was achieved. However, as indicated above, the number of acres actually expropriated and families benefitting were minimal. The situation has changed little since.

## Health

The specificity of the goals set forth in the field of health, education, and housing was truly remarkable considering the inexperience of the planners in the field of development and the poor historic record of Latin America in these sectors. Many of the countries in the region were dual societies, with the ruling elites paying little attention to the problems of poverty and the rural areas. In spite of that obstacle, the Charter of Punta del Este pledged major advances within the decade in improving mortality rates, sanitation, water supply, and disease control. Life expectancy was to be increased by five years. Considering that, on the whole, life expectancy levels were already respectable and that Latin America was already benefitting from many of the major advances in health care that had taken place in the postwar era, the goals in health appeared to be attainable. Indeed, the progress in the field of health during the decade of the 1950s in all of the countries was far more impressive than during the Alliance years, as is evident in Table 1.11.

The actual achievements, however, were spotty. Life expectancy continued on an upward trend, reaching a par with the major industrialized nations. The number of hospital beds increased, although hardly keeping pace with the expanding population (see Table 1.12). Similar targets were outlined for reducing infant mortality rates by half, a goal which remained elusive (see Table 1.13). However, the shortfall in this area masks important gains that continued to be made in the field. Because statistics in the rural areas were improving at the same time as environmental conditions, more reliable data on infant deaths were available than had been the case previously. Thus the numbers may not accurately reflect the overall reductions of infant mortality rates that continued throughout the Alliance years.

Potable water supply and sewage disposal were the focus of considerable effort. With the U.S. Agency for International Development and the Inter-American Development Bank establishing these as priority areas, most of the countries met

# Table 1.10
## Selected Countries of Latin America and the Caribbean: Area Affected by the Agrarian Reform and Number of Peasant Families Benefited

| Country | Forest and agricultural surface[a] (Thousands of hectares) | | | Number of farming families | | |
|---|---|---|---|---|---|---|
| | Total | Assigned | Percentage | Total | Benefited | Percentage |
| Bolivia | 3,275.0[b] | 2,730.0[c] | 83.4 | 516,200[d] | 384,560[c] | 74.5 |
| Chile | 28,759.0[e] | 2,940.0[f] | 10.2 | 412,000[d] | 38,000[f] | 9.2 |
| Costa Rica | 3,122.4[g] | 221.6[g] | 7.1 | 155,200[d] | 8,349[g] | 5.4 |
| Dominican Republic | 2,676.7[h] | 374.6[h] | 14.0 | 697,800[d] | 59,411[h] | 8.5 |
| Ecuador | 7,949.0[i] | 718.1[i] | 9.0 | 749,000[d] | 78,088[i] | 10.4 |
| Mexico | 139,868.0[i] | 60,724.0[k] | 43.4 | 4,629,400[d] | 1,986,000[k] | 42.9 |
| Panama | 2,253.9[i] | 493.2[m] | 21.9 | 132,800[d] | 17,703[m] | 13.3 |
| Peru | 23,545.0[i] | 9,255.6[n] | 39.3 | 1,419,400[d] | 431,982[n] | 30.4 |
| Venezuela | 26,470.0[i] | 5,118.7[o] | 19.3 | 561,800[d] | 171,861[o] | 30.6 |

[a]Corresponds to the total surface of the exploitations.
[b]1950 figures.
[c]Up to 1977, according to E. Ortega, "La agricultura y las relaciones intersectoriales: el caso de Bolivia", E/CEPAL/R.205, Santiago, Chile, 1979.
[d]According to FAO data.
[e]According to INE, "V Censo nacional agropecuario", Santiago, Chile, 1981.
[f]Up to 1982, according to A. Rojas, "Campesinado y mercado de alimentos en un modelo de economía abierta", Estudios e Informes de la CEPAL No. 35, Santiago, Chile, 1984.
[g]Corresponds to the peasant settlements created by the Instituto de Tierras y Colonización up to 1980. According to SEPSA, "Información básica del sector agropecuario y de recursos naturales renovables de Costa Rica, Número 2", Guadalupe, 1982.
[h]1983 data, according to S. Moquete, "La agricultura campesina y el mercado de alimentos: El caso de República Dominicana", Estudios e Informes de la CEPAL No. 39, Santiago, Chile, 1984.
[i]According to FAO, "Censo agropecuario mundial de 1970. Análisis y comparación internacional de los resultados del censo agropecuario mundial de 1970", Rome, 1981.
[j]Up to 1983, according to O. Barsky, "La reforma agraria ecuatoriana", Biblioteca de Ciencias Sociales, Vol. 3, FLACSO, Quito, 1984.
[k]1970 figures, according to Eckstein et al (1978, p. 11).
[l]According to R. Pérez, "Estudio sobre la ganadería bovina de carne de Panamá", mimeographed, undated.
[m]1977 data, according to PREALC, "La evolución de la pobreza rural en Panamá", Santiago, Chile, 1983.
[n]Up to 1982, according to the Ministry of Agriculture, "Informe sobre la marcha de las actividades en el sector de la reforma agraria y el desarrollo rural en el Perú" (for the FAO Conference of 1983), Lima, 1983.
[o]Up to 1979, according to S. Marta, "La pobreza agrícola y rural en Venezuela", Caracas, 1983.
Source: Prepared by the ECLAC/FAO Joint Agricultural Division.

Source: IDB, *Economic and Social Progress in Latin America*, 1986.

Table 1.11
Latin America: Life Expectancy at Birth for Selected Countries[a]—
1950, 1960, and 1968

|  | Around 1950 | | Around 1960 | | Around 1968 | |
| --- | --- | --- | --- | --- | --- | --- |
| Country | Period | Life expect- ancy | Period | Life expect- ancy | Period | Life expect- ancy |
| Argentina | 1946-48 | 60.6 | 1959-61 | 65.5 | 1967 | 66.3 |
| Barbados | 1950-52 | 55.7 | 1960 | 66.9 | 1968 | 68.8 |
| Chile | 1951-53 | 54.0 | 1959-61 | 57.2 | 1968 | 62.0 |
| Colombia | 1950-52 | 52.2 | 1964 | 60.2 | 1967 | 60.9 |
| Costa Rica | 1949-51 | 56.5 | 1963 | 65.3 | 1967 | 68.3 |
| El Salvador | 1949-51 | 51.4 | 1960-62 | 59.4 | 1968 | 62.6 |
| Guatemala | 1949-51 | 43.6 | 1964 | 49.4 | 1966 | 48.8 |
| Jamaica | 1952-54 | 59.1 | 1961 | 68.3 | 1968 | 66.6 |
| Mexico | 1949-51 | 48.8 | 1959-61 | 58.9 | 1968 | 61.2 |
| Panama | 1950 | 62.2 | 1959-61 | 65.8 | 1968 | 67.3 |
| Trinidad and Tobago | 1945-47 | 54.1 | 1959-61 | 64.2 | 1967 | 66.3 |
| Uruguay | 1949-51 | 68.8 | 1963 | 68.7 | 1968 | 68.4 |
| Venezuela | 1950-51 | 58.0 | 1960-62 | 66.1 | 1968 | 65.6 |

a. The countries selected are those for which death registration is considered complete enough to provide a reliable estimate of life expectancy at birth and for which statistics on distribution of deaths and population are available by age group.
Source: OAS-CIES.

or exceeded the goals in the urban areas, although few attained the goals in rural areas (see Table 1.14). Sewage disposal programs were apparently less successful (see Table 1.15), although information regarding the rural areas was virtually nonexistent.

## Education

The goals in education were also surprisingly specific and ambitious for a ten-year span, considering the massive problems that confronted the planners in this sector. But this was an objective in which the magnitude and import of the task mandated ambitious goals. The target for the nations of the hemisphere, set forth in the Charter of Punta del Este, was to eradicate adult illiteracy within the decade and to ensure a minimum of six years of primary education for every school-age child. Virtually all of the countries made substantial gains (Table 1.16).

The data on illiteracy, affected by numerous intangible factors such as retention, are notoriously misleading. Nonetheless, two things seemed clear regarding the Alliance efforts. First, the goal of eradicating illiteracy was not met. Second, programs in literacy patently increased and the region's traditional disregard of the problem was reversed (see Table 1.17). Education at the secondary and higher levels experienced a marked increase during the Alliance years, with the number of people going on to higher education doubling and tripling in many countries (see Table 1.16). An important indicator of the changes wrought by the Alliance was the patterns of government expenditures (see Table 1.18). In almost every case, the percentages of governmental revenues allocated to education and health were substantially increased.

The major impetus, especially in education for science and technology, came after the 1967 Meeting of the Presidents in which two new regional programs were added to the agenda of the Alliance. The Regional Program in Education and the Regional Program in Science and Technology were both aimed at increasing educational exchanges and the establishment of regional centers of excellence serving many countries. Felipe Herrera spoke at the time of creating a "common market of education" and pioneered in steering the Inter-American Development Bank toward the support of educational lending. New centers were established for the training of teachers in curricula development, for educational administrators, and for the utilization of new educational technologies and research. In the basic disciplines, such as languages and science, where the curricula had many common elements, the joint programs promised substantial cost savings for the smaller nations.

The essential need to compete in an increasingly complex technological world prompted new programs in the transfer of technology. Special centers were financed in applied technology covering industry (metallurgy, petrochemicals, chemicals) and the industrialization of agricultural and animal products (plant genetics, utilization of pesticides, tanning, etc). These did not get underway until the latter years of the Alliance, however, and were never funded at levels commensurate with the ambitious rhetoric. However, the basic efforts were impressive, with major gains registered throughout the hemisphere until the debacle of the debt brought many of them to a halt in the early 1980s.

## Housing

Housing was the other social sector that was earmarked for special achievement in the decade. Throughout the hemisphere, hundreds of thousands of people were moving from rural to urban areas in search of an improved standard of living. While debates continue to rage over whether their expectations were eventually realized, they came to live in vast slums and their lives were affected by major social disorientation. Better housing was perceived as vital to the long-term stability of the cities. It was also a prime generator of employment. A wide range of institutional initiatives were taken to provide incentives for housing construction, especially in the low and middle ranges. Institutional infrastructure was created, such as housing investment guarantees, savings and loan associations, mortgage banks, discounting facilities, and housing cooperatives. These were supplemented

Table 1.12
Latin America: Number of Hospital Beds with Ratios per Thousand Population
by Country, 1960–1968

| Country | Around 1960 | | Around 1964 | | Around 1968 | |
|---|---|---|---|---|---|---|
| | Number | Ratio per 1 000 Pop. | Number | Ratio per 1 000 Pop. | Number | Ratio per 1 000 Pop. |
| Argentina | 131 772 [a] | 6.4 | 129 435 [b] | 6.1 | 142 000 | 6.0 |
| Barbados | — | — | — | — | 2 625 | 10.4 |
| Bolivia | 6 184 | 1.8 | 7 371 [b] | 2.1 | 9 381 | 2.1 |
| Brazil | 233 503 [a] | 3.4 | 236 930 [b] | 3.2 | 254 000 | 2.9 |
| Chile | 37 869 | 5.0 | 36 290 | 4.3 | 38 230 [d] | 4.0 |
| Colombia | 44 696 | 3.2 | 46 507 | 2.7 | 46 009 [c] | 2.4 |
| Costa Rica | 5 746 [b] | 5.1 | 6 186 | 4.5 | 6 441 | 3.9 |
| Dom. Rep. | 8 024 [t] | 2.7 | — | — | 10 620 [e] | 2.8 |
| Ecuador | 8 803 [a] | 2.1 | 11 199 | 2.3 | 13 021 [e] | 2.4 |
| El Salvador | 5 211 [f g] | 2.0 | 6 375 [h] | 2.3 | 6 966 | 2.1 |
| Guatemala | 10 627 | 2.8 | 11 053 [d] | 2.6 | 11 754 | 2.5 |
| Haiti | 2 316 | 0.7 | — | — | 3 329 | 0.7 |
| Honduras | 3 531 [i] | 2.0 | 4 155 | 2.0 | 4 226 | 1.8 |
| Jamaica | — | — | 6 907 | 4.0 | — | — |
| Mexico | 45 844 [j] | 1.4 | 39 011 | 0.9 | 40 000 | 0.8 |
| Nicaragua | 2 660 [k] | 1.8 | 3 600 | 2.1 | 4 795 | 2.5 |

| | | | | | |
|---|---|---|---|---|---|
| Panama | 3 964 | 3.8 | 4 304 | 2.8 | 4 570 | 3.4 |
| Paraguay | 1 397 · | 0.8 | 4 297 | 2.2 | 4 795 | 2.0 |
| Peru | 23 086 ª | 2.2 | 23 850 ᵇ | 2.2 | 30 507 | 2.4 |
| Trinidad & Tob. | — | — | — | — | 5 209 | 5.1 |
| Uruguay | 11 006 ·ʰ | 3.9 | 16 935 | 6.4 | 13 311 | 4.7 |
| Venezuela | 26 029 | 3.6 | 27 873 | 3.3 | 31 207 | 3.2 |

a. 1959
b. 1962
c. 1967
d. 1969
e. 1966
f. Totals include only beds in government hospitals
g. Totals do not include 500 beds in social security, military and private hospitals.
h. 1963
i. 1957
j. 1958
k. Total does not include the number of beds in mental hospitals
— Not available

Source: OAS-CIES

Table 1.13

Latin America: Achievements in Reducing Child Mortality Rates in Relation to Goals of the Charter of Punta del Este, 1960–1968

| | Under one year | | | | 1-4 years | | | |
| | Death rate per 1 000 live births | | | | Death rate per 1 000 population | | | |
| Country | Average 1960-62 | 1968 | Goal [a] 1968 | Percent of decrease achieved | Average 1960-62 | 1968 | Goal [a] 1968 | Percent of decrease achieved |
|---|---|---|---|---|---|---|---|---|
| Argentina | 61.0 | 60.8 [b] | 42.7 | 2 | 4.3 | 2.6 | 3.0 | 131 |
| Barbados | 65.9 | 45.4 | 42.8 | 89 | 3.7 | 1.8 | 2.4 | 146 |
| Bolivia | 103.0 | 101.6 | 67.0 | 4 | 16.8 | n.a. | n.a. | n.a. |
| Brazil | n.a. | n.a. | n.a. | n.a. | n.a. | n.a. | n.a. | n.a. |
| Chile | 117.8 | 86.6 [a] | 76.6 | 76 | 8.2 | 3.2 | 5.3 | 172 |
| Colombia | 92.8 | 78.3 [b] | 65.0 | 52 | 15.4 | 11.7 | 10.8 | 80 |
| Costa Rica | 66.1 | 62.3 | 46.3 | 19 | 7.5 | 5.3 | 5.2 | 96 |
| Dom. Rep. | 94.1 | 72.6 | 61.2 | 65 | 10.4 | 7.1 | 6.8 | 92 |
| Ecuador | 99.4 | 87.3 [b] | 69.6 | 41 | 22.2 | 14.7 | 15.5 | 112 |
| El Salvador | 72.5 | 59.2 | 47.1 | 52 | 17.1 | 10.0 | 11.1 | 118 |
| Guatemala | 89.3 | 93.8 | 58.0 | n.a. | 32.4 | 27.6 [c] | 24.3 | 59 |
| Haiti | n.a. | n.a. | n.a. | n.a. | n.a. | n.a. | n.a. | n.a. |
| Honduras | 43.4 | 35.5 | 33.9 | 89 | 14.1 | 10.9 | 9.9 | 76 |
| Jamaica | 49.1 | 34.7 | 31.9 | 81 | 6.8 | 5.4 | 4.4 | 58 |
| Mexico | 71.4 | 64.2 | 46.4 | 28 | 13.8 | 9.8 | 9.0 | 83 |
| Nicaragua | 63.1 | 53.2 | 41.0 | 45 | 8.6 | 8.2 | 5.6 | 13 |
| Panama | 51.1 | 39.2 | 33.2 | 66 | 7.9 | 7.3 | 5.1 | 21 |
| Paraguay | 89.7 | 102.8 | 58.3 | n.a. | 9.4 | 11.3 | 6.1 | n.a. |
| Peru | 92.9 | 75.3 [b] | 65.0 | 56 | 15.7 | 9.0 | 11.0 | 143 |
| Trinidad & Tob. | 42.9 | 35.8 [b] | 30.0 | 55 | 2.5 | 1.7 | 1.8 | 114 |
| Uruguay | 44.6 | 49.8 [b] | 31.2 | n.a. | 1.3 | 1.4 | 0.8 | n.a. |
| Venezuela | 52.1 | 44.3 | 33.9 | 43 | 5.7 | 5.2 | 3.7 | 25 |

a. "Goal 1968" refers specifically to the proportion of the goal of the Charter for the Decade, to reduce the present mortality rate of children less than five years of age by at least one-half, achieved as of 1968.

b. 1967.

c. 1966.

by public sector housing and by the involvement of labor organizations in housing programs. The effort resulted in an impressive new infrastructure that has indelibly altered patterns in the housing field.

In housing construction, however, the programs had to contend with the ordeals of Sisyphus, since population growth and improved incomes boosted demand far higher than could be met by official programs. At the end of the Alliance years, the OAS reported that the housing deficit in Latin America grew during the period, with overcrowding and slum areas remaining as intractable problems, seemingly insoluble without a substantial slowdown in population growth.[15] The infrastructure put into place during the Alliance years, however, promised continuing growth in the sector, as the decades following have demonstrated to be true.

### Economic Infrastructure

An impressive variety of measures were employed simultaneously in the concentrated effort to improve economic performance. These included the implementation of national economic planning, the reform of tax structures, the expansion of exports, measures to address the problem of fluctuating commodity prices, the creation of new credit facilities, and the initiation of steps leading to the establishment of a Latin American common market. The latter goal was given further impetus during the 1967 Meeting of Presidents, at which the specific target date of 1985 was set for the achievement of economic integration for all of Latin America.

Performance was mixed, as might have been expected from so ambitious an agenda. Perhaps the greatest success, on paper, came with the almost universal adoption of the concept of national planning. By 1973, the OAS reported that all of the Latin American countries had central planning offices, most at the presidential level, and a number of ministries had established sectoral planning mechanisms. The creation of planning offices and the implementation of national plans, however, were two distinct matters. It was no secret that the effectiveness of the planning efforts were not generally given high marks. Most serious Latin American planners were well aware of the problems.[16] While the Charter of Punta del Este went into considerable detail regarding what a national plan should include, the absence of a political consensus and the diverse perceptions of development strategies were inherent difficulties. Plans could not be abstractions. Unless the major actors in the economic life of the nation participated in the process, the results were more likely to be a wish list than practical prescriptions for development.

This shortcoming was particularly acute regarding the participation of the private sector, whose interest and investment were critical to the attainment of the economic goals. Notwithstanding the widespread perception of the monolithic, impersonal corporations, when the corporate facade is pierced, the private sector stands as a conglomerate of all too human motivations. Their responsiveness to

Table 1.14
Latin America: Number and Percentage of Population Served by Piped Water Supply Systems, 1961–1970
(population in thousands)

| Country | Year | Urban Population [a] | | | Rural Population | | |
|---|---|---|---|---|---|---|---|
| | | Total Population | Total served Number | Percent | Total Population | Total served Number | Percent |
| Argentina | 1961 | 15 531 | 10 146 | 65.3 | 5 570 | 75 | 1.3 |
| | 1970 | 17 783 | 12 700 | 71.0 | 5 650 | 854 | 15.0 |
| Barbados | 1961 | n.a. | n.a. | n.a. | n.a. | n.a. | n.a. |
| | 1970 | 116 | 116 | 100.0 | 138 | 138 | 100.0 |
| Bolivia | 1961 | 1 448 | 808 | 55.8 | 2 367 | n.a. | n.a. |
| | 1970 | 1 072 | 976 | 91.0 | 3 230 | 31 | 1.0 |
| Brazil | 1961 | 32 963 | 18 031 | 54.7 | 40 125 | n.a. | n.a. |
| | 1970 | 50 300 | 28 210 | 56.0 | 46 475 | 2 000 | 4.3 |
| Chile | 1961 | 4 874 | 1 285 | 73.6 | 2 486 | 400 | 16.1 |
| | 1970 | 6 400 | 5 950 | 93.0 | 2 870 | 250 | 9.0 |
| Colombia | 1961 | 6 289 | 1 334 | 78.7 | 8 663 | 3 492 | 40.3 |
| | 1970 [b] | 12 002 | 11 700 | 97.5 | 8 617 | 4 100 | 47.6 |
| Costa Rica | 1961 | 421 | 412 | 97.8 | 766 | 179 | 23.4 |
| | 1970 | 859 | 859 | 100.0 | 894 | 501 | 56.0 |
| Dom. Republic | 1961 | 867 | 375 | 56.7 | 2 095 | 376 | 17.9 |
| | 1970 | 1 604 | 1 225 | 76.3 | 2 408 | 271 | 11.0 |
| Ecuador | 1961 | 1 248 | 726 | 58.2 | 3 183 | n.a. | n.a. |
| | 1970 | 2 277 | 1 701 | 75.0 | 3 728 | 276 | 8.0 |
| El Salvador | 1961 | 799 | 467 | 50.9 | 1 675 | n.a. | n.a. |
| | 1970 | 1 364 | 946 | 70.0 | 2 170 | 583 | 27.0 |

| Country | Year | | | | | | |
|---|---|---|---|---|---|---|---|
| Guatemala | 1961 | 961 | 371 | 38.6 | 2 900 | 2 025 | 69.8 |
| | 1970 | 1 779 | 1 597 | 90.0 | 3 381 | 425 | 13.0 |
| Haiti | 1961 | 402 | 102 | 25.4 | 3 100 | n.a. | n.a. |
| | 1970 | 914 | 400 | 44.0 | 3 952 | 126 | 3.0 |
| Honduras | 1961 | 618 | 212 | 34.3 | 1 373 | 103 | 7.5 |
| | 1970 | 772 | 720 | 93 | 1 864 | 190 | 10.0 |
| Jamaica | 1961 | n.a. | n.a. | n.a. | n.a. | n.a. | n.a. |
| | 1970 | 557 | 543 | 98.0 | 1 422 | 368 | 26.0 |
| Mexico | 1961 | 18 398 | 10 082 | 54.8 | 17 490 | n.a. | n.a. |
| | 1970 | 27 851 | 23 490 | 84.0 | 20 462 | 5 770 | 28.0 |
| Nicaragua | 1961 | 568 | 215 | 37.9 | 950 | 3 | 0.3 |
| | 1970 | 785 | 742 | 95.0 | 1 163 | 120 | 10.3 |
| Panama | 1961 | 514 | 433 | 84.2 | 574 | n.a. | n.a. |
| | 1970 | 676 | 648 | 96.0 | 749 | 67 | 9.0 |
| Paraguay | 1961 | 624 | 172 | 27.6 | 1 146 | n.a. | n.a. |
| | 1970 | 874 | 285 | 33.0 | 1 505 | 88 | 6.0 |
| Peru | 1961 | 4 878 | 3 361 | 68.9 | 5 487 | n.a. | n.a. |
| | 1970 | 5 831 | 4 200 | 72.0 | 7 021 | 840 | 12.0 |
| Trinidad & Tob. | 1961 | n.a. | n.a. | n.a. | n.a. | n.a. | n.a. |
| | 1970 | 358 | 356 | 99.4 | 702 | 666 | 95.0 |
| Uruguay | 1961 | 1 750 | 1 290 | 73.7 | 620 | 15 | 2.4 |
| | 1970 | 2 106 | 2 042 | 97.0 | 732 | 127 | 17.3 |
| Venezuela | 1961 | 4 653 | 2 318 | 49.8 | 2 709 | n.a. | n.a. |
| | 1970 | 6 900 | 6 820 | 99.0 | 3 500 | 2 283 | 65.0 |

a. "Urban" usually refers to cities of 2000 or more inhabitants except for Colombia and Venezuela, where "urban" includes 5000 or more inhabitants.

b. 1969.

n.a. Not available.

Source: OAS-CIES.

31

**Table 1.15**

**Latin America: Number and Percentage of Population Served by Sewerage Systems, 1961–1970 (population in thousands)**

| Country | Year | Urban Population [a] Total Population | Total served Number | Total served Percent | Rural Population Total Population | Total served Number | Total served Percent |
|---|---|---|---|---|---|---|---|
| Argentina | 1961 [b] | 16 410 | 5 600 | 34.1 | n.a. | n.a. | n.a. |
|  | 1970 | 17 783 | 6 200 | 34.9 | n.a. | n.a. | n.a. |
| Barbados | 1961 | n.a. | n.a. | n.a. | n.a. | n.a. | n.a. |
|  | 1970 | 117 | n.a. | n.a. | 138 | n.a. | n.a. |
| Bolivia | 1961 | n.a. | n.a. | n.a. | n.a. | n.a. | n.a. |
|  | 1970 | 1 072 | 320 | 29.8 | 3 230 | n.a. | n.a. |
| Brazil | 1961 | n.a. | n.a. | n.a. | n.a. | n.a. | n.a. |
|  | 1970 | 50 300 | 13 440 | 26.7 | 45 489 | n.a. | n.a. |
| Chile | 1961 | 4 874 | 2 899 | 59.5 | n.a. | n.a. | n.a. |
|  | 1970 | 6 400 | 2 430 | 37.9 | 2 870 | 185 | 6 |
| Colombia | 1961 | 5 932 | 3 645 | 61 | n.a. | n.a. | n.a. |
|  | 1970 [c] | 12 002 | 8 600 | 71.7 | 8 617 | 1 800 | 20.9 |
| Costa Rica | 1961 | 421 | 121 | 28.7 | n.a. | n.a. | n.a. |
|  | 1970 | 859 | 206 | 23.9 | n.a. | n.a. | n.a. |
| Dom. Rep. | 1961 [c] | 918 | 158 | 17.2 | n.a. | n.a. | n.a. |
|  | 1970 | 1 604 | 258 | 16.1 | n.a. | n.a. | n.a. |
| Ecuador | 1961 [c] | 1 248 | 664 | 53.2 | n.a. | n.a. | n.a. |
|  | 1970 | 2 277 | 1 311 | 57.5 | 3 728 | 40 | 1.1 |
| El Salvador | 1961 | n.a. | n.a. | n.a. | n.a. | n.a. | n.a. |
|  | 1969 | 1 142 | 842 | 73.7 | 2 251 | 4 | 0.2 |

| | 1 | 2 | 3 | 4 | 5 | 6 |
|---|---|---|---|---|---|---|
| Guatemala 1961 | 865 | 255 | 29.5 | 2 813 | 1 | 0.0 |
| Guatemala 1970 | 1 779 | 728 | 40.9 | n.a. | n.a. | n.a. |
| Haiti 1961 | 402 | n.a. | n.a. | n.a. | n.a. | n.a. |
| Haiti 1970 | 914 | 75 | 8.2 | n.a. | n.a. | n.a. |
| Honduras 1961 | 618 | 126 | 20.4 | n.a. | n.a. | n.a. |
| Honduras 1970 | 772 | 387 | 50.1 | 1 864 | 2 | 0.1 |
| Jamaica 1961 | n.a. | n.a. | n.a. | n.a. | n.a. | n.a. |
| Jamaica 1970 | 557 | 113 | 20.3 | 1 422 | 8 | 0.5 |
| Mexico 1961 | n.a. | n.a. | n.a. | n.a. | n.a. | n.a. |
| Mexico 1970 | 27 851 | 14 040 | 50.4 | n.a. | n.a. | n.a. |
| Nicaragua 1961 | 568 | 92 | 16.2 | n.a. | n.a. | n.a. |
| Nicaragua 1970 | 785 | 342 | 43.6 | n.a. | n.a. | n.a. |
| Panama 1961 | n.a. | n.a. | n.a. | n.a. | n.a. | n.a. |
| Panama 1970 | 676 | 460 | 68.0 | 749 | 54 | 0.5 |
| Paraguay 1961 b | 750 | 100 | 13.3 | n.a. | n.a. | n.a. |
| Paraguay 1970 | 874 | 125 | 14.3 | n.a. | n.a. | n.a. |
| Peru 1961 c | 4 878 | 2 500 | 51.3 | n.a. | n.a. | n.a. |
| Peru 1970 | 5 831 | 3 700 | 63.5 | 7 021 | 12 | 0.1 |
| Trinidad & Tob. 1961 | n.a. | n.a. | n.a. | n.a. | n.a. | n.a. |
| Trinidad & Tob. 1970 | 358 | 181 | 50.6 | 702 | 2 | 0.3 |
| Uruguay 1961 | 1 750 | 889 | 50.8 | n.a. | n.a. | n.a. |
| Uruguay 1970 | 2 106 | 1 200 | 56.9 | n.a. | n.a. | n.a. |
| Venezuela 1970 | 4 371 | 1 318 | 30.2 | 2 917 | 67 | 2.3 |
| Venezuela 1961 c | 6 900 | 3 272 | 47.4 | 3 500 | 100 | 2.8 |

a. "Urban" usually refers to cities of 2 000 or more inhabitants except for Colombia and Venezuela, where "urban" includes 5 000 or more inhabitants.
b. 1967.
c. 1960.
n.a. Not available.

Source: OAS-CIES.

33

Table 1.16
Latin America: Total Enrollment and Percentages of School-Age Population
Enrolled at the Different Levels of Education, 1950–1970 (in thousands)

| Country | Year | Primary | | Secondary [a] | | Higher | |
|---|---|---|---|---|---|---|---|
| | | Enrollment | % | Enrollment | % | Enrollment | % |
| Argentina [b] | 1950 | 2 212.0 | 85.1 | 322.2 | 17.5 | n.a. | n.a. |
| | 1960 | 2 947.7 | 90.4 | 776.2 | 32.0 [c] | 155.6 [d] | n.a. |
| | 1970 | 3 632.1 | 100.2 | 974.8 | 37.0 | 274.6 | 16.7 |
| Bolivia | 1950 | n.a. | n.a. | 16.7 | 5.1 | 12.0 | n.a. |
| | 1960 | 400.3 | 55.7 | 45.3 | 10.0 [c] | | |
| | 1970 | 612.5 | 69.8 | 128.9 | 22.8 [c] | 25.6 | 7.8 [f] |
| Brazil | 1950 | 4 352.0 | 41.8 | 540.7 | 7.9 | n.a. | n.a. |
| | 1960 | 7 458.0 | 52.8 | 1 076.2 | 13.6 [c] | 87.5 | 1.8 [g] |
| | 1970 | 13 413.8 [h] | 71.8 | 4 214.3 | 34.4 | 399.6 | 5.8 |
| Chile [i] | 1950 | 774.6 | 71.2 | 145.8 | 21.0 | n.a. | n.a. |
| | 1960 | 1 162.6 | 80.8 | 223.6 | 27.3 [j] | 19.1 | 3.6 [g] |
| | 1969 | 1 980.8 | 104.9 | 264.9 | 21.6 | 52.9 | 8.0 [c] |
| Colombia | 1950 | 808.5 | 36.7 | 74.9 | 5.0 | n.a. | n.a. |
| | 1960 | 1 690.4 | 49.8 | 224.3 [c] | 12.7 [c] | 19.2 | 1.9 [g] |
| | 1968 | 2 733.4 | 60.7 | 586.7 | 21.7 | 62.8 | 4.6 |
| Costa Rica | 1950 | 112.6 | 70.0 | 7.8 | 7.4 | n.a. | n.a. |
| | 1960 | 202.8 | 78.3 | 25.7 | 17.8 [c] | 3.1 | 3.8 [g] |
| | 1969 | 345.1 | 90.0 | 64.3 | 27.8 | 11.4 | 10.4 [c] |
| Dom. Rep. | 1950 | 229.0 | 51.2 | 10.7 | 3.7 | n.a. | n.a. |
| | 1960 | 496.9 | 74.9 | 19.9 | 5.1 [c] | 4.0 | 2.0 [g] |
| | 1967 | 725.9 | 78.9 | 89.5 | 16.2 [c] | 9.9 | 3.5 |

| Country | Year | | | | | | |
|---|---|---|---|---|---|---|---|
| Ecuador | 1950 | 314.7 | 53.9 | 29.1 | 7.2 | n.a. | n.a. |
| | 1960 | 596.0 | 67.2 | 48.3 | 9.7[d] | 77.4 | 2.4[k] |
| | 1969 | 975.5 | 78.1 | 194.7 | 25.7 | 21.5 | 5.4[o] |
| El Salvador | 1950 | 145.2 | 39.8 | 7.7 | 3.1 | n.a. | n.a. |
| | 1960 | 297.5 | 57.3 | 29.9 | 9.7[c] | 2.4 | n.a. |
| | 1969 | 516.9 | 73.8 | 84.6 | 19.7 | 4.5 | 2.0 |
| Guatemala | 1950 | 164.8 | 30.5 | 21.2 | 5.6 | n.a. | n.a. |
| | 1960 | 297.0 | 37.8 | 35.8 | 7.7[d] | 3.2 | 1.3[k] |
| | 1968 | 493.2 | 46.9 | 65.8 | 9.9[d] | 11.9 | 3.5 |
| Haiti | 1950 | 119.1 | 18.6 | 8.2 | 2.0 | n.a. | n.a. |
| | 1960 | 248.9 | 30.7 | 13.2 | 2.9 | 1.0 | 0.4[l] |
| | 1965 | 283.8 | 31.2 | 24.0 | 4.2 | 2.6 | 0.8 |
| Honduras | 1950 | 104.0 | 39.0 | 5.0 | 2.9 | n.a. | n.a. |
| | 1960 | 205.1 | 50.6 | 14.9 | 6.2[c] | 1.3 | 0.9[o] |
| | 1968 | 377.0 | 72.0 | 34.7 | 11.3 | 3.5 | 2.0 |
| Mexico | 1950 | 2 666.4 | 51.0 | 113.5 | 3.4 | n.a. | n.a. |
| | 1960 | 4 885.0 | 65.7 | 296.8 | 7.1[d] | 123.0 | 5.0[k] |
| | 1969 | 8 539.5 | 81.3 | 1 319.4 | 20.4 | 188.0 | 5.4 |
| Nicaragua | 1950 | 80.0 | 35.9 | n.a. | n.a. | n.a. | n.a. |
| | 1960 | 137.3 | 45.6 | 8.5 | 4.7[c] | 1.0 | 0.9[k] |
| | 1970 | 278.8 | 60.8 | 44.9 | 16.1 | 6.0 | 4.6[o] |
| Panama | 1950 | 110.0 | 75.2 | 18.6 | 20.4 | n.a. | n.a. |
| | 1960 | 161.8 | 78.2 | 37.0 | 27.4[c] | 3.3 | 4.6[k] |
| | 1968 | 222.5 | 82.7 | 66.7 | 39.5 | 10.1 | 10.2 |
| Paraguay | 1950 | 195.0 | 70.3 | 15.8 | 9.5 | n.a. | n.a. |
| | 1960 | 301.7 | 80.2 | 30.4 | 13.4[c] | 2.9 | 2.3[k] |
| | 1969 | 408.5 | 81.0 | 51.4 | 16.0 | 6.9 | 4.1[o] |
| Peru[1] | 1950 | 971.2 | 58.9 | 80.8 | 7.0 | n.a. | n.a. |
| | 1960 | 1 440.0 | 71.0 | 202.1 | 15.1[c] | 18.8 | 2.4[k] |
| | 1968 | 2 403.9 | 89.2 | 510.5 | 30.9[m] | 88.1 | 9.9[m] |

(continued)

Table 1.16 (continued)

| Country | Year | Primary Enrollment | Primary % | Secondary [a] Enrollment | Secondary [a] % | Higher Enrollment | Higher % |
|---|---|---|---|---|---|---|---|
| Uruguay | 1950 | 249.4 | n.a. | 34.2 | n.a. | n.a. | n.a. |
|  | 1960 | 301.0 | 84.1 | 55.0 | n.a. | 16.9 | n.a. |
|  | 1968 | 342.4 | 86.6 | 117.2 [m] | 42.5 [m] | 17.6 | n.a. |
| Venezuela | 1950 | 503.1 | 51.7 | 39.3 | 6.4 | n.a. | n.a. |
|  | 1960 | 1 223.0 | 78.7 | 108.0 | 13.5 [g] | 17.0 [g] | 3.6 [g] |
|  | 1968 | 1 639.5 | 76.0 | 430.2 | 32.7 | 72.6 [f] | 10.0 [f] |

a. In Costa Rica and Venezuela (1950), includes only general education.
b. Primary cycle of seven years.
c. 1959.
d. 1957.
e. 1968.
f. 1969.
g. 1958.
h. Estimate.
i. Primary cycle of six years until 1966, seven years in 1966, and eight years in 1967.
j. 1956.
k. 1955.
l. In Peru, primary enrollment includes pre-primary grades.
m. 1967.
n.a. Not available.

*Note:* The age ranges used to calculate the percentages of school-age population to which the enrollment figures correspond are the following:
Primary education: 7-14 years
Secondary education: 13-18 years
Higher education: 19-22 years.

Source:   OAS-CIES.

Table 1.17
Latin America: Adult Literacy Rates[1] — 1950, 1960, and 1970 (in percentages)

| Country | Data from Census of the Americas | | Estimated |
| | 1950 | 1960 | 1970 |
| --- | --- | --- | --- |
| Argentina | 86 [a] | 91 | 94 |
| Bolivia | 32 | 40 | 47 |
| Brazil | 49 | 61 | 71 |
| Chile | 80 [b] | 84 | 89 |
| Colombia | 49 [(E)] | 73 [d] | 78 |
| Costa Rica | 79 | 84 [e] | 89 |
| Dom. Rep. | 43 | 65 | 70 |
| Ecuador | 58 | 68 [f] | 73 |
| El Salvador | 38 | 49 [g] | 58 |
| Guatemala | 29 [c] | 38 [d] | 45 |
| Haiti | 11 | 20 [h] | 24 |
| Honduras | 35 | 47 | 57 |
| Mexico | 56 | 62 | 73 |
| Nicaragua | 38 | 50 [e] | 60 |
| Panama | 70 | 77 | 83 |
| Paraguay | 66 | 75 [f] | 78 |
| Peru | 47 [(E)] | 61 [g] | 71 |
| Uruguay | 85 [(E)] | 90 [e] | 93 |
| Venezuela | 51 | 63 [g] | 70 |
| Barbados [2] | 91 [i] | 98 [j] | 98 |
| Jamaica [2] | 74 [k] | 82 | n.a. |
| Trinidad & Tob. [2] | 74 | 88 | 93 |
| *LATIN AMERICA* | 52 | 67 | 73 |

1. Population 15 years of age and over.
2. Not a member of the OAS at start of Alliance for Progress.
E. Estimated.

| | | |
| --- | --- | --- |
| [a]1947 | [e]1963 | [i]1946 |
| [b]1952 | [f]1962 | [j]1967 |
| [c]1951 | [g]1961 | [k]1943 |
| [d]1964 | [h]1965 | n.a. not available |

Source:   IDB, Social Progress Trust Fund, *Socio-Economic Progress in Latin America*, 1969.

economic policies and incentives result either in generating confidence and in-creased economic activity or in capital flight. It was one of the most sensitive issues for national planners. Unfortunately, few of them had experience in the private sector or understood its motivations. Coupled with the traditional suspi-cion of the motives of the private sector that was built into the cultural percep-tions of Latin American society, the results of planning left much to be desired.

The measures taken to promote tax and agrarian reform were a major problem when taken together with the expressed desire of the Alliance planners to increase savings and investment. Placing these measures in juxtaposition with investment incentives in the same overall program was the epitome of contrasts. It was

Table 1.18
Latin America: Central Government Expenditures for Average Annual Effort Made in Each Sector, 1956–1969 (as a percentage of total annual expenditures)

| Country | Education | Health | Public Works | Defense | Interest on Public Debt |
|---|---|---|---|---|---|
| *Argentina* | | | | | |
| 1956-60 | 10.6 | 6.4 | 20.2 | 19.7 | 8.4 [a] |
| 1961-65 | 12.6 | 5.8 | 14.3 | 16.2 | 5.3 |
| 1966-69 | 13.9 | 10.2 [b] | 11.2 | 15.2 | 3.2 |
| *Bolivia* | | | | | |
| 1956-60 | 11.2 | 2.9 | | 8.1 | |
| 1961-65 | 23.9 | 3.0 | 5.5 | 13.9 | |
| 1966-69 | 31.6 | 3.4 | 7.8 | 15.1 | |
| *Brazil* | | | | | |
| 1956-60 | | | 23.5 | 25.7 | |
| 1961-65 | 6.7 | 2.9 | 22.1 | 16.5 | |
| 1966-69 | 7.0 | 10.4 | 16.2 | 21.2 | |
| *Chile* | | | | | |
| 1956-60 | 16.2 | 8.9 [d] | | 17.6 | 6.0 |
| 1961-65 | 14.1 | 9.3 [d] | | 10.5 | 8.8 |
| 1966-68 | 16.6 | 8.5 [d] | | 9.6 | 7.1 |
| *Colombia* | | | | | |
| 1956-60 | 8.4 | 4.9 | | 19.9 | 3.6 |
| 1961-65 | 14.4 | 5.3 | | 22.8 | 3.9 |
| 1966-69 | 14.5 | 5.0 | | 22.8 | 4.1 |
| *Costa Rica* | | | | | |
| 1956-60 | 23.5 | 2.6 | | 4.1 | 6.8 [c] |
| 1961-65 | 25.6 | 2.3 | | | 7.1 |
| 1966-68 | 29.5 | 3.7 | | | 7.5 |
| *Dominican Republic* | | | | | |
| 1956-60 | | | | | |
| 1961-65 | 9.9 | 6.9 [e] | 14.9 | 20.6 | |
| 1966-69 | 14.8 | 11.0 [e] | 14.0 | 14.4 | |
| *Ecuador* | | | | | |
| 1956-60 | 11.3 | 3.3 | | 20.8 | 3.7 |
| 1961-65 | 15.7 | 4.0 | | 16.3 | 7.0 |
| 1966-69 | 19.3 | 2.9 | | 14.7 | 8.2 |
| *El Salvador* | | | | | |
| 1956-60 | 16.5 | 10.4 | 14.8 | 10.2 | 3.0 [c] |
| 1961-65 | 22.1 | 11.0 | 12.8 | 11.3 | 4.0 [c] |

(continued)

Table 1.18  (continued)

| Country | Education | Health | Public Works | Defense | Interest on Public Debt |
|---------|-----------|--------|--------------|---------|--------------------------|
| 1966-68 | 25.0 | 13.0 | 10.0 | 10.8 | 2.8 ° |
| *Guatemala* | | | | | |
| 1956-60 | 20.8 | | 30.0 | 8.7 | 1.5 ° |
| 1961-65 | 23.2 | | 17.5 | 9.6 | 3.2 ° |
| 1966-68 | 24.5 | | 13.3 | 10.7 | 4.6 ° |
| *Haiti* | | | | | |
| 1956-60 | 10.9 | 9.6 | | 18.7 | 9.6 ° |
| 1961-65 | 10.7 | 11.5 | | 23.4 | 7.2 ° |
| 1966-68 | 11.4 | 12.3 | | 25.3 | 8.3 ° |
| *Honduras* | | | | | |
| 1956-60 | 12.3 | 4.4 | 21.5 | 10.6 | |
| 1961-65 | 21.5 | 6.0 | 20.3 | 11.6 | 3.4 ° |
| 1966-69 | 22.4 | 8.0 | 21.4 | 8.7 | 3.1 ° |
| *Jamaica* | | | | | |
| 1956-60 | | | | | |
| 1962-65 | 15.9 | 11.8 | 2.9 | | 9.2 |
| 1965-68 | 15.4 | 11.0 | 2.5 | | 11.0 |
| *Mexico* | | | | | |
| 1956-60 | 13.9 | 5.2 | | 9.1 | 2.8 |
| 1961-65 | 15.8 | 4.4 | 5.7 | 7.2 | 5.6 ° |
| 1966-68 | 15.6 | 3.8 | 5.0 | 5.5 | 14.5 ° |
| *Nicaragua* | | | | | |
| 1956-60 | | | | | |
| 1961-65 | 16.6 | 4.9 | 16.7 | 17.1 | |
| 1966-68 | 17.5 | 6.7 | 20.5 | 13.3 | 1.8 |
| *Panama* | | | | | |
| 1956-60 | 19.0 | | 17.0 | | 12.4 ° |
| 1961-65 | 28.7 | 17.5 ᶠ | 10.1 | | 5.6 |
| 1966-68 | 29.5 | 16.0 ᶠ | 9.8 | | 6.0 |
| *Paraguay* | | | | | |
| 1956-60 | 15.3 | 5.5 | 2.3 | 27.0 | 7.6 ° |
| 1961-65 | 17.0 | 4.7 | 1.9 | 22.0 | 10.5 ° |
| 1966-69 | 16.1 | 3.6 | 3.4 | 21.5 | 5.2 ° |
| *Peru* | | | | | |
| 1956-60 | 23.3 | 4.1 | 4.7 | 22.4 | |
| 1961-65 | 23.1 | 7.2 | 10.6 | 18.1 | |
| 1966-70 | | | | | |

(continued)

Table 1.18    (continued)

| Country | Education | Health | Public Works | Defense | Interest on Public Debt |
|---------|-----------|--------|--------------|---------|-------------------------|
| *United States* | | | | | |
| 1956-60 | | | | 60.3 | 10.5 |
| 1961-65 | 1.2 | 22.7 * | | 46.0 | 7.4 |
| 1966-69 | 3.7 ᵈ | 4.5 | | 43.9 | 8.2 |
| *Venezuela* | | | | | |
| 1956-60 | 7.1 | | | 10.0 | 0.0 |
| 1961-65 | 11.8 | 11.7 | 15.5 ʰ | 9.7 | 0.7 |
| 1966-69 | 14.0 | 12.4 | 13.1 ʰ | 10.1 | 0.8 |

a. Includes debt amortizations in 1956/58.
b. Includes "other social services."
c. Covers all public debt services.
d. Includes labor.
e. Includes social work.
f. Includes social work and labor.
g. Includes labor and welfare.
h. Covers transportation and communications.

Source:   OAS-CIES.

virtually impossible to discuss and implement meaningful tax and agrarian reform and, in the same breath, try to calm the nerves of investors. In that sense, the attempts to encourage private investors during the period were a vital expression of overall policy and good will. At least the political debate recognized the issues and there was some balance in the messages that reached the ears of the investors.

The results of the tax reform efforts were impressive. The Charter of Punta del Este called for the reform of tax structure, both for the purposes of fiscal soundness and also for social equity. For too long the brunt of prevailing Latin American systems of indirect taxation had fallen upon the lower-income groups. At the beginning of the decade there were few taxes on overall income. The traditional structure involved taxes on the source of the income—scheduled taxes—which were related to the occupation of the taxpayer, not to his ability to pay. By the end of the decade, virtually all of the governments had changed the philosophy behind their tax structures and had implemented new legislation. A major tax reform program operated by the OAS, with the backstopping of the Harvard taxation program, assisted 20 countries to draft new tax codes and improve fiscal administration, including the training of tax officials and auditors. Internal revenues improved in all of the countries (see Table 1.19). The effort resulted in a substantial change in the sources of revenue available to support government operations. The importance of customs taxes (both export taxes (!) and import duties) declined, while income and sales taxes increased (see Table 1.20).

Table 1.19
Latin America: Average Tax Coefficient—1950–1960, 1961–1965, and 1966–1970

| Country | 1950-60 | 1961-65 | 1966-70 |
|---|---|---|---|
| Argentina | 16.2 [a] | 17.4 | 21.7 |
| Barbados | 20.4 [b] | 24.5 | n.a. |
| Bolivia | 11.6 [c] | 12.0 | 12.3 [d] |
| Brazil | 17.5 | 19.0 | 26.6 |
| Chile | n.a. | n.a. | n.a. |
| Colombia [a] | 9.3 | 9.2 | 12.0 [e] |
| Costa Rica | 12.2 [f] | 11.5 | 11.2 [g] |
| Dominican Republic | n.a. | 20.5 | 16.5 [e] |
| Ecuador | 14.2 | 16.1 | 16.8 |
| El Salvador | 11.5 | 10.1 | 9.8 [g] |
| Guatemala | 8.2 [f] | 7.0 | 7.8 [g] |
| Haiti | n.a. | n.a. | n.a. |
| Honduras | 8.0 [f] | 8.6 | 10.2 [g] |
| Jamaica | n.a. | 14.7 | 16.1 [g] |
| Mexico | n.a. | 10.5 | 11.7 [h] |
| Nicaragua | 10.3 [f] | 9.4 | 8.8 [g] |
| Panama | n.a. | n.a. | n.a. |
| Paraguay | n.a. | 8.6 [i] | 10.4 [j] |
| Peru | 12.5 | 15.4 | 15.1 [k] |
| Trinidad and Tobago | n.a. | 16.9 [i] | 16.9 [d] |
| Uruguay | 15.1 [a] | 14.9 | 14.9 [g] |
| Venezuela | 19.4 [b] | 20.6 | 19.5 |

    a. 1955-60.
    b. 1960.
    c. 1958-60.
    d. 1966-67.
    e. 1966-68.
    f. 1953-60.
    g. 1966-69.
    h. 1967.
    i. 1962-65.
    j. 1967-69.
    k. 1966.
    n.a. Not available.

Source: OAS-CIES.

Perhaps the most utopian of all the Alliance plans came in the field of economic integration, where the ambitions of the planners openly challenged the underlying realities. The concept of integration was firmly ensconced in Latin American development thinking long before the Alliance came into being. Both the Central American Common Market and the Latin American Free Trade Association predated the Alliance, indicative of the directions of Latin American planners even before the U.S. got into the picture. The Andean Group and Caribbean Common Market came into being at a later time.

The rhetoric for integration was always impressive, culminating in full verbal support at the highest political levels, as evidenced by the Declaration of the

Table 1.20
Latin America: Composition of Central Government Revenues, 1956–1970
(sources of revenue expressed as percentages of total, with total expressed in millions of each country's monetary unit)

| Country | Export Tax | Import Tax | Tax on Goods & Services | Income Tax | Tax on Net Worth | Other Taxes | Nontax Revenues | Total (National Currency) |
|---|---|---|---|---|---|---|---|---|
| **Argentina 1/** | | | | | | | | |
| 1958-60 | 26.4 | 3.3 | 21.9 | 9.8 | 3.0 | 0.8 | 35.0 | 68.6 |
| 1961-65 | 18.4 | 3.0 | 21.3 | 12.8 | 2.6 | 0.6 | 41.8 | 200.4 |
| 1966-69 | 17.2 | 0.8 | 25.1 | 12.9 | 3.8 | 0.8 | 39.5 | 701.7 |
| **Barbados** | | | | | | | | |
| 1956-60 | | | | | | | | |
| 1961-64 | | 35.1 | 10.3 | 33.2 | | | 21.4 | 28.5 |
| 1965-68 | | 36.3 | 7.0 | 31.4 | | | 25.2 | 42.9 |
| **Bolivia** | | | | | | | | |
| 1961-62 | 16.8 | 43.1 | 11.0 | 13.9 | | | 15.2 | 445 |
| 1962-67 | 8.2 | 48.0 | 22.6 | 14.9 | 2.0 | 3.7 | | 665.2 |
| 1968-69 | | 47.4 | | | | 44.9 | 7.7 | |
| **Brazil** | | | | | | | | |
| 1956-60 | | 7.7 | 34.0 | 29.5 | | | 28.8 | 123,145.6 |
| 1961-65 | | 8.8 | 40.3 | 25.4 | | 12.4 | 13.2 | 1,477.4 |
| 1966-68 | | 6.0 | 38.2 | 20.2 | | 11.5 | 24.1 | 8,392.3 |

| | A | B | C | D | E | F |
|---|---|---|---|---|---|---|
| **Chile** | | | | | | |
| 1956-60 | 16.7 | 40.4 | 31.9 | 5.3 | 5.8 | 313.4 |
| 1961-65 | 16.2 | 41.2 | 29.8 | 7.5 | 5.3 | 1,655 |
| 1966-68 | 11.0 | 42.5 | 35.1 | 6.7 | 4.7 | 6,656 |
| **Colombia** | | | | | | |
| 1956-60 | 27.8 | 11.6 | 50.3 | | 10.3 | 1,286 |
| 1961-65 | 24.4 | 11.9 | 49.3 | | 14.4 | 3,411 |
| 1966-69 | 25.0 | 21.0 | 44.5 | | 9.5 | 8,565 |
| **Costa Rica** | | | | | | |
| 1956-60 | 4.7 | 53.0 | 14.5 | 16.6 | 11.2 | 320.1 |
| 1961-65 | 5.0 | 48.2 | 11.5 | 20.4 | 15.0 | 407.9 |
| 1966-68 | 5.2 | 32.5 | 28.5 | 23.9 | 10.1 | 577.5 |
| **Dominican Republic** | | | | | | |
| 1959-60 | 15.2 | 31.5 | 22.8 | 15.5 | 15.0 | 142.8 |
| 1961-65 | 4.8 | 35.7 | 23.6 | 16.0 | 19.9 | 155.9 |
| 1966-69 | 3.7 | 41.7 | 18.7 | 24.3 | 11.7 | 185.1 |
| **Ecuador** | | | | | | |
| 1956-60 | 6.6 | 40.7 | 29.1 | 14.5 | 9.0 | 1,326.8 |
| 1961-65 | 8.3 | 40.4 | 23.4 | 15.6 | 12.4 | 1,773 |
| 1966-69 | 5.3 | 47.8 | 17.5 | 15.1 | 14.4 | 2,665 |
| **El Salvador** | | | | | | |
| 1956-60 | 21.2 | 36.1 | 21.6 | 12.0 | 9.0 | 171.8 |
| 1961-65 | 13.8 | 31.9 | 27.1 | 16.4 | 10.8 | 194.8 |
| 1966-69 | 12.0 | 24.9 | 32.4 | 23.6 | 8.2 | 245.3 |

(continued)

Table 1.20  (continued)

| Country | Export Tax | Import Tax | Tax on Goods & Services | Income Tax | Tax on Net Worth | Other Taxes | Nontax Revenues | Total (National Currency) |
|---|---|---|---|---|---|---|---|---|
| **Guatemala** | | | | | | | | |
| 1956-60 | 13.9 | 31.4 | 27.1 | 8.7 | | | 19.0 | 89.3 |
| 1961-65 | 7.1 | 27.0 | 32.0 | 8.8 | 2.2 | | 22.9 | 102.8 |
| 1966-68 | 5.0 | 20.6 | 43.2 | 10.9 | 3.4 | | 16.9 | 129.2 |
| **Haiti** | | | | | | | | |
| 1957-60 | 17.1 | 35.9 | 14.4 | 10.9 | | | 11.5 | 151.6 |
| 1961-65 | 15.7 | 33.6 | 28.1 | 9.1 | | | 9.7 | 138.3 |
| 1966-68 | | | 30.2 | 9.3 | | | 11.4 | 140.6 |
| **Honduras** | | | | | | | | |
| 1956-60 | 4.3 | 43.8 | 23.4 | 16.1 | | | 12.3 | 69.9 |
| 1961-65 | 4.8 | 42.8 | 26.1 | 14.8 | | | 11.4 | 85.6 |
| 1966-69 | 4.0 | 30.4 | 30.1 | 27.1 | | | 8.4 | 137.0 |
| **Jamaica** | | | | | | | | |
| 1956-60 | | 29.0 | 18.0 | 35.2 | | | 17.8 | 94.4 |
| 1962-65 | | 23.7 | 23.3 | 33.5 | | | 19.5 | 137.7 |
| 1966-69 | | | | | | | | |
| **Mexico** | | | | | | | | |
| 1956-60 | 12.2 | 14.0 | 26.4 | 27.6 | | 2.8 | 19.8 | 10,814.1 |
| 1961-65 | 7.4 | 14.1 | 26.7 | 33.3 | | 2.6 | 15.6 | 16,643 |
| 1966-68 | 4.2 | 15.7 | 26.3 | 36.8 | | | 14.0 | 27,959 |

| | | | | | | | | |
|---|---|---|---|---|---|---|---|---|
| **Nicaragua** | | | | | | | | |
| 1957-60 | 5.7 | 50.4 | 15.9 | 8.9 | 4.7 | 6.3 | 9.9 | 245.9 |
| 1961-65 | 1.9 | 40.6 | 23.9 | 13.1 | 7.3 | 4.3 | 15.6 | 340.3 |
| 1966-68 | 1.8 | 30.1 | 31.0 | | | 5.2 | 11.5 | 464.5 |
| **Panama** | | | | | | | | |
| 1956-70 | 0.3 | 31.7 | 20.2 | 23.2 | | 10.0 | 24.8 | 52.4 |
| 1961-65 | 0.4 | 27.3 | 15.0 | 22.4 | | 9.4 | 24.9 | 73.1 |
| 1965-68 | | 22.8 | 15.2 | 30.4 | | | 21.8 | 110.8 |
| **Paraguay** | | | | | | | | |
| 1956-60 | 6.8 | 22.1 | 10.4 | 11.3 | 5.6 | 24.0 | 36.5 | 2,128 |
| 1961-65 | 2.9 | 23.2 | 6.0 | 11.2 | 5.1 | 20.0 | 22.7 | 3,692 |
| 1966-69 | | 21.0 | | | | 27.1 | 26.6 | 4,910 |
| **Peru 2/** | | | | | | | | |
| 1956-60 | 0.8 | 17.1 | 27.2 | 35.0 3/ | | 36.8 | 28.2 | 3,970 |
| 1961-65 | 1.1 | 25.0 | 33.3 | 32.2 | | | 22.7 | 10,346 |
| 1966-69 | | | | 28.6 | | | 12.1 | 22,212 |
| **Trinidad & Tobago** | | | | | | | | |
| 1956-60 | | 24.5 | | 32.3 | | | 43.3 | 224.7 |
| 1961-65 | | 22.1 | | 33.1 | | | 44.8 | 292.8 |
| 1966-68 | | | | | | | | |
| **United States** | | | | | | | | |
| 1958-60 | 1.1 | | 23.7 | 66.2 | 1.7 | | 7.4 | 86,210 |
| 1961-65 | 1.1 | | 25.9 | 63.9 | 2.1 | | 6.9 | 107,762 |
| 1966-69 | 1.3 | | 27.0 | 64.7 | 2.1 | | 5.0 | 155,490 |

(continued)

Table 1.20 (continued)

| Country | Export Tax | Import Tax | Tax on Goods & Services | Income Tax | Tax on Net Worth | Other Taxes | Nontax Revenues | Total (National Currency) |
|---|---|---|---|---|---|---|---|---|
| **Uruguay** 4/ | | | | | | | | |
| 1956-60 | 8.8 | | | 37.5 | | 23.9 | 29.8 | 956.5 |
| 1961-65 | 5.8 | | 19.0 | 28.9 | | 19.0 | 27.4 | 4,175 |
| 1966-69 | 5.4 | | 20.6 | 26.0 | | 19.5 | 28.5 | 35,623 |
| **Venezuela** | | | | | | | | |
| 1959-60 | 36.3 | 14.2 | 8.4 | 8.2 | | | 32.9 | 5,203.5 |
| 1961-65 | 40.3 | 7.2 | 8.0 | 10.3 | | | 34.3 | 6,478 |
| 1966-69 | 35.7 | 5.9 | 8.6 | 13.5 | | | 36.4 | 8,437 |

Source: OAS-CIES

1/ Export tax includes surcharges on exports and imports
2/ Excludes use of loans
3/ Direct taxes
4/ Data on income taxes include all direct taxes

Chiefs of State in their meeting of 1967. Financial support was forthcoming from the Inter-American Development Bank, which became, in effect, a bank for integration, financing projects that contributed to intra-regional trade. The U.S. Agency for International Development played a minor role, except in Central America where integration was one of the priority issues.

While the record of the failure to achieve integration is well known and widely discussed, the impact on intra-regional trade was significant. Trade among the Latin American nations, negligible at the start of the integration drive, expanded considerably during the Alliance years and the decade that followed. The increases in intra-regional trade were impressive. In 1962, intra-Central American trade stood at $40 million, or 8.5 percent of the region's total exports of $468 million. By 1973, trade among the Central American nations had increased to $388 million, or 23.5 percent of a total export trade of $1.6 billion (see Table 1.21). By 1980, regional trade in Central America had reached $1.161 billion (Table 1.22). The nations involved in the Latin American Free Trade Association (LAFTA), which was later restructured into the Latin American Integration Association (ALADI), also saw significant increases in intra-zonal trade, which rose from $624 million or 7.6 percent of total exports of $8.2 billion in 1962 to $2.2 billion, or 11.4 percent of total exports of $19.2 billion in 1973 (see Table 1.23). By 1980, the LAFTA member nations had reached total intra-regional trade of $8.5 billion (Table 1.24).

The record for the Andean Group, established in 1969, is equally impressive. Intra-regional trade stood at $77 million in 1970, shortly after the formation of the association, and increased to $1.1 billion by 1980, a growth of almost 1,500 percent within the decade (see Table 1.25). The overall record of all of the nations now demonstrates an average intra-regional trade level of 20–30 percent in the basic trade patterns of each of the nations involved in the common markets (see Table 1.26). Whether this trade pattern would have evolved without the impetus

Table 1.21
Central American Exports: Total and Intra-zonal—1960–1962, 1972, and 1973 (millions of dollars)

| | Annual average 1960-62 | | | 1972 | | | 1973ᵃ | | |
|---|---|---|---|---|---|---|---|---|---|
| | Total | Intra-zonal | % Intra-zonal | Total | Intra-zonal | % Intra-zonal | Total | Intra-zonal | % Intra-zonal |
| Costa Rica | $ 88.1 | $ 1.9 | 2.2 | $ 284.0 | $ 50.1 | 17.6 | $ 342.4 | $ 69.2 | 20.2 |
| El Salvador | 120.1 | 15.2 | 12.7 | 278.7 | 85.9 | 30.8 | 358.4 | 106.8 | 29.8 |
| Guatemala | 116.3 | 10.3 | 8.9 | 327.5 | 105.6 | 32.2 | 436.2 | 137.6 | 31.5 |
| Honduras | 73.6 | 9.8 | 13.3 | 187.9 | 6.7 | 3.6 | 236.8 | 13.2 | 5.6 |
| Nicaragua | 69.8 | 2.8 | 4.0 | 250.1 | 56.3 | 22.5 | 276.7 | 61.5 | 22.2 |
| **Total** | **$467.9** | **$40.0** | **8.5** | **$1,328.2** | **$304.7** | **22.9** | **$1,650.5** | **$388.3** | **23.5** |

Source: IDB, *Economic and Social Progress*, 1974

Table 1.22
Central American Exports: Total and Intra-zonal, by Country —
1980 (thousands of dollars)

| Exports Countries | Total Exports | Imports Countries | | | | |
|---|---|---|---|---|---|---|
| | | Guatemala | El Salvador | Honduras | Nicaragua | Costa Rica |
| Guatemala | | | | | | |
| 1979 | 309,898 | — | 162,487 | 47,726 | 30,158 | 69,527 |
| 1980 | 438,664 | — | 193,984 | 60,591 | 93,247 | 90,842 |
| El Salvador | | | | | | |
| 1979 | 263,616 | 172,364 | — | — | 23,471 | 67,781 |
| 1980 | 296,391 | 171,478 | — | — | 56,012 | 68,901 |
| Honduras | | | | | | |
| 1979 | 59,819 | 31,562 | — | — | 14,146 | 14,111 |
| 1980 | 84,839 | 38,233 | — | — | 28,874 | 17,732 |
| Nicaragua | | | | | | |
| 1979 | 90,066 | 21,467 | 17,893 | 13,313 | — | 37,393 |
| 1980 | 75,014 | 15,602 | 8,921 | 12,766 | — | 37,725 |
| Costa Rica | | | | 84 | | |
| 1979 | 176,668 | 61,875 | 48,616 | 26,368 | 39,809 | — |
| 1980 | 266,443 | 65,323 | 49,633 | 28,174 | 123,313 | — |
| Central America | | | | | | |
| 1979 | 900,067 | 287,268 | 228,996 | 87,407 | 107,584 | 188,812 |
| 1980 | 1,161,351 | 290,636 | 251,538 | 101,531 | 301,446 | 215,200 |

Source:  IDB, *Economic and Social Progress*, 1980–81, Table IV.3, p. 115.

Table 1.23
LAFTA: Total and Intra-zonal Exports, by Country, 1962–1973[1]
(millions of dollars)

| Country | Annual average 1962-64 | | | 1972 | | | 1973 | | |
|---|---|---|---|---|---|---|---|---|---|
| | Total | Intra-zonal | % Intra-zonal | Total | Intra-zonal | % Intra-zonal | Total | Intra-zonal | % Intra-zonal |
| Argentina | 1,330 | 196 | 14.7 | 1,941 | 484 | 24.9 | 3,266 | 797 | 24.4 |
| Bolivia[a] | 92 | 3 | 3.3 | 240 | 28 | 11.7 | 257 | 67 | 26.1 |
| Brazil | 1,350 | 99 | 7.3 | 3,991 | 408 | 10.2 | 6,199 | 557 | 9.0 |
| Chile | 486 | 9 | 1.9 | 845 | 102 | 12.1 | 1,084 | 99 | 9.1 |
| Colombia | 567 | 50 | 8.3 | 855 | 101 | 11.8 | 944 | 127 | 13.5 |
| Ecuador[b] | 125 | 8 | 6.4 | 326 | 37 | 11.3 | 544 | 91 | 16.7 |
| Mexico | 832 | 33 | 4.0 | 1,581 | 141 | 8.9 | 2,451 | 172 | 7.0 |
| Paraguay | 41 | 12 | 29.3 | 86 | 19 | 22.1 | 127 | 24 | 18.9 |
| Peru | 583 | 58 | 9.9 | 944 | 74 | 7.8 | 1,050 | 88 | 8.4 |
| Uruguay | 166 | 13 | 7.8 | 214 | 27 | 12.6 | 322 | 32 | 10.0 |
| Venezuela | 2,678 | 143 | 5.3 | 2,960 | 158 | 5.3 | 3,023 | 142 | 4.7 |
| **Total** | **8,253** | **624** | **7.6** | **13,983** | **1,579** | **11.3** | **19,267** | **2,196** | **11.4** |

[1] Bolivia and Venezuela began to negotiate in LAFTA in 1968. To facilitate comparison of the figures, their trade flows with the other LAFTA countries prior to 1968 have been taken into account.
[a] 1962 through 1964, **América en Cifras**, Inter-American Statistical Institute, OAS, Washington, D.C., 1965 and 1970.
[b] For 1973, **Boletín del Banco Central del Ecuador**, January-April 1974.

Source: IDB, *Economic and Social Progress*, 1974, Table IV.1, p. 118.

Table 1.24
LAFTA: Intra-zonal Trade, 1978–1979 (millions of dollars)

| | 1978 | | | | 1979[a] | | | |
|---|---|---|---|---|---|---|---|---|
| | Exports (fob) | % | Imports (cif) | % | Exports (fob) | % | Imports (cif) | % |
| I. ABRAMEX | 3,512.5 | 60.2 | 2,751.6 | 47.4 | 4,904.2 | 56.0 | 4,492.1 | 52.3 |
| Argentina | 1,512.9 | | 832.2 | | 2,011.6 | | 1,460.1 | |
| Brazil | 1,619.3 | | 1,570.3 | | 2,474.7 | | 2,463.2 | |
| Mexico | 380.5 | | 349.1 | | 417.9 | | 568.8 | |
| II. ANDEAN GROUP | 1,462.2 | 25.0 | 2,031.1 | 34.9 | 2,508.4 | 28.6 | 2,393.1 | 27.9 |
| Bolivia | 193.7 | | 184.3 | | 228.1 | | 259.4 | |
| Colombia | 355.2 | | 475.6 | | 659.5 | | 717.9 | |
| Ecuador | 229.2 | | 168.2 | | 316.1 | | 235.4 | |
| Peru | 235.0 | | 219.5 | | 664.0 | | 231.0 | |
| Venezuela | 449.1 | | 983.5 | | 640.7 | | 949.4 | |
| III. OTHERS | 864.4 | 14.8 | 1,030.8 | 17.7 | 1,346.5 | 15.4 | 1,701.7 | 19.8 |
| Chile | 605.7 | | 666.1 | | 927.2 | | 1,052.1 | |
| Paraguay | 66.8 | | 143.3 | | 104.0 | | 209.8 | |
| Uruguay | 191.9 | | 221.4 | | 315.3 | | 439.8 | |
| TOTAL(I + II + III) | 5,839.3 | 100.0 | 5,813.7 | 100.0 | 8,759.1 | 100.0 | 8,586.9 | 100.0 |

[a] Preliminary estimates.

Source:   IDB, *Economic and Social Progress*, 1980–81, Table IV.1, p. 106.


Table 1.25
Andean Group: Intra-regional Exports by Type of Products —
1970, 1979, 1980 (thousands of dollars)

| Type of Product and Country | 1970 | 1979 | 1980[a] |
|---|---|---|---|
| Type A[1] | 47,601 | 143,100 | 131,238 |
| Bolivia | 4,907 | 14,686 | 12,800 |
| Colombia | 15,947 | 31,355 | 15,238 |
| Ecuador | 7,079 | 32,612 | 22,500 |
| Peru | 13,085 | 46,309 | 58,100 |
| Venezuela | 6,583 | 18,138 | 22,600 |
| Type B[2] | 30,132 | 902,684 | 982,186 |
| Bolivia | 33 | 7,416 | 10,600 |
| Colombia | 18,277 | 520,907 | 441,936 |
| Ecuador | 1,941 | 63,697 | 86,300 |
| Peru | 6,487 | 276,746 | 390,850 |
| Venezuela | 3,394 | 33,918 | 52,500 |
| Total | 77,733 | 1,045,784 | 1,113,424 |

[1] Type A: Traditional products excluding petroleum and petroleum derivatives.

[2] Type B: Non-traditional products.

[a] Estimated on the basis of figures for the first half of the year, provided by the Statistical Unit of JUNAC and the trends of earlier years.

Source:   IDB, *Economic and Social Progress*, 1980–81, Table IV.2, p. 109.

Table 1.26
Intra-Regional Exports as a Percentage of the Total Exports
of Latin American Countries — 1962, 1965, 1970, 1975, 1979

| Country | 1962 | 1965 | 1970 | 1975 | 1979 | Most recent year |
|---|---|---|---|---|---|---|
| *LAIA* | | | | | | |
| Argentina | 13.0 | 16.8 | 21.0 | 25.9 | 26.3 | 20.3[a] |
| Brazil | 6.4 | 12.8 | 11.6 | 15.6 | 17.1 | 15.0[a] |
| Chile | 8.5 | 8.3 | 11.2 | 23.8 | n.a. | 24.7[c] |
| Mexico | 5.0 | 8.2 | 10.4 | 12.6 | 6.7 | n.a. |
| Paraguay | 32.6 | 30.7 | 38.5 | 36.0 | 34.4 | n.a. |
| Uruguay | n.a. | n.a. | 12.6 | 28.8 | 40.2 | 28.7[b] |
| *Andean Group* | | | | | | |
| Bolivia | 4.1 | 2.7 | 8.5 | 35.0 | 31.5 | n.a. |
| Colombia | 5.5 | 11.1 | 13.5 | 20.8 | 17.9 | 20.7[a] |
| Ecuador | 6.0 | 10.6 | 11.1 | 37.8 | 24.1 | n.a. |
| Peru | 9.6 | 9.4 | 6.4 | 16.9 | 21.3 | 15.6[a] |
| Venezuela | 10.1 | 12.6 | 12.5 | 12.3 | 11.7 | 16.9[b] |
| *CACM* | | | | | | |
| Costa Rica | n.a. | 19.8 | 23.3 | 29.2 | 25.4 | 34.2[b] |
| El Salvador | n.a. | 23.5 | 32.7 | 29.0 | 26.6 | 44.2[b] |
| Guatemala | n.a. | 20.9 | 36.7 | 29.8 | 27.0 | 38.2[b] |
| Honduras | n.a. | 18.4 | 16.6 | 21.2 | 11.6 | 12.2[b] |
| Nicaragua | n.a. | 9.2 | 28.3 | 25.9 | 17.0 | 18.4[a] |
| *CARICOM members* | | | | | | |
| Bahamas | n.a. | n.a. | n.a. | 4.2 | n.a. | n.a. |
| Barbados | n.a. | n.a. | 6.5 | 12.7 | 18.5 | 20.7[c] |
| Guyana | n.a. | n.a. | 13.5 | 13.3 | 23.3 | n.a. |
| Jamaica | 3.7 | n.a. | n.a. | 5.4 | 11.5 | 10.8[b] |
| Trinidad and Tobago | n.a. | n.a. | 12.8 | 11.2 | 13.7 | 18.6[a] |
| *Non-associated countries* | | | | | | |
| Dominican Republic | n.a. | n.a. | n.a. | 1.0 | 7.7 | 7.4[a] |
| Haiti | n.a. | n.a. | 1.5 | 1.3 | 1.1 | n.a. |
| Panama | 13.0 | 3.0 | 4.9 | 7.8 | 15.9 | 16.0[a] |
| Suriname | 4.1 | n.a. | n.a. | n.a. | n.a. | n.a. |

[a] 1982.    [c] 1980.
[b] 1981.    n.a. Not available.

Source:  IDB, *Economic and Social Progress*, 1984, Table II.6, p. 106.

provided by the Alliance for Progress is one of those "what if" questions that are
the bane of humanity. It is clear, however, that intra-regional trade did increase,
and the foundations exist for a continuation of the pattern.

The greatest disappointments in the economic arena were registered in the
efforts to stabilize commodity exports. The major achievement was the implementation of the International Coffee Agreement, which was initiated during the
Eisenhower Administration and signed in 1962. It brought together the major
producing and consuming countries and stands even today as a major contribution
to the elimination of some of the excesses in that historically volatile market. In
virtually no other areas, however, were multilateral commodity price agreements
effective. Even with the "burst of energy" provided by the OPEC nations in 1973,
which prompted the producing nations to pay renewed attention to arrangements
in other commodities such as copper and tin, no agreements were possible.

## THE INTER-AMERICAN INFRASTRUCTURE
## OF THE ALLIANCE

The feature that most distinguished the Alliance for Progress was the extraordinary and elaborate intergovernmental machinery that was accepted by the participating nations as part of the effort. Only Europe, in its moves toward the European Community, was comparable. And there is some question whether the American nations, in their zeal, may not have created even more institutions than the Europeans.

The tone was set in the original Charter of the Alliance which established a panel of experts to assist the countries in the new venture of preparing national plans. Nine experts, soon to be called the "Nine Wise Men," were chosen on the basis of individual technical competence, not as representatives of governments. They were given "unquestioned autonomy" in the accomplishment of their tasks, which included interpreting their own terms of reference. Governments, however, were given the option of presenting their plans to the panel "if they wished," a rather timid expression but a necessary compromise between those who felt annual reviews were essential to stimulate serious preparation of the plans and a number of countries who were reluctant, to say the least, to have any mechanism of this type established. The latter viewed it as the forerunner of a type of supranational "Inter-American Tribunal on Development Planning." The Panels were attached to the Inter-American Economic and Social Council (CIES) of the OAS for administrative purposes, which was a polite way of giving the OAS credit for the effort, while keeping the governments at arm's length. CIES was also given the responsibility of submitting an annual report to the OAS member nations on the progress of the Alliance.

It didn't take long for the machinery to start to multiply. Ostensibly concerned that the Alliance was perceived as a U.S. aid program when, in fact, the original concept had originated with the Latin American nations, the first CIES report pointed out that the United States government had begun to establish "extensive machinery" of its own to administer Alliance aid on a bilateral basis. It also noted that few U.S. officials stationed in Latin American countries "understood the multilateral concepts on which the Alliance was based," which severely affected political support in Latin America. In addition, the resistance of several countries to submitting their development plans to the "Nine Wise Men," and the lack of leverage on the international financial institutions that failed to follow the panel's recommendations, prompted a call for a general review of the "political direction and coordination" of the program. In the first annual review of the Alliance, CIES agreed to set up a special committee composed of the two former presidents who had most to do with the conceptualization of inter-American cooperation, Alberto Lleras Camargo of Colombia and Juscelino Kubitschek of Brazil. The major concern was to decide how the inter-American system could be adapted to play a more effective and "dynamic" role in the Alliance.[17]

The result of the study of the two former presidents was the creation of a new permanent body to coordinate and exercise "executive functions" over the Alliance. Thus emerged the Inter-American Committee on the Alliance for Progress, better known by its Spanish acronym CIAP, as the official intergovernmental body composed of seven members representing all of the governments participating in the Alliance. The governments chose former Colombian Finance Minister Carlos Sanz de Santamaría to chair the group, a post which he held until his resignation in 1973. He was CIAP's only chairman, as the entity was disbanded or "merged," to use the phrase of the time, into a standing committee of the CIES upon his departure.

The most important and precedent-shattering function given to CIAP was that of making an annual estimate of each country's external financial requirements. This function became the source of the annual "country reviews"—the fulcrum of the Alliance and the principal mechanism that gave it multilateral substance. As the Alliance gained momentum, the country reviews, taking place almost on a weekly basis, brought together the representatives of all of the major national and multilateral lending agencies to hear the presentations and questions of the national officials responsible for the development planning and finance, as José Luis Restrepo describes in more detail in Chapter 12. The U.S. Agency for International Development, the Inter-American Development Bank, the World Bank and the International Monetary Fund all participated. United Nations specialized agencies such as the FAO and ILO set up special offices attached to CIAP in Washington in order to coordinate their activities and participate in the country reviews. The principal industrialized nations cooperating with Latin America also participated regularly, including Canada, Spain, Italy, France, Great Britain, Japan, and Israel. It was almost the epitome of what the architects of the inter-American System had dreamed of for decades—an authentic coordinating mechanism that brought the various interested agencies and nations together around a substantive function. In its later years, CIAP also obtained the unprecedented agreement of the United States to undergo a "country review" of its economic aid objectives and their relationship to the goals of the Alliance. In a controversial gesture to CIAP, the U.S. Congress adopted an amendment to its foreign aid legislation in 1966, proposed by Senator William Fulbright, which made CIAP's positive recommendation mandatory for bilateral loans under the Alliance.

Given the need to review 19 countries per year, the country review mechanism was an intense and vigorous one. The reviews lasted one week and were conducted on the basis of the presentations of the countries and the "observations" of the Secretariat. The yearly cycle was announced each September and in virtually every case, until the last years of the Alliance in the early 1970s, the countries appeared and the reviews were held without postponement. The historic achievement of the meetings was the fact that they took place. To borrow a phrase from Marshall McLuhan, the process of the meetings was its message. The interchanges that were made possible by the disciplined discussions were more important than any formal evaluation of the country plans. Under the able and sensitive leadership of Carlos Sanz de Santamaría, the Committee steered away from resolutions and pronouncements, concentrating on more informal approaches to improve the level of communication and coordination among the various governments and agencies. As Dr. Sanz de Santamaría points out in Chapter 8, he regarded the moral authority and "ombudsman" function as most important to the success of CIAP's mission. The principal goals were to expedite the dialogue among the agencies and the national governments, make each agency aware of the other agencies' plans to participate in the national development programs, and inform the national authorities of the response of the financial community to their goals. The process impelled the discussion of controversial issues and served to reduce misunderstandings, enabling the development process to continue as smoothly as possible under the circumstances.

In all, CIAP was a noteworthy achievement. Never before, nor since, have the American nations agreed to allow an inter-American body to exercise such functions in regard to predominantly domestic issues. The reactions of the smaller countries to the process, however, differed from those of the larger nations. The larger nations didn't need the CIAP, resisted it all along, and were finally responsible for its quiet demise as the momentum of the Alliance petered out in the early 1970s. They had the ability and staffing to carry on their own discussions with the international funding agencies as they pleased. For the smaller nations, however, it was a boon. While they had difficulty in compiling the data and projects for the national plans, it gave them, for the first time, a method to reach all of the relevant agencies and to get feedback in a form to which they could relate rapidly and effectively. Not only was this process cost-efficient, it was highly doubtful that they could otherwise have reached many of the agencies and European governments even if they chose. They simply didn't have the manpower. Thus, the perpetual and traditional divergence between the needs and perceptions of the large nations and those of the smaller nations regarding the usefulness of international agencies was again forcefully articulated in this arena.

Another concern of all of the countries was that there were three major international agencies whose mandates overlapped in the various tasks emanating from the Charter of Punta del Este: the OAS, the new Inter-American Development Bank (IDB), and the United Nations Economic Commission for Latin America (ECLA). Potential competition among them could create chaos and waste scarce resources. Consequently, a number of attempts were made to establish interagency mechanisms to coordinate policies and implement sectoral programs. Most important of these was the joint committee on agricultural development, which was set up as a semi-autonomous agency and composed of staff members of the OAS, IDB, FAO, ECLA, and the Inter-American Institute for Agricultural Cooperation (IICA), a specialized organization of the OAS. Known by its Spanish acronym CIDA, the Inter-American Committee on Agricultural Development operated until 1967. It had authority to finance special studies on issues related to agricultural development and agrarian reform and to coordinate technical assistance to the nations in the field of agriculture. After 1967, when most of the initial studies it had commissioned were completed, its status was reduced and it became an advisory committee to CIAP on agricultural matters.

Similarly, the Joint Tax Program in which the OAS, IDB and ECLA participated, was a unique and highly successful effort. It was the focus of a coordinated effort in the critical field of tax and fiscal reform. Considering the painful process of tax reform and the enormous political resistance it inevitably engenders, the coordinated efforts of the three agencies in this sensitive area helped to mobilize the most capable teams of experts, pooling their financial and intellectual resources. To these joint efforts were attributed responsibility for the successful achievements in this field.

Not as successful, however, was a coordinating committee set up with a much broader mandate. A Tripartite Committee composed of representatives of the three major agencies, OAS, IDB and ECLA, worked to assist the countries in the process of planning. The different foci of the participating institutions, however, and their differing criteria for programs and projects, made their joint missions unproductive. The issues were too sensitive to leave to roving bureaucrats in the field. The Tripartite Committee was dissolved in 1963 and replaced by a more coherent instrument for the training of planners, the Latin American Institute for Economic and Social Planning (ILPES), which was established in 1963 and was closely related to ECLA in Santiago, Chile.

For the purpose of more effective follow-up to loan disbursements in accordance with the country reviews, CIAP established an Inter-Agency Advisory Group (IAAG) composed of senior level representatives of the major aid-giving agencies: the IDB, World Bank, IMF and USAID. The group reviewed special region-wide development problems. As a result of the work of the IAAG, CIAP representatives were included in the loan review process of both USAID and the IDB, and an agreement was reached with the World Bank to coordinate and reduce duplication of staff work by utilizing the data collected by the World Bank as the basis for the country review process.

By the conclusion of the Alliance, the institutional machinery for international and institutional cooperation reached as high a level as was ever thought possible when the Alliance began with nothing on the books in 1961. Much was due to the discreet and informal mechanisms fashioned by CIAP under the leadership of Carlos Sanz de Santamaría. No judgments were made, no declarations as to which countries were performing well or badly, no public officials put on the spot for their policies. It was no easy task to maintain this stance. Intense pressures were exerted on CIAP to be more controlling. Many of the criticisms levelled at CIAP were precisely that it failed to come out with the kind of "judgments" that would justify the positions of certain bureaucratic interests. The final results, however, were in keeping with the patterns that had proven successful over the years in the inter-American system; that is, an informal approach based on persuasion and consensus.[18] This achieved a higher measure of cooperation among the nations than anyone thought possible.

The Alliance got a last shot of adrenalin toward the end of the decade. In 1967, when spirits began to falter as a result of the preoccupation of the United States with the Vietnam War, President Lyndon Johnson agreed to an Argentine initiative for a meeting of the presidents of the hemisphere to "give a more effective political impulse toward achieving the goals of the Alliance for Progress." The session spelled out a series of mutual commitments from the Latin American and U.S. sides, with the Latin American nations pledging to take all necessary measures to achieve full economic integration by the year 1985, while the U.S., for the first time, agreed to consider a system of nondiscriminatory trade preferences for developing nations. This initiative led within a few years to the adoption of the general system of trade preferences (GSP) by the U.S. Congress. The Latin American commitment to economic integration was based largely on the report prepared a year previously by the major figures of the Alliance of the period: Felipe Herrera, president of the Inter-American Development Bank, Carlos Sanz de Santamaría, Raúl Prebisch, then director of the new UNCTAD, and José Antonio Mayobre, then director of ECLA. Their report was known as the Report of the Group of Four.

Unfortunately, the major commitments made at the meeting were honored more in the breach than in the achievement. Total economic integration was never a realistic possibility at the time, and few steps were ever taken to facilitate it. New regional programs in education and technology were funded at about a third of their targeted amounts of $25 million a year, and, with the new U.S. President Richard Nixon articulating a policy of "benign neglect," the programs never developed momentum. Indeed, the OAS reported that the failure to follow through on these recommendations created an atmosphere of skepticism that permeated the Alliance and undermined the entire spirit of the inter-American cooperative effort.[19]

The culmination of the institutional aspects of the Alliance years at the close of the decade came in the form of two initiatives that had widely diverse impacts: the creation of CECLA and the reform of the OAS Charter. CECLA, the Spanish acronym for the Special Coordinating Committee for Latin America, was established in 1963 by CIES as the vehicle to coordinate a Latin American position on trade issues for the first meeting of the United Nations Conference on Trade and Development. In the spirit of the Alliance, the Latin American nations felt it was important that they act as a bloc in the meeting to help protect their interests. The United States was invited to participate in the CECLA meetings as an observer. Initially established only for that first meeting of UNCTAD, CIES subsequently maintained CECLA to coordinate Latin American positions on global trade matters. It was CECLA that produced in 1969 the major statement of Latin American goals in response to President Nixon's request to the Latin American nations for their recommendations for the future development of the hemisphere. The CECLA report, known as the Consensus of Viña del Mar, was interestingly called by the OAS the "first coherent and fully coordinated formulation of Latin America's position on inter-American and international cooperation . . . within the spirit of the Alliance for Progress."[20] The document covered all aspects of trade, finance, investment, and technical cooperation and was presented to President

Nixon in March 1969. Subsequently the movers of CECLA began to think of a new Latin American organization for economic matters without the participation of the U.S. By 1973, the Latin American Economic System (SELA) was formally constituted with headquarters in Caracas and CECLA passed into history.

The reform of the OAS Charter at the meeting in Buenos Aires in 1967 incorporated into the Charter most of the principles of the Alliance for Progress and many of the institutional mechanisms that had evolved to implement them. Consideration of the reforms began during the formative years of the Alliance, with two preliminary drafting conferences held in 1964 and 1966. Adopted in 1967, the amendments came into effect in 1970 — just in time for the phasing out of the Alliance. In one sense it was a fortunate occurrence, since it preserved in the Charter of the OAS many of the measures for inter-American cooperation in the field of economic and social reform that were integral to the Charter of Punta del Este. In another sense the new political strength given to the development institutions — the Inter-American Economic and Social Council (CIES) and the Inter-American Council on Education, Science and Culture (CIECC) — elevating them to a hierarchical level equal to the political Permanent Council, came just as the interest in these bodies was waning. With the gathering momentum of the Inter-American Development Bank in financial matters and IDB annual disbursements soaring over the $1 billion mark, as compared to the OAS' $50 million in technical assistance, the finance ministers simply did not come to the OAS forum. Policy, such as there was, was articulated in the loan priorities of the Bank. Within a short time thereafter, as noted above, the enormous flow of financial resources through the commercial banks diverted everyone's attention and no policy or agency was relevant; only the capacity to repay mattered.

While the CIECC fared somewhat better for a while, largely because the education ministers had no other forum, it soon degenerated into a grandiose budgetary exercise to divide up a pie, with little attention paid to the underlying policy issues in the field of technology and education and little effort to establish any regional regimes to ensure the long term institutional continuity of the effort. In the absence of financial resources to back up the pronouncements, the pragmatic instincts of the ministers prevailed and the concept of regional policy in this eminently domestic arena was never heard from again.

## CONCLUSIONS

The Alliance for Progress was a commitment to a long-term program to facilitate social and economic reforms essential to the establishment of the foundations for democratic growth in Latin America. The framers of the Charter of Punta del Este were well aware of the magnitude of the task and the obstacles. Democracy was more the aberration than the rule in the 150 years since independence in Latin America, and the historical record hardly demonstrated social justice to be a compelling concern of the nations. The traditional social and cultural institutions of the region were built on a foundation of centralization and statism established over generations of Spanish rule as well as the pervasive authoritarianism represented by the Church and the military. In a real sense, as Tad Szulc pointed out in his book on the Alliance at the time, it was a development program in which everyone was learning together.[21]

Given this background, the accomplishments, viewed in the light of 25 years of history, were truly remarkable. While the hemisphere fares little better today than it did a quarter of a century ago, as many of the writers in the volume attest, the cause of the present adversity lies not in the failures of the Alliance but in its successes. The Alliance gave birth to a sense of self-confidence and pride that resulted in Latin America becoming inundated with financial resources far greater than anyone ever imagined possible. While the inflow of capital resulted from the accumulation of resources in a few Middle Eastern countries in the OPEC cartel, it served as an effective instrument for the redistribution of wealth. The oil consumers paid an increased tax and the funds were recycled to investment projects. Unfortunately, the continent was still not ready to employ the resources as wisely as it might have. A few countries, such as Brazil, struggling to free itself of its dependency on imported oil, invested in building a productive financial and industrial base that has subsequently enabled the country to meet its enormous debt service obligations. Colombia and Venezuela also applied considerable resources toward building a more diversified economic base. Mexico did not fare as well, although significant economic progress was chalked up in many sectors during the two decades. The decade of easy money following the Alliance distorted national economies accustomed to deficit finance, so that harsh adjustment policies must now be implemented. Countries that run deficits must either borrow or print money to make up the difference. They can no longer borrow and the alternative—printing money—results in the other familiar disaster of debasing the currency and inflation. The Alliance bred the confidence that the future was manageable. But it wasn't, at least not in the context of the events of the 1970s.

The Alliance could boast of a number of impressive achievements that indelibly altered the pattern of political and social development in Latin America. Carlos Sanz de Santamaría reported in his final message in 1973 that the experience produced changes in the countries that could not be statistically expressed or accurately measured. Institutions such as mortgage banks, private universities, and rural cooperatives have established the bases for continuing growth in sectors that, prior to the Alliance, were virtually ignored. By the end of the decade, continuing until the oil shocks of the mid-1970s, the Alliance began to foster impressive growth. While the lack of success of the integration efforts were a disappointment to many, the decade had a powerful influence in altering regional trade patterns. In 1960, no nation in the hemisphere had more than 10 percent of its exports in manufactures. In 1986, most had over 30 percent and some, such as Brazil, exceeded 50 percent. More important, a new generation is coming into power that has a level of training and skills unprecedented in the history of the continent. Forces have been set into motion that no Latin American will be able to contain.

There were setbacks. The Alliance was never able to stop the unsettling trends in population growth, and the resulting overwhelming problems of housing, education and health, urban migration, and sprawl. It also reinforced a massive bureaucracy, as Daniel Sharp points out in Chapter 15, that set about to expand the role of the state in the productive sectors. Region-wide, the role of the state in GNP increased from about 25 percent in 1960 to about 45 percent in 1984. Ironically, this trend was accelerated by the role of the commercial banks, which insisted on government guarantees for their loans to industry.

But the vision that this generation has received and the institutions that are now implanted will not easily be denied. Carlos Sanz de Santamaría points out in Chapter 8 that new stronger mechanisms may be necessary along the lines of the old OEEC in Europe to surmount Latin America's current crisis. In achieving such innovations, however, the problem of coordination with the United States is a double-edged sword. The overwhelming economic power of the U.S. is essential for the success of an effective economic plan. However, the very presence of the United States is an inhibiting factor on the self-reliance of the Latin American nations; many politicians prefer the short-term rewards of working out their best arrangements bilaterally with the U.S. rather than entering into any long-term inter-American cooperative arrangements. Extraordinary sensitivity and leadership are needed to overcome the psychological barriers to genuine hemispheric cooperation in this regard.

The results on the political side are more difficult to assess. On balance, the nations of the region have come out well, with an unprecedented and universal resurgence of democracy and growing awareness of the significance of human rights and freedom of the press. The awareness did not come easily. It was partially the result of horrendous experience. By the 1970s, virtually every major country in the hemisphere was subject to increasing terrorism and growing military repression. Some observers argue that the repression was the result of the collusion of the middle class, which was fearful of a growing radicalism and felt helpless before seemingly runaway demands of an awakening underclass. In any event, the threat that unlawful elements posed to stability in some of the nations was real. The impact of the terrorism, kidnapping and brazen violence that grew in the early 1970s can hardly be judged by people who did not live through it. But the people of the hemisphere learned a hard lesson. The military, which stepped in to reverse the terror, had no magic solutions. More important, they had few governing skills. Finally, with government accountable to no one, corruption ran amok and, by the 1980s, the cycle was ready to begin again.

The most remarkable achievements of the Alliance were the most short-lived. Plagued for decades by the growing asymmetry of power between the United States and the rest of the hemisphere, for a few brief moments the Latin American nations began to evidence some will to cooperate in multilateral institutions to compensate for their individual vulnerabilities. The inter-American institutions began to serve their appointed functions of building confidence and of increasing the responsibility of the Latin American nations for their own destiny. By the end of the decade of the 1960s, Latin America was vigorously trying to forge unity and a common agenda. CECLA and its soon-to-be-formed successor, the Latin American Economic System (SELA), from which the U.S. was excluded, expressed an important, if naive, view of Latin America's role in the global scene. Unfortunately, Latin America was soon to discover that, while it cared a great deal about the rest of the world, the rest of the world cared little about it. The discovery came too late, and the solid, albeit rudimentary, multilateral institutions built in the 1960s were left to atrophy before the new-found cornucopia brought by the commercial banks.

Many of the concepts presented in this volume are colored by the urgency of the times in which they are written. The magnitude of Latin American debt appears overwhelming. Stagnation has set into the global economy and the terms of trade continue their adverse patterns. Talk of increasing protectionism, despite the existence of the General Agreement on Tariffs and Trade (GATT) and UNCTAD, is frustrating. Latin America finds it difficult to see how to increase exports in order to earn hard currency. But there are lessons from the Alliance years, and the experience gained during that decade offers many models for the Americas' current crisis. In sum, the principal concepts that emerge from the analyses set forth in this volume are:

1. The Alliance was predominantly a Latin American initiative deriving from the work of Raúl Prebisch in ECLA and sparked by the proposal for an "Operation Pan-America" by President Juscelino Kubischek of Brazil (see Chapters 6–8).

2. The primary U.S. interest in accepting the Alliance concept was not only to counter Cuban influence, but to combat a rising demagogic populism in Latin America, which was feeding on underdevelopment and was "a prescription for continuing economic stagnation" (Chapter 4).

3. The concept of the Alliance in the U.S. was bipartisan in origin and execution, the need having been acknowledged and the general approach designed during the Eisenhower Administration. The Inter-American Development Bank was approved and the legislation for the Social Progress Trust Fund sent to Congress during the Eisenhower period (Chapter 2). It was one of the major attempts in U.S. history to link strategic interests with humanitarian and social justice concerns (Chapter 7).

4. The strength of the Alliance was rooted in both concept and process. The concept was the commitment, for which leadership was the key ingredient. The U.S. provided that. The process was the machinery which, without the commitment, was nonfunctional (Chapters 13 and 21).

5. Major achievements, aside from basic sectoral advances which were amply reflected in the statistics, were:

   – Psychological: Latin America's development economists were given a major boost in acceptability. The concept of peaceful revolution was given legitimacy (Chapters 8, 13, and 21).

   – Development planning was raised to a higher level and made the principal item on Latin America's agenda (Chapters 4, 6, 13, and 21).

   – Important infrastructure was created, most of which worked as well as could be expected in this period of history. CIAP was useful in strengthening confidence and altering the balance of forces within some countries. It worked even though, or

perhaps because, it was noncoercive. Integration efforts gained an important foot-
hold and spurred a major increase in intra-regional trade (Chapters 6 and 8).

– The agreement regarding coffee renewed confidence in the potential for alleviating
unstable commodity prices, although it did not prove to be replicable in other areas
(Chapters 8 and 13).

– The confidence generated in Latin America was a direct influence in the decisions of
the commercial banks to channel unprecedented financial flows in the following
decade (Chapters 13 and 21. But see Point 8).

6. The Alliance was effective primarily because Latin America was poised for a "Rostovian" take-off. All it needed was a little push to become self-generating (Chapter 4). It
helped Latin America bridge the transition of the period in which some of the
momentum toward a take-off of the previous period had been lost (Chapter 24). Its
success was most evident in strengthening the economic and social infrastructure.

7. The major difficulties encountered were the flaws in basic assumptions regarding the
realities of Latin American culture and society and the support which could be
generated to alter the balance of political power. There were intractable problems
related to:

– the predominance of a statist philosophy which generated a ponderous, intransigent
bureaucracy (Chapter 24)

– a protected private sector with enormous built-in disincentives to investment (Chapter 15)

– social injustice

– population increases

– unrealistic trade policies (Chapter 18)

– unrealistic agricultural policies

– the inability to develop sufficient political mystique to overcome vested interests
(Chapters 4 and 7), or deep-rooted Latin American cultural attitudes that impede
effective development management (Chapter 23).

8. The infrastructure of the Alliance was lost in the free flow of funds of the 1970s when
the commercial banks flooded Latin America with money regardless of an effort to
plan or program. There was no longer any incentive or need to cooperate. However,
the spirit and reality of pragmatic cooperation fostered by the Alliance still prevails and
is evident in persistent efforts to restructure integration efforts and to coordinate
policies to deal with the debt issue (Chapters 6, 13, and 21).

9. The major lessons of the Alliance relate to the imbalance in Latin America's capital
flows, which are more complex than the problems that were faced in the 1960s
because of different perceptions of the roots of the problem (Chapter 13). There is no
need to overload the system with ambitious new machinery, since the people and
institutions are now in place that can deal with these problems (Chapter 21). But
mechanisms that allow partial debt repayment in local currency, if monitored by CIAP-
type inter-American machinery, would be politically more acceptable (Chapter 17).

10. The other major issue, which is of prime importance for policy makers throughout the
hemisphere, is technology and the need to ensure the hemisphere's resource base.
Technology requires:

—a shift from the state bourgeoisies, which are clumsy, inefficient, and unable to absorb new technology, to a private sector base. This is a responsibility Latin Americans must take on.

—radical changes in educational policy. This too is the responsibility of the Latin Americans themselves, but is an area where U.S. help could be crucial (Chapter 24).

11. In retrospect, the fear that Latin America was ripe for revolutionary upheavals under-estimated the structural rigidities, the inertia of the system, and the impact of populist rhetoric. Nationalism is a far more potent political emotion in Latin America than class revolution (Chapter 3).

12. The new efforts that are required are in the hands of a maturing Latin America which must look to genuine cooperative institutions. Latin America must find ways to involve the legislatures of the new democracies, devise regional and subregional judicial bodies, and create monetary machinery. This is the challenge to Latin America to meet the exigencies of increasingly competitive global markets and rapidly evolving production technology (Chapter 6).

Perhaps the real tests of the Alliance, and the intangible spirit and sense of confidence that it attempted to reinforce, are still to come. The most important is the depth to which the respect for human rights and representative government has permeated the thinking of the people of the Americas. Did the Alliance and ensuing events plant sufficient seeds to make freedom really flourish, or will the old patterns of indifference and elitism reassert themselves? Will the region have the foresight and capability to marshal its resources to meet, as Walt W. Rostow reminds us in Chapter 24, the challenge of the new technological revolution that is sweeping the industrialized world? This is by far the most ubiquitous and severe challenge in the history of the hemisphere. As strong as the arguments of dependency and the Raúl Prebisch thesis on periphery capitalism were, the accelerated changes that result from the new technologies dwarf those of the past. If the nations of the region do not mobilize to absorb and master the new technologies, they will become more dependent and more marginalized in coming generations than they ever imagined possible. Meeting that challenge will take a prodigious effort of a magnitude equivalent to or greater than the Alliance for Progress. It is improbable that the smaller nations will be able to manage it alone. Thus, the need for cooperation between northern and southern partners is more pressing than ever before. If any lessons are learned from the Alliance, this is the time to apply them.

Partly as a result of the successes and the failures of the Alliance, Latin America has moved on to a new stage of its development, a movement that was accelerated because of the Alliance efforts. Major adjustments are still needed, as they always will be. The task will never be finished. The principal lesson of the Alliance is that, in the final analysis, the nations of the region have demonstrated that they can assume the responsibility which, ultimately, is theirs. It also teaches that the commitment of the U.S., marginal as it is, generates an enormous amount of collateral energy, which motivates and fosters confidence throughout the hemisphere. It teaches that the U.S. can pursue its national objectives not by use of military force, but in cooperation with the enlightened sectors of Latin American society to strengthen the foundations of social justice and freedom. This commitment is most critical for U.S. policymakers to take into account as they consider how to meet the challenges ahead.

## NOTES

1. Harvey S. Perloff, *The Alliance for Progress* (Baltimore: Johns Hopkins Press, 1969), p. 149.

2. Jerome Levinson and Juan de Onis, *The Alliance that Lost Its Way* (Chicago: Quadrangle Books, 1970). See also Senator Edward M. Kennedy, "Beginning Anew in Latin America," *Saturday Review*, October 17, 1970.

3. William D. Rogers, *The Twilight Struggle* (New York: Random House, 1967), p. 266.

4. Flight capital was not systematically tracked at the time. Some estimates of the amounts in the first two years of the Alliance reach $25 billion. See: *The OAS and the Alliance for Progress*, unpublished speech of William Sanders, Assistant Secretary General of the OAS, February 7, 1963.

5. Bela Balassa, Gerardo Bueno, Pedro-Pablo Kuczynski, and Mario Henrique Simonsen, *Toward Renewed Economic Growth in Latin America: Summary* (Washington, D.C.: Institute for International Economics, 1986), p. 21.

6. Albert O. Hirschman, *The Principle of the Hiding Hand* (Washington, D.C.: Brookings, 1967). See also: A. O. Hirschman, *Journeys Toward Progress* (New York: Twentieth Century Fund, 1963).

7. Inter-American Development Bank, *Socio-Economic Progress in Latin America* (Washington, D.C.: 1970).

8. Organization of American States, *Latin America's Development and the Alliance for Progress* (Washington, D.C.: CIES Doc. 1636, 1973).

9. Perloff, *The Alliance for Progress*, p. 77.

10. OAS, *Latin America's Development*, p. 223.

11. Ibid., p. 346.

12. Ibid., p. 225.

13. U.S. Congress, *New Directions for the 1970s*. Report of the Sub-Committee on Inter-American Affairs (Washington, D.C.: USGPO, July 22, 1969).

14. OAS, *Latin America's Development*, p. 225.

15. Ibid., p. 238.

16. Perloff, *The Alliance for Progress*, pp. 150 ff.

17. OAS, *Latin America's Development*, pp. 157–159.

18. See the discussion of the history of informal machinery in the inter-American system as applied in the area of peaceful settlement of disputes in L. Ronald Scheman and John Ford, "The OAS as Mediator," in *International Mediation in Theory and Practice*, eds. Saadia Touval and William Zartman. SAIS Papers in International Affairs, no. 6 (Westview, 1984).

19. OAS, *Latin America's Development*, pp. 196–7.

20. Ibid., p. 179.

21. Tad Szulc, *The Winds of Revolution* (New York: Praeger, 1963).

# 2
## *The Prelude*

### *C. Douglas Dillon*

The best contribution I can make to a retrospective of the Alliance for Progress would be to offer my recollections of the years immediately preceding its birth, when I was in charge of economic affairs in the Department of State.

My connection with the economic problems of Latin America dates back to August 1957, when a meeting between the ministers of economic affairs of the hemisphere took place in Buenos Aires. The head of the United States delegation was Robert Anderson, the newly appointed Secretary of the Treasury; I was the deputy head of our delegation. Since Secretary Anderson only stayed in Buenos Aires for three or four days, I was in charge of the U.S. delegation for the remainder of the conference, which lasted about three weeks.

After World War II, United States economic policy toward Latin America was based on the premise that the countries of Latin America had prospered during the war and, with the sole exception of technical assistance, needed no economic aid that could not be provided by hard loans from the World Bank or from our own Export-Import Bank. This policy formed the basis of our delegation's instructions as we went to Buenos Aires. It was contrasted sharply with U.S. policy toward other areas of the world and was the cause of considerable resentment throughout Latin America as being unfairly discriminatory.

The conference was a revelation to me. I was much impressed by the arguments put forward by other heads of delegations, particularly the delegates from Mexico and Brazil. All of them called for a more active and forthcoming policy on the part of the United States. I, for one, was convinced. Although my instructions prevented any major agreements, I was able to commit the U.S. to restudying the need for both a coffee agreement and a new development bank for the Americas. As a result, the conference ended on a note of hope.

A few months after my return to Washington, the U.S. agreed, for the first time, to negotiate an international agreement to regulate the sale of coffee. This was of great importance to many countries of the Americas, especially Brazil, Colombia, and the countries of Central America. The agreement was successfully concluded and marked the first step toward a more cooperative U.S. role in inter-American economic affairs.

The second step was a bit more difficult, as it involved a major shift in U.S. policy. Accordingly, one of the most gratifying moments of my four years in the State Department came when I was able to announce to the delegates to the Inter-American Council assembled in Washington that the United States was prepared to work with our Latin friends to create an inter-American development bank.

This change in policy was only possible because Treasury Secretary Anderson was a native Texan who fully understood the importance of Latin America, and Mexico in particular, to the United States. Anderson was an early supporter of the Bank, having been encouraged to take this position by his Assistant Secretary for international affairs, T. Graydon Upton. It was Mr. Upton, a former college classmate of mine, who was in charge of the U.S. negotiations on the Bank's charter. He later joined the staff of the Inter-American Development Bank where he played a distinguished role as Chief Deputy to the Bank's President, Felipe Herrera.

Despite these advances, it was not long before it became clear that more was required of the United States. The President of Brazil, Juscelino Kubitschek, put forth his visionary proposal "Operation Pan-America," which called for substantial direct aid from the United States along general lines of the Marshall Plan that had been so successful in Europe.

An inter-American economic meeting at the ministerial level was scheduled for late August and early September of 1960 to consider the Brazilian proposal and other economic matters. It was to be held in Bogota. After much consideration, we in the State Department decided in the late spring of 1960 that the time had come for another, even more radical change in U.S. policy. We formulated a plan calling for a $600 million fund for grants to promote social justice in Latin America. This was not too different in principle from the concept of Operation Pan-America, though far more modest in size. It represented, however, a complete reversal of our long-standing policy of not making development grants to the countries of Latin America.

Obtaining approval of this idea prior to the Bogota Conference, first from the President and then from the Congress, became our objective. But this time the Treasury Department opposed us, maintaining the stance that no grant aid was needed in Latin America. Thus, the matter went to President Eisenhower for decision.

I well remember the occasion. It was early July and there had been a routine National Security Council meeting at Eisenhower's summer White House in Newport, Rhode Island. Secretary Anderson and I stayed afterward to meet with the President and obtain his decision. This was not unusual; we had quite often taken questions regarding foreign aid to President Eisenhower for decision when we had been unable to agree among ourselves.

This time, before we could start our discussion, the President said jokingly, but with a slight note of exasperation: "I wish you two fellows could exchange jobs for a while—then you might have fewer disagreements." Little did either President Eisenhower or I suspect what fate had in store for me less than seven months later, when I found myself serving as Secretary of the Treasury.

At the end of our meeting, the President approved the State Department proposal, and we were half-way home. I should say here that President Eisenhower had a deep interest in Latin America. He had sent his brother Milton on a number of fact-finding trips, and he later sent then Vice-President Richard Nixon on a similar mission. None of the changes in U.S. policy that I have mentioned would have been possible without his interest and support. I should also say here that I felt that Secretary Anderson's opposition to our social justice fund for the Americas was more in the nature of *pro forma* support of earlier Treasury positions than of deep-seated opposition. Once the President had made his decision, Secretary Anderson wholeheartedly supported the new proposal.

But we still had to get congressional approval in time for the conference in order to make our proposal plausible. Latin American officials were fully aware of the vagaries of what they and other countries considered to be our eccentric and unpredictable form of government. They had learned that presidential decisions or governmental agreements with the United States were meaningless without congressional approval, and they knew that, as often as not, this was not forthcoming.

By the time we were ready to push for congressional action it was August, and a presidential campaign was getting underway. Senator John F. Kennedy had just been nominated by the Democratic Party, which controlled the Congress. I was told that the fate of our legislation depended on him and that, if it were to pass, I must have his support. I was concerned that this might not be forthcoming because by this time he had made clear his interest in a new, all-encompassing effort to improve economic conditions in Latin America, an effort that was to become the Alliance for Progress. I was worried that he might feel that our more modest proposal stole some of his thunder on this issue, and he would have been clearly justified in such feelings.

So it was with some trepidation that I went to see him at the Senate. Although I had met Senator Kennedy occasionally at meetings of the Senate Committee on Foreign Relations, I had never dealt with him on a matter of substance. When I came in he was obviously under great pressure and made very clear his distaste for the timing of my request. Why couldn't it wait until after the election?

When I explained the situation to him—the importance of the Bogota meeting, which had been scheduled well before he had taken a major position approach on Latin America, and the need for the United States to have a positive approach at the conference—he relented and most magnanimously made me a compromise proposal. He would support legislation authorizing the fund and would work to get it passed in time for the conference, but the actual appropriation of funds would have to come later, in early 1961. In this way, if elected, he could include it as part of his overall proposal for the Alliance.

I thanked him profusely and left, feeling that here was a man who could and would put the nation's interest above his own personal political ambitions. Senator Kennedy was as good as his word, and the needed legislation received final approval while the conference was still meeting in Bogota. At the conference we offered to accept and support the Brazilian concept if it could be modified to fit with our new proposal. This was done. Everyone was delighted and the conference ended on a friendly note. The way had been paved for the arrival of the Alliance for Progress.

# 3

# Myth and Reality

*Arthur Schlesinger, Jr.*

Let us begin by recalling how the Alliance for Progress received its name. During the 1960 campaign, Senator Kennedy called for a new United States approach to the western hemisphere. Sitting in the campaign bus as it rolled across Texas in September, Richard Goodwin groped for a phrase that would express for Kennedy what the phrase "Good Neighbor policy" had expressed for Franklin Roosevelt. As he pondered, his eye caught the title of a Spanish-language magazine someone had left on the bus: *Alianza*. Senator Kennedy readily agreed that "alliance" should be part of the new phrase; but alliance for what? Goodwin called Karl Meyer, then on the *Washington Post*, who called Ernesto Betancourt, then at the Pan American Union. Betancourt had two thoughts: *Alliance para el Desarollo* and *Alianza para el Progreso*. And that is how the Alliance for Progress was, if not born, at least christened.

The actual birth was more complicated. Contrary to the latter-day myth that the *Alianza* was a Yankee idea arrogantly imposed by the Kennedy Administration on Latin America, the essential elements were not only Latin American in origin but had been urged on Washington by Latin American governments to little avail, at least until Douglas Dillon came on the scene in the late 1950s. I need not remind this audience of the proposals in the 1950s of Raúl Prebisch and the Economic Commission on Latin America, and Juscelino Kubitschek and Operation Pan-America. A thoughtful memorandum in March 1961 from ten leading Latin American economists had particular impact on President Kennedy's decision to launch the Alliance for Progress 25 years ago. His speech of March 13, 1961 gave more comprehensive, more evangelical, and no doubt more pretentious form to ideas that had been circulating for a long time in Latin America.

Under the prodding of Douglas Dillon, Milton Eisenhower and, more especially, Fidel Castro, the Eisenhower Administration had come by 1960 to support the

Act of Bogota and had asked Congress to appropriate $500 million for social development in Latin America. The *Alianza* went considerably beyond this to lay down three goals for the hemisphere: long-term economic development, structural reform, and political democratization. This was what Kennedy proposed in that eloquent address to the Latin American diplomatic corps in the East Room of the White House 25 years ago. I remember Ambassador Mayobre of Venezuela taking my arm afterward and saying urgently, "We have not heard such words since Franklin Roosevelt."

Kennedy's very eloquence on that and subsequent occasions has led to a second latter-day myth that the *Alianza* was a classic case of overselling; that it promised easy accomplishment of unattainable goals; that, by exciting hopes that could not possibly be realized, it inevitably ended in resentment and disillusion. Instead of trumpeting forth bold new programs and pledging to get all Latin America moving again within a decade, the United States, we are told, should have worked without fanfare for modest and attainable ends.

Very likely Kennedy ran an often over-rhetorical administration. Still there are moments when there is no substitute for eloquence. What the hemisphere needed in 1961 was less a new aid program than a new political consciousness. The ten Latin American economists had insisted to Kennedy that the new effort must, above all, "capture the imagination of the masses." Conceptions as well as acts were necessary to create new moods and purposes, to signal breaks with the past, and to inspire fresh initiatives. In this sense, words became acts.

Kennedy, moreover, was approaching the problem with the ardor characteristic of his countrymen. As Emerson said long ago and as North Americans still believe, "Nothing great was ever achieved without enthusiasm." Would there have been a New Deal without "overselling" by Franklin Roosevelt? Would we have mobilized as swiftly for World War II without FDR's "overpromising" 50,000 planes? Enthusiasm has its legitimate role in politics. Without passion, without eloquence, the *Alianza* would have shrunk into just another U.S. aid program.

Nor did Kennedy at any point suggest that the task would be easy. Quite the contrary: In speech after speech and press conference after press conference he emphasized the difficulties that lay ahead. In June 1962 he warned against the expectation "that suddenly the problems of Latin America, which have been with us and with them for so many years, can suddenly be solved overnight." "We have, in a sense, neglected Latin America," he said in September, "so that we are engaged in a tremendous operation with insufficient resources." "We face extremely serious problems in implementing the principles of the Alliance for Progress," he told the Economic Club of New York in December. "It's trying to accomplish a social revolution under freedom under the greatest obstacles. . . . It's probably the most difficult assignment the United States has ever taken on." In the speech he delivered before the Inter-American Press Association at Miami in November 1963, four days before he went to Dallas, Kennedy repeated that "the task we have set ourselves and the Alliance for Progress is a far greater task than any we have ever undertaken in our history."

A third latter-day myth indicts the *Alianza* on the ground that it gave the United States too large a role in what had to be, in the nature of things, a Latin American enterprise. No doubt the fact that the *Alianza* was proclaimed in a White House speech created an impression, in Latin America as well as in North America, that the United States would do more than it could possibly do—an impression that may have persuaded some Latin American governments that they would not have to apply themselves to the task with full rigor. But Kennedy was acutely conscious of this problem and did his best to counter it.

Kennedy had few illusions about the ability of the United States to solve the problems of other countries. The United States' role, as he saw it, was to strengthen the hand of Latin Americans in pursuing the *Alianza*'s objectives. "They and they alone," he emphasized in the March 13 speech, "can mobilize their resources, enlist the energies of their people and modify their social patterns so that all, and not just a privileged few, share in the fruits of growth. If this effort is made, then outside assistance will give vital impetus to progress; without it, no amount of help will advance the welfare of the people." The United States' role was marginal—a point he made from start to finish. The task, as Kennedy said in his last word on the subject (at Miami in November 1963), rested essentially on the shoulders of the people of Latin America. It was they who must undergo "the agonizing process of reshaping institutions," who must "bear the shock wave of rapid change," who must "modify the traditions of centuries."

A fourth latter-day myth, much cherished on the Left, sees the *Alianza* as a neocolonial maneuver, a Wall Street plot, an instrument of United States imperialism designed to make Latin America more dependent and subordinate than ever in a world market ruled and looted by North American capitalism. This was hardly the way that North American capitalists or their friends in Latin American oligarchies saw the *Alianza* at the time. Kennedy constantly reiterated the need for land, tax, and educational reform, for the distribution of the fruits of growth to the *campesinos* and the workers, for political democracy, for human rights. "Those who make peaceful revolution impossible," he said on the first anniversary of the *Alianza*, "will make violent revolution inevitable." If the *Alianza*'s secret purpose was to lock Latin America more firmly than ever into U.S. capitalist hegemony, presidential speeches stimulating and legitimizing Latin American ambitions for economic independence and structural change seemed an odd way of going about it.

Ellis Briggs, who served as U.S. ambassador to Uruguay, Peru, and Brazil, spoke for many when he denounced the *Alianza* as a "blueprint for upheaval throughout Latin America" and offered his sympathy to those "hard-pressed" Latin chiefs of state to whom Kennedy's exhortations "sounded suspiciously like the Communist Manifesto in reverse. . . . If there is a more pernicious doctrine than one which impels the sponsor of an economic and social program to throw lighted gasoline into his neighbor's woodshed, it has yet to come to the attention of history," Briggs concluded.

The Administration's attitudes on private investment provoked Harold Geneen of International Telephone and Telegraph into the campaign that resulted in the 1962 passage of the notorious Hickenlooper Amendment. This amendment, which Kennedy opposed, required the suspension of United States economic assistance when Latin American governments took strong measures—nationalization or even discriminatory taxation—against United States corporations.

The strongest witness against the idea that the *Alianza* was an instrument of Wall Street imperialism is Fidel Castro himself. "In a way," he remarked to Jean Daniel in 1963, "it was a good idea; it marked progress of a sort. Even if it can be said that it was overdue, timid, conceived on the spur of the moment . . . despite all that I am willing to agree that the idea in itself constituted an effort to adapt to the extraordinarily rapid course of events in Latin America." This remains Castro's assessment. "The goal of the Alliance," he told Frank Mankiewicz a dozen years later, "was to effect social reform which would improve the condition of the masses. . . . It was a politically wise concept put forth to hold back the time of revolution . . . a very intelligent strategy." In a 1985 interview with the Spanish news agency EFE, he observed that "Kennedy promoted the Alliance for Progress as an antidote to social convulsions and undoubtedly the measures were imaginative." I might add that Castro reaffirmed this view of the *Alianza* when I had a couple of those five-hour talks with him in May and October of 1985.

Castro also predicted the fate of the *Alianza* with a certain astuteness. "Kennedy's good ideas aren't going to yield any results," he assured Jean Daniel. Historically, the United States had been committed to the Latin oligarchs. "Suddenly a President arrives on the scene who tries to support the interests of another class (which has no access to the levers of power)." What happens then? "The trusts see that their interests are being a little compromised (just barely, but still compromised); the Pentagon thinks the strategic bases are in danger; the powerful oligarchies in all the Latin American countries alert their American friends; they sabotage their new policy, and soon Kennedy has everyone against him."

Kennedy certainly had a good many people against him. The Latin American oligarchs, with notable exceptions, resented and detested the *Alianza*. They felt that Kennedy had wantonly lined up the United States with radicals who wanted to dispossess them in their own countries. The United States business community, again with notable exceptions, was unenthusiastic about the *Alianza*. Foreign private investment in Latin America actually declined in 1961. The Pentagon, the CIA and, to a degree, the State Department, when they thought about Latin America at all, thought most of the time about 'hemispheric security.' Though the security concern was far from pointless, as the Cuban missile crisis showed, it was too often reduced to a simple-minded reading of every decision in terms of an exaggerated communist threat.

The unrelenting pressure of the national-security bureaucracy generated a set of programs plausibly intended to protect the development process from disruption and sabotage, but which soon acquired a life, momentum, and horrid impact of their own. From the Bay of Pigs through the counterinsurgency infatuation of 1962 to the State Department's International Policy Academy and the public safety programs of the Agency for International Development, these efforts freely dispensed anti-riot instruction, gas guns and grenades, helicopters and small arms to Latin American internal security forces. In the end, United States police training provided the Latin American status quo with ugly weapons that were used promiscuously against all forms of dissent. Washington thus inadvertently contributed to the militarist assault on democracy that disfigured Latin America in the later 1960s. It is evident, I believe, that national-security pressures did more in the early years than capitalist pressures to deform the *Alianza*.

Strictly speaking, there were only those early years. The *Alianza* came to an end with Kennedy's death. Subsequently another program by the same name struggled on after the political and social components of the original *Alianza* — that is, its heart — had been removed. For the new Administration moved rapidly to liquidate two of the three Kennedy goals: structural change and political democratization. Economic development remained a central objective, but even this was often subordinated to the use of the *Alianza* as a political arm of the United States business community.

In Peru, for example, the Johnson Administration stopped aid to the democratic, pro-*Alianza* Belaude government in the hope of coercing Lima toward a favorable settlement with the International Petroleum Company, a Standard Oil of New Jersey subsidiary.

In 1965 Senator Robert Kennedy, about to leave on a trip to Latin America, asked the assistant secretary for inter-American affairs to explain the point of stopping aid to a government in Lima dedicated to the goals of the *Alianza* and at the same time increasing aid to the new military dictatorship in Brazil. After receiving the usual palaver in response, Robert Kennedy finally said, "You're saying that what the Alliance for Progress has come down to is that if you have a military takeover, outlaw political parties, close down the congress, put your political opponents in jail, and take away the basic freedoms of the people, you can get all the American aid you want. But, if you mess around with an American oil company, we'll cut you off without a penny. Is that right? Is that what the Alliance for Progress comes down to?" The assistant secretary said, "That's about the size of it."

"The Alliance for Progress is dead," Victor Alba wrote in Mexico. "What is left is a bureaucratic structure, mountains of mimeographed paper, a sarcastic smile on the lips of the oligarchs, and pangs of guilt on the part of the politicians of the left who did not take advantage of the Alliance and make it theirs."

Was the *Alianza* a failure? Who knows? It was never really tried. It lasted around a thousand days, not a sufficient test, and thereafter only the name remained. Even that disappeared in the Nixon years. Could it have succeeded? What lessons does the aborted experiment offer us 25 years later?

Looking back, I believe that both Kennedy and Castro were wrong in the early 1960s in supposing that Latin America was ripe for revolution. We all underestimated the dead weight of vested interests, of structural rigidities, and of popular inertia — a weight so deadly and so pervasive that some Latin American idealists desperately conclude that the only way to throw it off is through revolutionary violence. But the most potent political emotion in Latin America, then and now, is not class revolution but nationalism. "Unless the Alliance is able to ally itself with nationalism," Arturo Morales-Carrion wrote 20 years ago, " . . . the Alliance will be pouring money into a psychological void." This is an alliance the United States has not made, perhaps cannot make; for how is Latin American nationalism to define itself except by defiance of the United States?

Yet let us not be too tragic about the problems of the hemisphere. History offers numerous examples of nations that have achieved modernization without violence and tyranny. Latin America has its absolutist and centralizing past. But I retain the conviction that the passion for human rights and democratic choice is strong and real. That passion finds its primary expression in the progressive democratic parties, whether of social democratic or Christian democratic tendencies.

The original *Alianza* was a wager on the capacity of progressive democratic governments, with carefully designed economic assistance and political support from the United States, to carry through a peaceful revolution. Latin America today has a greater number of moderate and democratic governments than it has had for a long time. It is true that the problems they face are graver than those the hemisphere faced when the *Alianza* began: the population is twice as large today, the external debt 18 times greater. Still, a new hope is alive throughout the Americas.

The challenge to the United States is to reinforce that hope. I have no time to discuss ways and means, but I am sure that the worst way to go about it is to keep on doing what we are doing today. The present course of military intervention in Central America can only rouse and unite Latin American nationalism against the United States. It might be added that the Latin American external debt, with its potential for bringing down many leading United States banks, is a greater threat to the United States than the beleaguered Sandinistas in Managua. What is required is not the return of Rambo, the Yanqui bully, but a hemisphere-wide revival of the humane and cooperative spirit that animated the Alliance for Progress.

In the end, however, the fate of Latin America depends only marginally on the United States. "Latin America," Octavio Paz has written, "is a continent full of rhetoric and violence—two forms of pride, two ways of ignoring reality." The Latin American future depends on the capacity of Latin Americans themselves to confront and change their own reality. As they do this, I believe that they will find themselves reclaiming the ideas of the *Alianza*—ideas Latin in their origin and early formulation—and making them at last their own.

# 4

# The Alliance at Birth: Hopes and Fears

## Lincoln Gordon

Twenty-five years ago, on March 13, 1961, the Alliance for Progress was launched by President Kennedy in a highly publicized White House address to the Latin American diplomatic corps and many members of Congress. It had been foreshadowed in his Inaugural Address and his first message on the State of the Union. The substantive content had been drawn from the report of a transition period task force chaired by Adolf Berle, which dealt with all aspects of inter-American relationships—political, security, cultural, and economic. As a task force member, I was responsible for the economic chapter, in which the basic concepts of the Alliance were officially formulated for the first time.

I have never claimed originality for those concepts. They had emerged over several years in the form of proposals by Latin Americans in the Inter-American Economic and Social Council of the OAS, studies by ECLA (the UN Economic Commission for Latin America), academic thinking both North and South, and most recently, the 1960 Act of Bogota. But as the economic policy specialist on the task force, the author of Kennedy's March 14 message to Congress requesting funding for the Act of Bogota, and an active member of the U.S. negotiating team at Punta del Este, I can speak with some authority about our hopes and fears a quarter century ago.

### WHY THE ALLIANCE?

Some geopolitically inclined historians, preoccupied with superpower relations as the be-all and end-all of foreign policy, interpret the Alliance simply as a reaction to the revolution in Cuba—a prophylactic program to negate Che Guevara's prediction of "many Sierra Maestras" in Central and South America. That is a grossly oversimplified assessment. Admittedly, the March 13 speech did point to "the alien forces which once again seek to impose the despotisms of the Old World on the people of the New," and later coupled Castro with Trujillo in expressing the hope that Cuba and the Dominican Republic would soon rejoin "the society of free men." Fear of communist expansion also helped to secure warm bipartisan support for the Alliance in Congress. But there was also the more generalized concern about nationalist anti-Americanism and demagogic populism, crystallized by the hostile reception of Vice-President Nixon in 1958 and the subsequent sober evaluation by Milton Eisenhower. It was evident that the good-will in Latin America generated by Franklin Roosevelt's "Good Neighbor" policy and collaboration during World War II had been dissipated by several years of neglect in favor of Europe, Japan, and Korea. It was felt that the resulting resentments and frustrations might jeopardize American interests well short of an expansion of the so-called "Sino-Soviet bloc." And nationalist populism, as *Peronismo* in Argentina had demonstrated, was also a prescription for economic stagnation and continuing political instability.

Alongside these negative motivations was the positive side—the hopes for a major advance in social and economic development in a region of long-standing special interest to the United States. For me and for most North American initiators of the Alliance, these positive expectations were the dominant force behind our actions. That may surprise listeners in the 1980s when superpower rivalries are again so prominent. It can be understood only against the background of the Kennedy Administration's wider policies of aid for the world's underdeveloped regions—in part ideological, but also, in the famous phrase of the Inaugural Address, "because it is right." A wave of intellectual interest in economic development had swept over the academic world during the 1950s, amply supported by the great philanthropic foundations. Among officials and policymakers dealing with foreign aid, there had been a continuous broadening of involvement, both geographical and functional. Thinking in both academic and official circles had been deeply influenced by Walt Rostow's *Stages of Economic Growth*, with its concepts of "preconditions" and "take-off into sustained growth." The underlying national interest was not identified with either superpower rivalry or global missionary do-goodism. It was the conviction that American values of freedom, responsible government, and equality of opportunity, together with American economic prosperity, would be more likely to flourish at home if they were widely shared abroad. We had benefitted from the revival of Europe and Japan, and would benefit similarly from the modernization of the underdeveloped world.

Those of us interested in Latin America saw special opportunities for accelerating development in this hemisphere. We believed that most of the region, especially the larger countries of South America and Mexico, were on the threshold of a Rostovian take-off. We knew that there were institutional and social obstacles, but not cultural ones such as Oriental fatalism, sacred cows, or caste systems. There was a base of substantial urbanization, industrialization, and modernization of agriculture and animal husbandry. Although there were extremes of wealth and poverty, there were also substantial middle classes. There had been a gratifying recent wave of democratization, with dictators being displaced in Colombia, Venezuela, Argentina, and Peru (soon to be followed in the Dominican Republic). Economic development and modernization seemed to be at the top of the Latin American political agenda. Juscelino Kubitschek's *desenvolvimientismo* (developmentalism) in Brazil, with its slogan "Fifty Years in Five" and its fuzzy but appealing call for *Operacao Pan-Americana*, seemed to embody all of these characteristics. There were similar priorities in the Democratic Action parties of Romulo Betancourt and Pepe Figueres, the Christian Democrats in Chile and Venezuela, the *Radicales* in Argentina, the Liberals in Colombia, and the Diaz Ordaz wing of Mexico's PRI. All this was in sharp contrast to most of Africa, which still lacked the preconditions for take-off, and South and Southeast Asia, which would have to overcome ancient cultural obstacles. So Latin America appeared ripe for a big push, in which ten years of intensive effort, with substantial but not unthinkable volumes of external capital and technical assistance, might engender self-sustaining further growth and bring most of the region within sight of southern European levels of production and income.

What of U.S. economic interests, which, according to Leninist doctrine – and much discourse in Latin America at the time – should have dominated American foreign policy? In the minds of those who created the Alliance, they were distinctly subordinate to the broader political and economic objectives. We saw trade and investment as a positive-sum game with Latin America, beneficial to both parties and indispensable to a successful developmental push. Being acutely aware of Latin American nationalist concern about foreign domination of the region's economies, I was a strong proponent of joint ventures as the most effective vehicle for transferring technology and developing badly needed export markets. But there was no narrow notion of buying protection for existing American investments – and no Hickenlooper Amendment – in the original legislative proposals.

Thus concerns and opportunities, hopes and fears converged on the goal of a peaceful but revolutionary transformation aimed at democratic political stability, accelerated economic growth, broad participation in the benefits, and enhanced social justice. That was an ambitious agenda. Some pitfalls were obvious from the start and others soon emerged.

## THE CONCEPT OF REVOLUTIONARY
## BUT NONVIOLENT TRANSFORMATION

It was common in the 1960s to compare the Alliance with the Marshall Plan. That comparison was invited by Kennedy himself, when he said on March 13 that the United States "should help provide resources of a scope and magnitude sufficient to make this bold development plan a success – just as we helped to provide, against equal odds nearly, the resources adequate to help rebuild the economies of Western Europe." In fact, however, the odds against success in Latin America were much heavier.

We were well aware of the quintessential differences, both in the base conditions and in the actions required. Europe had suffered great physical damage and its markets had been disrupted, but it did not need changes in social structure. It did not lack technical and administrative skills. Its basic requirements in 1947 were for a large input of foreign exchange during the phase of intensive reconstruction, together with an energizing impulse to remove the trade and payments restrictions that had been erected due to the foreign exchange shortage. Europe's governments and political leaders, except for the communists, had a single-minded dedication to rapid economic recovery. In practice, the momentum of the Marshall Plan carried Europe well beyond mere recovery and helped to spark major productive innovations in both governmental and business practices. But the foundations for success of the Marshall Plan were already in place long before the war.

The challenge for the Alliance was far more profound. The new program called for new industries, new ways of farming, new systems of education and health care, new attitudes toward government and community responsibility, new relationships between city and country, landlord and peasant, manager and worker. The analogy with the Marshall Plan was valid only in two respects: the promise of large-scale aid from the United States and the concept of a partnership between the United States and Latin American nations. On this latter front, however, the initial institutional arrangements were weak. A closer fit to the Marshall Plan pattern was achieved only with the establishment of the Inter-American Committee on the Alliance for Progress (CIAP) at the end of 1963.

Why did we believe in the possibility of economic and social progress amounting to a nonviolent revolutionary transformation? On this central issue, my own thinking leaned heavily on the example of Sao Paulo (both city and state), which I had come to know as a researcher on Brazilian development. Sao Paulo in 1960 seemed to me much like New York in 1900 — or perhaps even 1920. There was a steep social pyramid. At the top, New York's Gilded Age "Four Hundred" were matched by the *gran fino* "four-century Paulistas." At the bottom, masses of refugees from drought in Brazil's northeast corresponded to New York's recent immigrants from Southern and Eastern Europe. In between was a substantial and growing middle class, mixing people of all origins. Literacy was spreading. The University of Sao Paulo was shifting from French-style pedantry to education and training directly relevant to development, somewhat like City College and New York University early in the century.

Social mobility was extraordinary in Sao Paulo. The most famous examples were rags-to-riches immigrant families from Italy, Lebanon, and Eastern Europe. But there were also well-paid foremen in automobile factories, formerly illiterate northeastern peasants who were self-educated and trained on the job. Several smaller cities spread about the state were emulating the metropolis. In the countryside, nearby the large coffee *fazendas* were thousands of family farms and the fantastically successful cooperatives founded by Japanese immigrant horticulturalists. The state government had moved away from *clientelismo* to well-administered infrastructure development, planned by competent technocrats. Political influence, once monopolized by the larger coffeegrowers, was now shared with industrialists, trade union leaders, small businessmen, and others. There was an atmosphere of energy, dynamism, and opportunity fostered by a constructive symbiosis of government, private business, and foreign investment. In short, Sao Paulo had already experienced a revolutionary transformation without violent revolution.

No one would claim that New York in 1920 (or even in 1960!) was a perfect society. But there was surely the capacity there for continuing economic and social progress that could extend its benefits to successive layers of the society, until all could participate. So it also seemed in Sao Paulo. Of course Sao Paulo was in a class by itself in Latin America. But why should it not be replicable? Within Brazil, Belo Horizonte, Curitiba, and Porto Alegre were moving in similar directions, although this was not the case in Recife or Fortaleza. Were there not hopeful beginnings in Mexico City, Medellin, Caracas, Santiago de Chile, Lima, and even Buenos Aires, if the stagnating miasma of Peronism could be dissipated? With the right kind of push from the above and help from outside, could not these beginnings be built on? Some of Washington's Latin specialists in the State and Treasury Departments were very skeptical, but others joined the Kennedy team enthusiastically in trying to give operational content to this kind of vision. In our view, history taught that such gradual transformations were generally more durable than the spectacular violent revolutions so often followed by reaction and tyranny.

While it eschewed violent means, in most of Latin America the Alliance would require extensive social, political, and economic reforms. Land reform, it was thought, could be promoted through taxation of nonproductive land and limitations on *latifundia*. Tax, institutional, and administrative reforms would also be necessary parts of the package. And thoroughgoing reform of educational systems at all levels was a prerequisite to the basic goal of widespread popular participation. To avoid zero-sum games in which the potential loser would make such reforms politically impossible, they would have to be carried out in an environment of rapid overall economic growth. Thus the program envisaged a new and more equitable distribution of the gains from development, but—in the terminology of Hollis Chenery, one of the "Nine Wise Men" of the Alliance's early structure—it has to be redistributed with growth. Otherwise, given the low average incomes prevailing in the region, the program would merely redistribute poverty.

## SOME REFLECTIONS

Others will assess what happened to the Alliance for Progress, why it happened, whether there were successes along with the obvious failures, and the lessons for today and tomorrow. I will conclude with a few personal reflections, 25 years later, on the hopes and fears at the launching.

The fears were not overdrawn. The Soviet model of economic development has by now been so thoroughly discredited that one easily forgets how many Latin Americans, especially intellectuals, were attracted to the notion of affiliation with the USSR. Marxist philosophy remains quite popular in Latin America, but not, in most cases, as a guide to action. The danger of spreading demagogic nationalist populism was even greater. The Alliance helped to avert this threat for a time, but it takes on renewed strength in each period of North American neglect, up to and including the present.

As to the hopes, there have been profound disappointments. First and foremost were the long interruptions in democratic institutions and civil liberties in all of South America beyond Colombia and Venezuela. On the economic and social side, even after making large discounts in the overambitious goals and timetables of the Charter of Punta del Este, results were far below expectations and considerably short of realistic possibilities. Should we then conclude that the hopes were simply a naive and impossible dream? Was the Alliance misconceived from its very beginnings?

I believe not. In my judgment, the diagnosis in 1961 and the array of proposed policies, reforms, and outside assistance were correct in their essentials. But there were two critical errors. On the Latin American side, as I noted in a speech as early as August 1962, the Alliance never generated a sufficient political mystique to overcome the resistance of vested interests and the obstacles of traditional political rivalries. On the United States' side, we erred in not promoting from the very beginning arrangements appropriate to a more genuine partnership.

Having accepted President Kennedy's invitation to lead our embassy in Brazil in order to help implement the Alliance there, I became deeply frustrated by the growing realization that the central purposes of two successive presidents—Janio Quadros and Joao Goulart—were not economic and social progress, but rather the pursuit of personal and illegitimate power. Fortunately, numbers of Brazilian cabinet ministers and state governors did share the goals of the Alliance, and we were able to cooperate with them. Elsewhere in Latin America, there were bright periods with Frei and Carlos Lleras and Diaz Ordaz, and dark periods too numerous to mention. At the inter-American summit of 1967, we hoped to reinvigorate the Alliance in both spirit and substance, but that opportunity passed with Johnson's withdrawal. Then the Alliance was repudiated by Nixon and Kissinger in favor of a new era of neglect. For that mistake, all the Americas—North, Central, and South—continue to pay a heavy price.

I nonetheless believe that the balance sheet of the Alliance for Progress remains on the positive side. Between 1960 and 1980, Latin America did make significant advances in the continuing transformation from Third World dependency to independent action on the world stage—a transformation that will somehow surmount today's international debt crisis. During the 1960s, the Alliance helped lay the foundations for the surge in production of the 1970s, and for notable improvements in literacy, health, and life expectancy. Above all, its investments in human resources—in technical and administrative skills to complement the region's humanistic tradition—has made possible an ongoing modernization, looking ultimately to full incorporation into the First World. Recent political develop-ments have vindicated those of us who were confident that the underlying support for democratic institutions would outlast military authoritarianism, even though it took longer than we hoped. The great misfortune is that the opportunity of 1961 was not fully used. But the enterprise we set in motion a quarter century ago was not merely another plowing of the seas.

# 5

# The Will to Economic Development

*Teodoro Moscoso*

Having been called upon frequently to discuss the implications of President Reagan's Caribbean Basin Initiative, I often recall our experience with the Alliance for Progress. Thinking of the Alliance fills me with nostalgia and pain for what might have happened but did not. Memory of the few successes fills me with joy; the errors and failures generate much regret.

Twenty-five years ago I thought there were solutions to the problems taken on by the Alliance, and that given time and patience—and less negativism from the U.S. power structure—we would be able to work out solutions. Perhaps this optimism, or if you will, idealism, was misplaced. Yet I still remember the old saying about the aerodynamic certitude that a bumblebee cannot fly—yet it does.

Since the memory span in Washington is brief, and its interest in Latin America is as durable as yesterday's newspapers, I would like to note here that there were important tangible results in the first four years of the Alliance: 6,000 miles of roads were built; 130,000 dwelling units were constructed; 530,000 kilowatts of power-generating capacity were installed; 136,000 new acres of farmland were irrigated; classrooms were built for an additional 1 million students; 450 new health facilities were constructed; financing was provided for over 5,000 private industrial firms, and so on.

Many of these achievements have been duly noted by historians and others who choose to defend the Alliance. I would like to examine an area that has not received the attention, analysis, and understanding that is both merited and sorely needed: the relationship between culture and economic growth. By culture, I mean basically the values of a people, their priorities and their mode of thinking, of seeing themselves and the world.

To say that economic development in the final analysis is dependent on the will, the determination, of a people to lift themselves from poverty, seems obvious to the point of being trite. But that is precisely the point that I want to make. If we look at the western hemisphere, if we look coldly, objectively, at what has happened in North America—the United States and Canada—and at what has happened in the Caribbean, Central and South America, at the core of the enormous economic differences is a crucial difference in what I could call "the will to economic development."

And this will is a manifestation, I believe, of culture. Why has North America achieved such a high degree of economic and social development, and why haven't the Caribbean, Central and South America? I hope that I will not be accused of racism, or of being anti-Iberian, or anti-Spanish when I say that the answer lies in the different cultures. In one there is the will to economic development while, in the other, with a few exceptions, this is not the case.

I want also to make another point. The decisive element in the relation between culture and economic development is political leadership. This is crucial because the last thing that I want to imply is that Spanish America will always be what it has been because it is *Spanish* America. Political leadership can play a decisive role precisely because it can ignite in a people the will to economic development. It can do so even when it must overcome other powerful and deeply imbedded cultural characteristics that impede, or even denigrate, economic growth.

Puerto Rico, I believe, is a good example. All the elements have long existed in Puerto Rico that seemed to make economic development, not difficult, nor even unlikely, but impossible. Puerto Rico is a very small island, one-twelfth the size of Cuba. It is enormously overpopulated (nearly 1,000 people per square mile), lacking in natural resources, with very little arable land, and perhaps worst of all, permeated by a centuries-old state of mind aptly called by Oscar Lewis the "culture of poverty."

We were extremely poor for four very long centuries under Spain and only a bit less poor for half a century under the United States. Suddenly, toward the end of the 1940s something strange happened in Puerto Rico. It became known among the economists of the world as a "miracle." We had an economic take-off. It was indeed a wonderous thing since Puerto Rico not only achieved economic growth, it achieved one of the highest rates of growth in the world for a sustained period of time. The London *Economist* described our peaceful revolution as a "century of economic development in a single decade."

What happened in Puerto Rico?

All the elements that seemed to doom Puerto Rico to extreme poverty were still there. Our hard-core realities were unchanged. What did change was the quality of our political leadership.

Puerto Rico was blessed with a great political leader, Luis Muñoz Marín. If you were to ask me out of all of the elements that made Operation Bootstrap such a success, of all of the ingredients that produced our economic miracle, which was the most important, I would answer this way: Certainly it would not have taken place without our special economic and political relationship with the U.S., especially our free access to the U.S. market combined with our full exemption from U.S. taxes.

I would add that it probably would not have happened without the contribution, I believe sadly ignored, of the last American governor of Puerto Rico, Rexford Tugwell, who created the governmental structure that made possible what Charles T. Goodsell has correctly described as the "administration of a revolution."

But I would answer that the most fundamental cause of our economic take-off was the political leadership of Muñoz Marín, who turned our culture of poverty into a will to economic development. He changed the state of mind of the Puerto Rican people. He changed the culture.

I noted at the outset that the relation of culture to economic development has not received the attention that is needed. But what inspired me to bring up this point here today is a recently published book by Lawrence Harrison based on precisely that theme. The title of the book could not be more appropriate: *Underdevelopment is a State of Mind: The Latin American Case*. The launching platform for Harrison's thesis (see Chapter 23) is a statement by a Peruvian intellectual, Augusto Salazar:

Underdevelopment is not just a collection of statistical indices which enable a socio-economic picture to be drawn. It is also *a state of mind*, a way of expression, a form of outlook and a collective personality marked by chronic infirmities and forms of maladjustments.

Harrison proceeds to analyze what makes development happen and how little development has occurred in the Latin part of the western hemisphere. His studies convince him that culture is indeed the principal determinant of the course and pace of development. To reinforce his point, Harrison argues that where Latin American countries have strayed from the mainstream of traditional Hispanic-American culture and the underlying influence of Spain and its institutions, they have progressed further in the journey toward realization of social and economic progress.

Now, if I am correct in saying that economic development is fundamentally a matter of will — or, in negative terms, if Harrison is right in his thesis that "underdevelopment is a state of mind" — the obvious conclusion is that Latin American attitudes, culture, and politics are to blame for Latin American underdevelopment.

Needless to say, this contradicts the conventional wisdom of a great number of Latin American political leaders, economists, and intellectuals who claim that the essential cause of underdevelopment in Latin America is American imperialism. Harrison goes to great lengths to refute what has become known as the dependency theory: that Latin America is poor because the United States is rich. The root cause of underdevelopment, according to the theory, is the nature of U.S. capitalism, which depresses the price of Latin American export products while inflating prices of U.S. exports to Latin America and which "exploits" Latin American workers through the monopolies of U.S. multinationals.

Again, allow me to draw on our experience in Puerto Rico. For nearly the first half of this century, our "culture of poverty" was wrapped in the ideological argument that the impediment to Puerto Rico's development was "U.S. colonialism." We must first rid ourselves of our colonial relationship to the U.S. in order to attack our tragic economic and social ills, it was argued. Muñoz Marín's genius was his ability to liberate Puerto Rico from the culture of poverty by making a truly astounding discovery: It was precisely our unique relationship to the U.S. that gave us the powerful instrument to lift the entire island from extreme poverty. If you will, that unique relationship became our great natural resource – it allowed us to attract thousands of industries that created hundreds of thousands of jobs. Muñoz' political wisdom consisted in not falling victim to egocentric nationalism that would have destroyed what became the powerful industrial incentives that produced our economic miracle.

Once again, this was an example of political leadership changing a cultural attitude – the escapist argument that what is wrong in Puerto Rico is the fault of the United States and a collective surrendering to impotency and hopelessness.

Now, one reason that Harrison's book struck such a strong chord in my heart is that I have long admired an outstanding Latin American thinker who has been saying exactly this for a long time, but who has been largely ignored in the U.S. and, needless to say, who has been denounced as a "lackey of American imperialism" by his Latin American peers.

Carlos Rangel, the Venezuelan scholar and journalist, wrote an extraordinary book ten years ago in which he cried out to his Latin American brothers: "Look, look, let's stop blaming the North Americans for our own failures."

This book, *From the Noble Savage to the Noble Revolutionary*, is truly the first contemporary essay on Latin American civilization in which a new and probably correct interpretation is offered. Rangel begins by dissipating the litany of untrue descriptions, complacent excuses, and false interpretations that dominate so much of Latin American writing. Throughout his work Rangel continuously confronts Latin America with its myths and its realities and underscores the discrepancies between what a society truly is and the image that society has of itself. For the 20th century Latin American (as Jean-Francois Revel, the French sociologist and an admirer of Rangel, puts it), North America is reactionary, Latin America is revolutionary. The insolent economic success of the United States (at least until lately) is resented bitterly as an insufferable scandal. Here was a bunch of Anglo-Saxons who arrived in this hemisphere much later than the Spaniards, lacking everything, wrongheadedly establishing themselves in such a severe climate as to raise doubts about their survival – and they have become the number one power in the world. Comparing the socioeconomic performance of the colonizers of the north and the south of this hemisphere hurts Latino pride. Furthermore, no Latin American leader worth his salt will ever deny publicly that all the ills that affect

Latin countries find their root cause in North American imperialism—all, that is, except Rangel, who makes this point:

It was Latin America's destiny to be colonized by a country that, though admirable in many ways, was at the time beginning to reject the spirit of modernism and to build walls against the rise of rationalism, empiricism, and free thought—that is to say, against the very bases of the modern industrial and liberal revolution, and of capitalist economic development. Imperialism has existed and still exists, but it is more a consequence rather than a cause of our [Latin America's] impotence.[1]

Rangel and his admirer Revel both agree that classifying Latin America as belonging to the Third World is incorrect. They contend that it is essentially Western, as attested by its culture, language, and world view. Their diagnosis of the problem is that underdevelopment in Latin America is first political and then economic, rather than the other way around as is the case with the Third World.

Rangel is particularly critical of the Catholic Church because of its absolutism, for influencing what Latin America has and has not become. Latin American Catholic society, he contends, is readily satisfied with appearances, with a show of religion. In Rangel's view only North American influence has in recent years allowed Latin American societies to become somewhat more tolerant of nonconformist behavior patterns. Protestant North American society, by way of comparison, puts far more stringent requirements on its citizens to give proof of what they really are, as against what they claim to be.

Rangel firmly believes that Latin American history has been determined mainly by its Spanish culture and that this history, in his view, is a "story of failure." He backs his conviction with a listing of indicators:

1. the disproportionate success of the United States in the same "New World" during a parallel period of history;
2. Latin America's inability to evolve harmonious and cohesive nations capable of redeeming, or at least reasonably improving, the lot of vast marginal social and economic groups;
3. Latin America's impotence in its external relations—military, economic, political, cultural—and hence its vulnerability to outside . . . influences in each of these areas;
4. the notable lack of stability of Latin American forms of government, other than those founded on dictatorships and repression;
5. the absence of noteworthy Latin American contributions in the sciences or the arts (the exceptions merely prove the rule);
6. Latin America's population growth rate, the highest in the world;
7. Latin America's feeling that it is of little, if any, use to the world at large.[2]

I have been profusely quoting Rangel and Harrison, not only because their analysis describes my own views on Latin American underdevelopment, but also because I believe that no U.S. economic policy or program can succeed in Latin America unless it is realistic, and it can be realistic only if it is grounded in a precise understanding of Latin American culture. Allow me one self-serving quote that appears in the introduction of Harrison's book.[3] As I said, we worked together in the early days of the Alliance for Progress. Harrison quotes from a speech I made in 1966, after I had served as the U.S. coordinator of the Alliance:

The Latin American case is so complex, so difficult to solve, and so fraught with human and global danger and distress that the use of the word "anguish" is not an exaggeration.

The longer I live, the more I believe that, just as no human being can save another who does not have the will to save himself, no country can save another no matter how good its intentions or how hard it tries.

Well, I have lived a little longer since saying those words, and I feel even more strongly today than I did then about this fundamental truth.

On a more pragmatic note, it is interesting to observe how, at least in some measure, the ideas of the Alliance for Progress are reflected in a current program, the Caribbean Basin Initiative (CBI). The CBI is really a mix of the Alliance, Operation Bootstrap, and a very positive new factor that we had hoped to achieve in the Alliance days—one-way free trade. Back in the 1960s, the entrenched bureaucracy in Washington did not welcome a deviation from the prevailing U.S. free trade policies.

Regional one-way free trade was frowned upon for Latin America and the Caribbean, even though European countries had already created trading blocs with their former African and Asian colonies. Proposals made in those days were rejected because, in the words of one of the protagonists, "The large interests of the free world are tied to the creation of a more dynamic trading system. Preferential blocs could tend to separate the world." The deluded State Department official who wrote those words eventually ate them and promptly fell in line 25 years later when President Reagan announced the CBI, which has one-way free trade as its shining centerpiece.

Of course there have been many protectionist amendments to the CBI, but actually the U.S. customs barrier has not been, over the past 25 years, the sinister obstacle to hard-currency earning that some enemies of the development have made it out to be. I recall that in 1960, the Inter-American Research Committee of the National Planning Association published an extensive, profusely documented report on the future of Latin American exports to the United States. The report proved that many manufactured products could be competitively produced in Latin America and sold in the U.S., provided adequate tax and other incentives were offered to prospective producers. So impressed was I by the potential for development implied in this report that, as a part of the Alliance effort, I had hundreds of copies distributed to leaders in all member countries. Not one letter of acknowledgement, let alone of interest, was ever received. Let's see if the bus isn't missed this time.

In conclusion, I would like to stress that the physical accomplishments of the Alliance for Progress were overshadowed by much more meaningful signs of socioeconomic and political progress. I turn again to Carlos Rangel, as a scholar and Latin American, to provide the ultimate evaluation of the Alliance:

Habitual references to the 'technical' hypotheses and measures recommended by the international experts have led us to lose track of the one important element: the very real success scored by the alliance. . . . Established ancestral habits were shaken, the self-satisfaction and inertia of Latin American leaders were disturbed, and hope was held out to the people. Today, Latin America as a whole, including such formerly staunch conservative sectors as the church and the army, rejects immobilism and has started thinking along dynamic lines. The concept of economic planning has been generally accepted. It is now tacitly accepted that it is important that these societies, which are anything but revolutionary as has been claimed, but rather desperately stable, if not static, need a good shaking up.[4]

The Alliance for Progress did succeed in at least shaking things up a bit in Latin America and I am glad that I was able to help. But Rangel also put his finger on one of the failings of the Alliance which brings me back, in closing, to my original point. He wrote: "The Alliance . . . failed to take into account the cultural impediments to development inherent in the ancestral customs and traditions of the Latin American societies."[5]

It all boils down to the ancient maxim: God helps those who help themselves. If, on the one hand, this leads us to lecture Latin Americans that they have essentially themselves to blame for their underdevelopment, the other side of the coin could not be more promising: Latin America's economic development, its future, is in Latin American hands — in the quality of its political leadership, and in the depth of its will.

## NOTES

1. Carlos Rangel Guevara, *The Latin Americans: Their Love-Hate Relationship with the U.S.*, tr. Ivan Kats. (New York: Harcourt, Brace Jovanovich, 1977).

2. Ibid.

3. Lawrence E. Harrison, *Underdevelopment Is a State of Mind* (Cambridge: Harvard Center for International Affairs and University Press of America, 1985).

4. Rangel Guevara, *The Latin Americans*.

5. Ibid.

*6*

# Principles and Performance

*Felipe Herrera*

By the end of the 1950s, President Eisenhower's policy toward Latin America had begun to reflect a U.S. position quite different from that of the earlier postwar period. In fact, there had not been an active inter-American policy during those years, due to Washington's priority toward Eastern and Western Europe. A clear example of the newly emerging interest in Latin America was the Eisenhower Administration's decision to sign the Constitutive Agreement of the Organization of American States in Bogota in 1948.

The change was a result, in part, of pressure by broad sectors in the United States who were conscious of the growing criticism of the U.S. in inter-American economic meetings, such as those held in Quintandinha, Brazil in 1954 and Buenos Aires, Argentina in 1957. The hostile reception of then Vice-President Richard Nixon when he toured several Latin American countries during this period also influenced the change of attitude.

In March 1958, Brazilian President Juscelino Kubitschek wrote a letter to Eisenhower in which he referred to these problems and called for an "Operation Pan-America." He said:

We cannot hide the fact that, in the world's opinion, the idea of pan-American unity is seriously undermined. Negative events, which we deplore, leave the impression that we do not live fraternally in the Americas. Corrective action . . . needs to be taken. We must truly examine our conscience toward pan-Americanism and determine whether we are on the right track.

In August of that year the government of Brazil sent a memorandum to all American countries defining the bases for a pan-American Operation and referring to Latin America's need for international cooperation. It should be pointed out that the foundations for the creation of an inter-American bank and of regional markets in the hemisphere were set forth in this document, similar to those that had been established for the European Economic Community in Rome in 1957.

In September, the U.S. agreed to support the creation of the Inter-American Development Bank, and negotiat'ons began shortly thereafter within the framework of the OAS. The bank began operations in early 1960. During the same year, a meeting that could be seen as the forerunner of the Alliance for Progress was called in Bogota.

This series of events helped the recently elected U.S. President, John F. Kennedy, to announce his new program, the Alliance for Progress, during a March 13 meeting at the White House. Many of President Kennedy's remarks did not come as a surprise to those attending the event. A group of Latin Americans had been preparing a memorandum about future relations and regional policies for the new President during the preceding weeks. Among the participants in this group were Raúl Prebisch, Juan Antonio Mayobre, Jorge Sol, and Enrique Perez-Cisneros.

The following excerpts from Kennedy's remarks that day are, I believe, completely valid today:

We should give our support to any economic integration process that truly opens markets and economic opportunity. The fragmentation of Latin American economies poses a serious obstacle to industrial development. Some projects, such as the establishment of a common market for Central America and of Latin American free trade areas, would facilitate development in this field. . . .

As it has well been expressed by the Government of Chile, the time has come to take the first steps towards the establishment of a reasonable limit to armamentism. . . .

I have just signed a request to Congress to approve an appropriation of $500 million as a first step towards the accomplishment of the document *Acta de Bogota*. This constitutes the first long-term inter-American step toward eliminating social barriers that obstruct economic progress.

Ninety days later, as president of the IDB, I had to co-sign with President Kennedy the document that created the Trust Fund for Social Progress. The latter facilitated the IDB's cooperation with social reform programs in Latin America affecting education, agriculture, sanitation, technology, and housing.

Kennedy put much emphasis on the consolidation of democratic systems within the new inter-American policy he was developing. This was clear when he stated: "Our Alliance for Progress is an alliance of the governments and one whose main objective is to eliminate tyranny in a hemisphere where there is no legitimate place for it."

Kennedy's concerns were echoed in the "Declaration to the People of the Americas," which precedes the Charter of Punta del Este into which the Alliance programs were incorporated in August 1961. In this regard, the Declaration says:

This Alliance is based on the principle that states that the desire for work, housing, land, school, and health is best achieved in freedom and through the institutions created in a representative democracy. There is not, and there cannot be, a system to guarantee true progress if there is no opportunity to assert the individual dignity that constitutes the foundation of our civilization. Therefore, the signing countries, in a sovereign act, promise for the years to come to hasten Latin American integration in order to invigorate the continent's economic and social progress, a process that has been initiated by the general Treaty of Central American Free Trade Association and, in other countries, by the Latin American Free Trade Association.

Following the introductory Declaration, the Charter of Punta del Este lists the following sections: objectives of the Alliance for Progress, economic and social development, economic integration of Latin America, and basic export products. I do not intend to enter into an analysis of the Charter, but rather to emphasize that the need for Latin American integration was being clearly acknowledged. In fact, we see in 1961 that Latin American countries stressed the importance of joint efforts in this direction and the United States pledged support of these efforts. These declarations, articulated for the first time in 1961, had far-reaching implications.

The second meeting at Punta del Este was held six years later in 1967, at the initiative of President Lyndon Johnson. His Administration had inherited Kennedy's views on Latin American problems, and Johnson believed a new rapprochement was needed in the region. Just as Kennedy had inspired the 1961 meeting, President Johnson decided to convene a second high-level meeting with the purpose of reformulating the Alliance for Progress program in the light of the six years that had passed. If Johnson had not taken the initiative, it is unlikely that the 1967 meeting of Latin American chiefs of state would have taken place, given the reluctance our governments have historically displayed toward such meetings.

As it turned out, the meeting was of great significance and far-reaching scope. The matters discussed point to its importance: agreement was reached regarding the creation of a Latin American Common Market between 1970 and 1985; the actual bases for Latin American economic integration through multinational projects to reinforce the programs of the IDB were debated; the goal of substantially increasing Latin America's foreign trade was set forth; the need to update living conditions in rural areas by increasing productivity in farming and animal husbandry was established; the urgent need to stress education, science, and technology as a function of development was declared; and programs to improve health care and eliminate unnecessary military expenditures were underlined.

Unfortunately, despite the extraordinary significance of this meeting, Latin American countries failed to employ profitably the new support offered to them by the United States toward the process of achieving integration. President Johnson took the initiative of sending a message to the Congress requesting authorization of a $500 million fund for Latin America when agreement was reached on the establishment of a Common Market. This point was never reached, and the events that took place after the Johnson Administration brought about profound changes within the United States, including a general withdrawal from its relations with Latin America.

Looking at Latin America in 1986, I think it can be said that the Alliance for Progress achieved some important successes. The main points of the Charter of Punta del Este have been put into effect, and there has been a new inter-American convergence. Even though a Latin American Common Market was never created, several schemes for economic integration have gotten under way. I point in particular to the establishment of the Andean Pact and the Caribbean Community (CARICOM). In the same context, there have been territorial agreements to spur multilateral growth in the River Plate Basin and Amazon River areas. Even if LAFTA has become ALADI, economic survival has clearly become a significant issue for the signatory countries. Similarly, it should be noted that despite Central America's political crisis, the various economic integration agreements existing among the five countries continue in full force.

Moreover, several financial institutions were created during the Alliance years to promote economic integration. Among them were the Central American Bank for Economic Integration, the Andean Development Corporation, and the Caribbean Bank. During the same period the Andean Reserve Fund and the Fund for the Cuenca del Plata were established, as well as the systems for multilateral payments used by ALADI, for Central America, and for the Agreement of Santo Domingo.

The decade of the 1960s also had a strong impact on cultural, academic, scientific, and technological matters, as several specialized regional organizations began to operate during those years. It would not be an exaggeration to say that from the 1960s onward, the level of exchanges in these fields increased twentyfold. This trend was clearly encouraged by the Punta del Este agreements.

Thus it can be concluded that a vast number of the Alliance's achievements occurred during the 1960s; during the next 15 years the process reversed and the trends weakened.

The programs undertaken under the aegis of the Alliance for Progress acquire even greater significance when we consider that they began falling apart by the early 1970s. In my opinion, the great political and economic challenges that Latin America has faced since the early 1970s constitute a major justification for the Alliance for Progress. I refer particularly to the erosion of democracy in Latin America—a situation that, luckily, has been overcome over the last few years as elections have taken place in Brazil, Argentina, Uruguay, and Peru—and to the increasing indebtedness of our countries, which currently totals around $360 billion. It is beyond the scope of this presentation to analyze in depth the Latin American debt program. My point, however, is that had the letter and spirit of the two Punta del Este agreements been respected when financial decisions were made regarding Latin America, we would not be facing our present dilemma.

Latin American integration, nonetheless, has had a new impetus not only because of historical interest, but also because integration provides a better alternative for Latin American countries in meeting the multiple political and economic challenges that face us today and tomorrow. We should mention in this context the creation of the Latin American Economic System (SELA) in 1975, and the importance for our countries of the recent incorporation of Spain and Portugal into the European Economic Community.

To conclude, I would like to suggest what I believe are the lessons of the Alliance for Progress that should constitute the outline of any future Latin American Community. Such a community would be open to all nations in the hemisphere that could be defined in socioeconomic terms as developing countries. It would be based on negotiated agreements and on the establishment of a general agreement that would set down the underlying and operational principles leading to the creation of a Community of Latin American States. The organization should be given a wide scope of operations and enough flexibility to enable it to respond not only to present goals but to future aspirations. The general agreement would not be viewed as a substitution of agreements already in force; subregional economic integration schemes would be recognized as steps in the achievement of this common market.

The main organ of the new organization would be an assembly of chiefs of state, taking into account the political characteristics of each country. In each signatory country, a council composed of cabinet members should be formed to deal with specific areas. The Latin American Community should have a parliament that could, at first, be formed indirectly by the national congress and later be elected directly through universal suffrage. This parliament would not supersede existing national legislative systems. Rather, its mandate would be to deal specifically with Community interests, undertake analysis, and pass legislation. A Latin American Supreme Court would be in charge of settling public or private disputes that emerge from the application of the new Community institutions.

The Organization of American States would constitute, under this plan, the central nucleus around which the various authorities, corporations, and multinational agencies would be organized to take charge of implementing specific functions and policies. These bodies would include, for example, a Latin American central bank; a planning coordinating committee; mechanisms for educational and cultural development and for scientific and technical advancement; a Latin American news agency; a corporation to defend basic products and natural resources of the region, and so on. These institutions should parallel an institutional/juridical system that would work toward making the various types of member country national policies—labor, fiscal, administrative—compatible. Some of the institutions and organisms mentioned above already exist; others are being created or have been proposed as sectoral responses to collective Latin American needs.

Clearly, the Alliance for Progress, a program of cooperation not only for the 1960s but also for the present and the future, has provided us with a better understanding of events and should constitute the decisive backdrop for all initiatives toward Latin American integration, as was suggested by Gabriela Mistral:

We must unite our homelands internally by means of education that will become a national conscience and of an allotment of well-being that will become an absolute balance; and we must unite these countries of ours in rather Pythagorean rhythm, according to which those twenty spheres will move without collision, in freedom and beauty. We are driven by a dark and still confused ambition that rolls in our bloodstream from the Platonic archtype reaching to the feverish and suffering face of Bolivar, whose utopia we wish to create from poetic compositions.

# 7

# Did the Alliance "Lose Its Way," or Were Its Assumptions All Wrong from the Beginning and Are Those Assumptions Still with Us?

*Howard J. Wiarda*

The title of this chapter is taken from the title of the well-known book by Jerome Levinson and Juan de Onis, *The Alliance that Lost Its Way: A Critical Report on the Alliance for Progress.*[1] That title, in turn, derives from a provocative essay on the Alliance by former Chilean President Eduardo Frei that appeared in *Foreign Affairs* in 1967.[2] The implication of both these titles is that while the Alliance for Progress began satisfactorily—maybe even nobly by some accounts—it somehow went astray, was perverted, and lost its direction.

The responsibility for the Alliance "losing its way" is variously assigned.[3] Some place heavy emphasis on the transition from Presidents Kennedy to Johnson to Nixon and thus on the dying interest in, or commitment to, the Alliance. Others assign blame to the Latin American oligarchies, or the Latin American militaries, or both together. Some place responsibility for failure on the internal mechanisms of the Alliance, on the lack of coordination between the various institutions, in both the U.S. and Latin America, charged with carrying out Alliance goals. Some blame the Latin American governments and others the U.S. government, especially the Department of State or at least some individuals in it. But in all these interpretations, the original goals and presumptions of the Alliance are assumed to be correct.

My own interpretation takes another direction. I believe the Alliance was well-

Janine Perfit assisted with the research for this chapter; Dr. Ieda Sigueira Wiarda commented on an earlier draft.

intentioned but that its assumptions, from the beginning, were erroneous. It is not just that subsequent implementation was faulty, in my view. Rather, I argue that the fundamental presuppositions of the Alliance were wrong and misconceived right from the start. Moreover, I fear that those mistaken assumptions of a quarter century ago are still with us, in the Kissinger Commission recommendations, the Caribbean Basin Initiative, and the Democracy Agenda. This chapter proceeds to examine the original assumptions of the Alliance, the degree to which we are still prisoners of those early assumptions, and whether anything can be done to change them or if we should just accept them as fundamental assumptions of American policy destined to remain with us forever.

## THE ALLIANCE: CONTEXT AND ORIGINS

The Alliance for Progress was a ten-year, multi-billion dollar assistance program launched in 1961 and designed, at least ostensibly, to aid the social, economic, cultural, and political development of Latin America. Though its institutional machinery was put in place by the Kennedy Administration, its roots lay in the preceding Eisenhower Administration, particularly in the report on Latin America prepared by Milton Eisenhower for his brother,[4] and in the revised thinking about Latin America that evolved during the last three years of the Eisenhower Administration. That reassessment suggested that the U.S. halt its coddling of dictators, stop taking Latin America for granted, and begin aiding its democratic forces—a major turnaround. Just as the "Good Neighbor" policy of Franklin D. Roosevelt had its origins in the preceding Hoover Administration, so the Alliance for Progress built upon, and greatly expanded, a policy reorientation that had actually preceded the inauguration of John F. Kennedy.

A powerful and earlier impetus to the Alliance had also come from Latin America. As early as 1955 President Juscelino Kubitschek of Brazil had begun to call for a vast program of assistance to and self-help for Latin America, which he called "Operation Pan-America" and which incorporated most of the main ingredients of the Alliance. He was later joined by President Alberto Lleras Camargo of Colombia in pushing for such a program. Other Latin American presidents advocated similar measures. The founding in 1959 of the Inter-American Development Bank, a regional, multilateral, but largely U.S.-funded assistance bank, was an integral part of this same campaign.[5] Indeed, one of the unique aspects of the Alliance as an assistance program was the degree to which it initially grew out of, and partially incorporated, ideas emanating from Latin America. One is tempted to suggest at this early point in the discussion that had the Alliance continued seriously to reflect Latin American input, it would likely not have gone in all the wrong directions that it did.

The election of John F. Kennedy in 1960 was a key turning point. It was Kennedy that actually proposed, spoke passionately for, shepherded through the Congress, and implemented the Alliance for Progress. President Kennedy had been prodded into taking this bold new initiative by the reports he had received on Latin America by such foreign policy advisers as Adolph A. Berle and General William Draper. Such White House intellectuals and policy advisers as John Dreier, John Kenneth Galbraith, Lincoln Gordon, DeLesseps Morrison, Walt W. Rostow, and Arthur F. Schlesinger, Jr., similarly played a strong role in the design and formulation of the Alliance.[6]

The question of the origins of the Alliance—and whether it was a U.S.- or a Latin American-designed program—is an important but very complicated one. Many Latin Americans who were active in the formulation of the Alliance in those early days claim that it was their creation, that at least eight of the ten points in the original Punta del Este agreement that served as the charter of the Alliance came from Latin America. On the other hand, the Alliance program of economic growth, social modernization, and political democratization and stability converged with U.S. strategic goals. Moreover, in those days economic growth, social modernization, and political democratization and stability were widely assumed in development literature and in U.S. foreign assistance programs to go hand in hand. That is, it was assumed that socioeconomic modernization would lead to and produce democracy of economic growth, and stability. On this agenda, for the most part, the Latin American counsellors and the U.S. advisers saw eye-to-eye—even though their emphases were somewhat different. The Latin Americans wanted economic growth largely for its own sake, while the U.S. saw economic development both as a good in its own right and as a path to stability.

But the problem is more complicated than this. The Latin Americans who helped set up the Alliance were a particular kind and generation of Latin Americans. Many had attended U.S. universities, they had read Lipset and Rostow, their writings were full of citations of the newest developmentalist literature. The U.S. participants were also a special group, followers of Gunnar Myrdal, believers (like their Latin American counterparts) in state-led and -directed development, often determinists who assumed that economic development would inevitably lead to political development. In this sense both parties claiming to have conceived the Alliance were correct: The Latin Americans formulated many of the early ideas, but they were Latin Americans who thought like North Americans. Moreover, their ideas were both compatible with what the U.S. officials believed almost as an ideology of development, and they could readily be subsumed under a broader U.S. strategic concept. Further, while these special Latin Americans had a strong hand in the early design of the Alliance, its implementation over the years—and increasingly its agenda of programs as well—became increasingly a U.S. activity.

The Alliance for Progress was formally inaugurated on August 17, 1961, when the so-called Charter of Punta del Este was signed by all the member states of the Organization of American States (OAS), with the exception of Cuba. The Alliance was a comprehensive program of social, economic, and political assistance sponsored in large part by the United States and designed to improve the life and welfare of the people of the Latin American republics. The Alliance aimed to stimulate economic growth in Latin America at the rate of at least 2.5 percent per year, and to provide for a vast array of social and political programs: agrarian reform, tax reform, improved water supplies, electrification, literacy programs, housing, health care, development banks, plans and planning agencies, technical assistance, educational reform, legal reform, family planning, military reform, labor reform, democratization, and a host of other activities.[7] It was a vast and ambitious program which, with hindsight, we know was too vast and too ambitious. Its aim was to promote change, under U.S. auspices, and presumably in the right direction. The program was launched with great fanfare; the rhetoric indicated that the United States would assist and itself help initiate, presumably with the recipient countries' cooperation, a democratic social and political revolution in Latin America.

The Alliance was greeted with great enthusiasm in both parts of the Americas. But contradictions were immediately apparent. Latin Americans saw it chiefly as a means to gain access to U.S. foreign aid and largesse and to improve their economies (and often, not coincidentally, themselves personally). The Latin American democratic left, whom the U.S. was then championing, saw it as an opportunity to achieve power; other Latin Americans wanted only the money, not the democracy. Within the U.S., many saw the Alliance as a noble and heroic initiative, a program designed to achieve democracy and social justice, as opposed to the aid to dictators the U.S. had provided in the past. For many of these persons, both in and out of government, the Alliance was the high point of their careers—a brief but glorious moment when the U.S. finally seemed to live up to its ideals. But others in the U.S. were more cynical (and, in part, this was how the Alliance was sold to the Congress), viewing the Alliance as basically a strategic design that used high-sounding rhetoric to achieve a new Cold War security policy. For a time these contradictory perspectives coexisted within the Alliance programs but eventually the strategic purpose that had always been there achieved predominance, much to the chagrin and disillusionment of the Alliance's "true believers."

It is important to sort out what was new and what remained the same in United States policy toward Latin America under the Alliance. Quite a number of the programs begun under the Alliance were clearly new. The sheer size and ambition of the effort was surely new. So was the enthusiasm, at least initially. Within the State Department bureaucracy, President Kennedy had brought in some new faces and shifted others around; these personnel changes signaled a considerable shift of emphasis under the new program.[8] There were also structural changes within the administrative machinery, most notably the considerable infrastructure created for the Alliance itself and the greater coordination now expected between the Department of State's Bureau of Inter-American Affairs and the Agency for International Development (AID). Finally, it is important to emphasize that the Alliance for Progress was a White House initiative and enjoyed the full backing of President Kennedy, which gave it added pizzazz and authority. As Arthur F. Schlesinger wrote in 1970, it would have been impossible, because of bureaucratic inertia, to expect such a large and ambitious program to emanate from the regular foreign policy departments.[9]

Lest one be carried away with enthusiasm for the democratic reformism incorporated in the Alliance, however, one must continue to bear in mind its fundamental strategic purpose. That purpose was the prevention of any additional Castro-like communist regimes in the hemisphere inimical to U.S. interests. At its root, once one strips away the high-flown rhetoric and the humanitarian aid programs (which, as we have seen, also acquired in some quarters a life of their own), the Alliance for Progress was an anti-communist and cold war strategy designed to serve U.S. strategic interests. What was new and ingenious about the Alliance was that humanitarian and social and political reformist goals could be served simultaneously, apparently, with the advancement of U.S. security interests. An economically developing, more socially just, and politically democratic and stable Latin America was now seen as the best protection for U.S. strategic interests in the region.

This was a considerable shift, at least in tactics, from the early Eisenhower Administration. Under Eisenhower the orientation had been that to prop up even right-wing dictators was the best way of preserving stability, protecting U.S. interests, and keeping out communism. But the revolution in Cuba changed all that. The Cuban experience demonstrated that rather than thwarting communism, dictatorships such as Batista's might instead make ripe the conditions under which communism can thrive. Batista's regime, after all, had just been replaced by the Marxist-Leninist regime of Fidel Castro, a fact that weighed heavily on strategic thinkers and policymakers and forced them to reassess past policies. Henceforth, under the Alliance the U.S. would be opposed to dictators of both the left and right and would work to advance development and democratization as the best means to achieve our primary goal of preventing communism. But the goal of pursuing a successful anti-communist strategy in Latin America and of providing for its handmaidens—stability, moderation, and middle-of-the-roadness—remained the same. Only the means, or tactics, had now changed.[10]

One central point must be acknowledged: The Alliance for Progress was a direct response to and outgrowth of the Cuban revolution. This was not just some starry-eyed, altruistic, humanitarian giveaway program, as it was sometimes portrayed at the cartoon level and as some of its supporters actually believed. Rather it was that plus, and more fundamentally, a whole lot more: a program designed to serve basic U.S. strategic purposes in Latin America. Or perhaps it could be said (and this helps account for its immense attractiveness) that the Alliance would enable the United States to serve both humanitarian and self-interest goals at the same time. That combination of appealing to U.S. moral concerns and serving fundamental strategic interests is of course typically American; it is also what enables programs like the Alliance to be "sold" to diverse constituencies and passed in Congress. But it also implies the possibility for future conflict when these diverse goals later prove contradictory, as was the case with the Alliance. The conflict between long-term developmentalist goals and shorter-term U.S. strategic interests was in fact one of the key reasons that the Alliance ultimately proved unsuccessful.[11]

Having hinted at some of the key contradictions that would plague the Alliance from the beginning, it must also be said that the Alliance was not designed by naive or incompetent persons. Having just reread all the early literature on the Alliance, I can attest that the Alliance architects were experienced experts in their respective fields. It is necessary to say this because the history of the Alliance was marred by so many failures and mistakes that one could easily conclude that the persons who conceived it must also have been incompetent. In fact, the Alliance's architects were among the most able people in the U.S. government. Where they failed was not in their experience, competence, or technical expertise in their respective fields, but in their sometimes woeful ignorance of or naivete toward Latin America. The designers of the Alliance knew history (or at least U.S. and European history), knew economics, knew about planning and taxes, the theoretical literature on development, agrarian reform and family planning from the Japanese and Taiwanese experiences. They knew their technical fields well. What they lacked was in-depth and specialized understanding of how all these programs that sounded wonderful on paper and in the general theoretical literature would actually be received or would play in Latin America.[12] Therein, I believe, lay the fundamental flaw in the Alliance. It is also the gap between general theory and Latin American reality that lies at the heart of the analysis in this paper.

## THE ASSUMPTIONS OF THE ALLIANCE:
## TEN FATAL FLAWS IN SEARCH OF A THEORY[13]

The fatal flaws in the Alliance, we argue here, were not in its implementation — although implementation often left a great deal to be desired. It was therefore not so much a problem of the Alliance "losing its way." Rather, the fatal flaws were conceptual. That is, the problems of the Alliance stemmed principally from the erroneous assumptions upon which the program was based. To the person inexperienced in, or unacquainted with, Latin America, and who thus relied on Western European or United States experience for models and examples, the Alliance assumptions looked quite coherent and rational. To the experienced Latin America specialists, however, the assumptions of the program appeared naive and wrong-headed. The Alliance in fact revealed a profound lack of knowledge and understanding of Latin America. One suspects that the reason for this is that the policy was designed by persons who had only very general knowledge about the region.[14] In fact, the program was designed by economists and foreign policy generalists, most of whom were located in the White House; very few of what we might call "experienced Latin America hands," either governmental or academic, were involved in the initial planning and program design.

Hence the Alliance was based not so much on actual Latin American realities (personalism and lack of institutionalization in politics, the continuing importance of family and patronage ties, clique and clan rivalries that defied neat ideological categories) but on abstract, theoretical, developmentalist schemes derived from other areas and superimposed ill-fittingly on the Latin American region. The model used was based on the developmental experiences of Western Europe (actually, Northwest Europe) and the United States, with some reference to Japan, Taiwan, or the countries of the British Commonwealth. It assumed that Latin America would follow the same developmental course as had these earlier modernizers. Alternatively, the formula derived from the general development literature then rising in currency, most of which was tied to the experiences of the "new nations" or the "non-Western areas"—more models and concepts that had little to do with Latin American realities. None of these models, and few of the corresponding assumptions of the Alliance, were based on actual Latin American realities, social structure, political dynamics, or culturally conditioned ways of doing things.[15] That is (or was) the fundamental problem with the Alliance: It had little to do with day-to-day realities of Latin America. As the Alliance was implemented, these flaws in the assumptions on which the program was based became more and more apparent. It is not, therefore, so much that the program went off track during the course of the 1960s (although that happened too). Rather, it was never on track to begin with, a fact that became entirely obvious only as the program went forward.

Let us review some of the major flawed assumptions on which the Alliance was grounded. I list ten such fatal flaws, but that, we shall see, will not exhaust the list, and some of these flawed assumptions need to be further subdivided into numerous flawed sub-assumptions. Each of these assumptions requires discussion in more detail than is possible here; my intention is to be both provocative and brief, raising the main issues but not presuming by any means to have exhausted the subject.

## Assumption 1: The "One-Minute-to-Midnight" Thesis

In the late 1950s and early 1960s, reflecting the fear that the Cuban revolution would be repeated throughout the length and breadth of the hemisphere, the Latin America issue was always posed in stark, immediate, and crisis terms. It was "one-minute-to-midnight in Latin America," as the title of one widely read study of the time put it,[16] and the clock was about to toll.

Posing the issue in such a dramatic way and using scare tactics is of course useful for galvanizing the bureaucracy, gaining public attention and support for the new program, and prying loose more funds from an otherwise reluctant Congress. But it had little to do with Latin American realities. Throughout the hemisphere in those years the local communist parties were weak and disorganized, there were no guerrilla movements in other countries that constituted much of a threat, and the possibility that all of Latin America would soon explode in a Cuba-like revolution was preposterous when examined more than superficially.[17] The organizational base and groundwork for launching such revolutions were simply not there. Even the Cuban revolution, if looked at closely, could be seen as a fluke, the product of such unusual circumstances on that island that they were unlikely to be repeated elsewhere. And of course Latin Americans are not themselves above – and in fact are quite good at – exaggerating their problems so as to secure greater attention and funds from the United States. Old-time Latin America hands know that in this sense Latin America is perpetually in "crisis," and therefore that we should not become unduly alarmed. That is a normal Latin American condition.

It is probably accurate to say that in 1961–62, at the time the Alliance was launched, not a single country in Latin America had even a slight possibility of going the way of Castro's Cuba. Even the Dominican Republic, to which the Administration in Washington at that time devoted so much attention because conditions superficially resembled those in pre-Castro Cuba (a poor nation, wide social gaps, one-crop economy, bloody dictator), was in fact quite different from Cuba and had no possibilities whatsoever at that time of "going communist." It had no strong Communist Party as Cuba did, no communist-dominated trade unions or peasant leagues, no guerrilla movement, no charismatic leader on the Left, no social infrastructure on which a serious Marxist-Leninist challenge could be based.[18] In fact, the bell was not about to toll anywhere in Latin America – or if it was, it was unlikely that it would lead to a Marxist-Leninist regime. The Alliance was in this sense vastly oversold, a product of bloated rhetoric and verbal overkill. And, of course, as this became increasingly apparent during the course of the 1960s, the program lost its appeal. The Alliance was gradually ignored by everyone from the President on down, became just another economic giveaway program, and was finally (though unofficially) abrogated in favor of a policy of "benign neglect," which did eventually contribute to the conditions in Latin America in which revolution would flourish a decade later.

Why was the "one-minute-to-midnight" thesis so widely accepted in the United States, even by persons whose education and experience should have led them to know better? One cannot know finally but one suspects that, in addition to the perceived immediacy of the Cuban threat, it also had much to do with the historic disparagement of Latin American institutions and ways of doing things that is so strong in the United States: the myth of Latin America's incapacity to solve any of its own problems by itself. Actually, Latin America has a considerable history of coping with its problems in its own ways, sliding through from crisis to crisis, and fashioning ad hoc, often crazy-quilt solutions to seemingly intractable difficulties. But if these processes and institutional arrangements, which are in fact highly "developed," are not recognized as such, or are disparagingly dismissed, then it is easy to see why the "one-minute-to-midnight" thesis would have some credibility. We will return to this issue later.

## Assumption 2: The "Economic Development Produces Political Development" Thesis

The Alliance for Progress became, finally, a United States strategic design that was largely based on economic determinist assumptions. It was designed and largely run by economists and economic historians. Initially, and sporadically thereafter, some limited attention was paid to political development,[19] which was almost universally (though much too simply and perhaps mistakenly) defined as meaning democratization along U.S. lines. But over time the political development efforts—by their nature much more complex and difficult to carry out—were shunted aside in favor of an agenda devoted almost exclusively to economic development.

Put in bold and only slightly oversimplified terms, the economic determinist argument dominant in the development literature of the time (and still present, as we shall see, in many U.S. programs today) is as follows: If only we can pour in enough capital, prime the pumps, and start the engines for take-off, meanwhile providing our advice and technical assistance, then not only will the Latin American economies develop but, even more importantly, certain social, political, and strategic concomitants will inevitably and universally follow as well.[20] A business elite will grow up alongside the old landed elite and presumably with a sense of social responsibility that the latter may lack; the middle class will grow and become a bastion of stability, moderation, and democracy; the lower classes will also become more affluent and therefore less attracted to the appeals of communism; trade unions will be oriented toward U.S.-style collective bargaining and will eschew more radical and divisive political action, and so on. Economic development would thus have ramifications in various social areas as well, producing a more literate and therefore a more participatory democratically oriented citizenry, expanding mass media and therefore producing freer and more pluralistic societies, enabling governments to expand social services and reduce the appeal of communism.[21] It is important to emphasize that these were not just theoretical formulations emanating from academics but, through Walter Rostow's position and influence in the State Department, these ideas pervaded the U.S. foreign assistance program as well.

The trouble with all these theories, which in fact sound quite plausible and even reasonable, is that they are all based on the previous developmental experiences of Northwest Europe and the United States and have very little relevance to Latin America. The new business elites in Latin America have, for the most part, precious little social responsibility; the middle class, as we shall see in more detail below, has not become a bastion of stability; and the lower classes have not become less radical or eschewed political action. Expanded literacy and other social mobilization programs did not produce more participatory and pluralist regimes in the 1960s, but rather prompted a series of military takeovers that were destructive to all this progress.[22]

In short, the social, political, and strategic concomitants that were supposed to follow automatically from economic development did not in fact follow. The end product of economic determinism was not happier, more stable, more democratic societies; in fact it produced quite the reverse. Two maxims therefore follow: Economic development is far too important to be left to economists, and we ignore or inadequately deal with social, cultural, and political determinants of behavior at great peril.

### Assumption 3: The "Latin America Couldn't or Wouldn't Do Anything on Its Own" Thesis

North American prejudices and biases about Latin America are strong and deeply ingrained. We tend to think of the area as unstable, backward, "less-developed," incompetent, and historically "unsuccessful." Our material progress in the United States has been so great and our democracy so stable that, assuming Latin America wants the same things and in the same ways, we label our history a success and theirs a failure. It follows that we would tend to assume that we can solve Latin America's problems for them. It also follows that in so doing, we would feel we could ignore – or not bother to learn – Latin American history.

We tend to think of Latin American leadership in much the same way: not very competent, unstable, quasi-infantile, children whom *we* must guide and lead.[23] True, in the Alliance's case, there was considerable Latin American input at least initially, and through the so-called Committee of Nine Wise Men, Latin American advice was sporadically sought, chiefly on procedural and technical matters. But the assumptions, overall plan, and program of the Alliance came more and more to be a U.S. operation. It was we who knew best and who would presumably bring the benefits of our civilization to Latin America. Both Latin American intellectuals and politicians were viewed in this superior and patronizing way.

This disparagement of Latin America and its leadership, and the belief that Latin America couldn't or wouldn't do anything on its own had deep roots in the United States. In part it stemmed from historic prejudice by Protestant, Anglo-Saxon civilization toward the fundamental assumptions of a Catholic, Thomistic, Latin, scholastic, maybe even inquisitorial civilization. In part it came from a general sense in the United States that Latin America and its leaders rank low in terms of talents and accomplishments. In part it stemmed from long-held assumptions in the social sciences, both Marxist and non-Marxist, about Latin America. Marx thought of Latin America, with its lack of industrialization or well-formed classes, as rather like "Asiatic societies," a label Marx used not just as a neutral scientific term but with scorn and derision. Hegel said that Latin America had "no history," a judgment that in the Hegelian metaphysic consigned the area to the most primitive of categories. Social Darwinism condemned Latin America, with its racially-mixed populations, to an inferior place on the evolutionary ladder; in the positivist hierarchy Latin America, because of its presumed lack of accomplishments and progress, also ranked low among the continents. More recently one thinks of Henry Kissinger's famous quip that the axis of the world flows through Moscow, Berlin/Bonn, Paris, London, Washington, and Tokyo – thus excluding Latin America entirely!

Building upon these earlier traditions and prejudices was the development literature that loomed so large in the early 1960s and from which many policy-makers took their categories, if not their cues.[24] In this influential body of writings Latin America and its institutions were consigned to the realm of the "traditional," which either had to be destroyed or altered "fundamentally" if the region was ever to modernize. Seldom in this literature or in the policy initiatives emanating from it were the notions advanced that traditional institutions such as those of Latin America might in fact be quite flexible and accommodative, that they could bend to change rather than be overwhelmed by it, that they were themselves capable of a great deal of modernization, and that sweeping them away or shunting them aside might well leave Latin America with the worst possible legacy: with neither "modern" institutions (that we presumably would implant) sufficiently well-rooted and institutionalized, nor with traditional institutions (even with their acknowledged problems) capable of providing coherence and holding political society together during the trauma of transition. I have written on these themes in more detail elsewhere.[25] Here let me simply say that if there is one primary cause of the Alliance's failures, it is these wrong assumptions of the literature on development that so strongly undergirded our policy initiatives, then and maybe now. By ignoring the realities of Latin American history and experience, we not only made manifest our ignorance of the region, but we also condemned worthwhile initiatives like the Alliance to failure.

### Assumption 4: The "Salvation Through the Middle Class" Thesis

Not all of the Alliance's assumptions were explicit in the actual language of the program. Nor were AID and other technicians and managers of the Alliance always fully aware of the theoretical literature upon which the program was based. Nevertheless, that literature was enormously important in shaping the assumptions of the Alliance and the kinds of programs it supported. Such was surely the case with the thesis of "salvation through the middle class."

The assumption, once again based on the Northwest European and North American experiences, was that a large and prosperous middle class was closely correlated with a stable, democratic, middle-of-the-road policy—precisely what the United States wanted to promote in Latin America.[26] The main arguments for this assumption were based on economic history as well as the emerging field of political sociology. There was even some writing, fatally flawed by errors of logic, reasoning, and history, from a prominent Latin Americanist that supported this thesis.[27] The argument was that if only we could create in Latin America more middle-class societies, then more stable, more just, more democratic, and more anti-communist attitudes would surely prevail. To that end we created programs in both rural and urban areas that would lead to a larger middle class: agrarian reform in the countryside that would presumably produce a class of medium-size family farmers who would then be able to resist the appeals of communism to the "peasants" (presumably what happened in Cuba; actually Cuba's was by no means a peasant revolution); and a variety of economic development and social service programs in the cities designed to swell the middle class there. Here the model was Western Europe or the New Deal in the United States.

It should be understood that the problem was not agrarian reform per se or any of these other programs. Rather, the problem was the assumption that by pursuing such programs we could create a moderate, middle-of-the-road, happy, bourgeois society that looked just like ours. For while the middle class has in fact grown in size in Latin America, it has taken on few of the presumed middle-class virtues that the literature based on Western Europe or the United States would lead us to expect. Rather, the literature from Latin America suggests that the middle class tends to ape upper-class ways and attitudes, lives way beyond its means, holds aristocratic attitudes even more strongly that the real aristocrat, is non-egalitarian and perhaps anti-democratic, disparages manual labor, disdains the peasant and working classes even more than the elites, holds very conservative attitudes, and is not above staging coups and supporting military regimes that freeze society in place and are repressive of progressive social forces.[28] That is not a set of attitudes designed to institutionalize a stable, moderate, pluralist, democratic, middle-of-the-road policy.

It may be that in the present circumstances—when the Latin American militaries have themselves been thoroughly discredited and when democracy is on the rebound—the middle class may, at least for the time being, be supportive of democratic rule. If for no other reason, this may occur because representative government is temporarily viewed as protecting their interests and providing stability better than military rule. But such expediency is not a very sturdy rock upon which to build one's hopes for the future. Certainly in the wave of coups and repression that swept Latin America in the 1960s it was—contrary to all the Alliance's hopes and assumptions—the middle class that urged and in some cases brought the military into power and supported the severe economic and political measures that the armed forces imposed on the lower classes.

### Assumption 5: The "Integration-as-Critical" Thesis

One of the key aspects of the Alliance—a part of its ten-point program—was its effort to achieve economic integration in Latin America. To this end the Latin American Free Trade Association (LAFTA) was organized; the Central American countries formed the Central American Free Trade Association; Venezuela, Colombia, Ecuador, and Peru (Chile's position was usually uncertain) organized the Andean Pact; and the small islands of the Caribbean later joined in the Caribbean Community (CARICOM). The theory and logic behind such organizations seemed sound enough: Larger markets for more products would thereby be created, industrialization could hence be expanded; the lowering of tariffs and increased trade would have a multiplier effect on the participating economies; affluence would spread, thereby diminishing the *Fidelista* threat; and presumably, again using Western Europe and the Marshall Plan as examples, economic integration might well lead to political integration or at least greater unity, which would help produce political stability. On this topic a great body of romantic and rather wishful literature was produced in the 1960s.

Latin American economic integration is another one of those grandiose schemes produced by abstract planners, economists, and technicians who often knew little of, or preferred to ignore, the realities and politics of the area. Actually, the integration movement has produced some rather notable results, if one focuses only on the economic statistics; but its more fundamental political goals were never realized. It would be difficult to argue, for example, that Latin America is any more unified now, as an anti-Soviet or any other kind of bloc, than it was in the early 1960s. One would be equally hard-pressed, looking at all the coups, military takeovers, and full-scale revolutions that have occurred in the last 25 years, to argue that the area is now, or in the foreseeable future will be, more stable. The political rivalries, petty jealousies, and nationalistic hatreds between the Latin American states are just as intense as ever. Now there is a great deal of evidence that they have become even more bitter, that Latin America may become the next area of international conflict and irredentism.[29]

Hence the movement toward integration foundered, by ignoring the political realities and simply hoping they could be superseded. Costa Rica never could get along with Nicaragua and still cannot; El Salvador and Honduras went to war; Brazil didn't fit anywhere; Chile and Argentina are rivals and sometimes enemies as are Chile, Bolivia, and Peru. Peru and Ecuador have long-standing border problems and a history of conflict in the Amazon basin; Venezuela was distrustful of Colombia and could not compete with Colombia's labor costs. The largest island in the Caribbean, Cuba, was excluded from CARICOM countries on political grounds; nor did the English-speaking Caribbean want to join forces with the Spanish-speaking Caribbean. And so it went.

The integration movement is one sad illustration among many that could be cited under the Alliance's auspices, of what happens when economists and technicians design programs that ignore political variables or assume that these can be overcome by brave acts of political will. Political scientists tend not to talk much about political will and many even doubt if there is such a thing; rather, they talk about the balance of political interest groups, the role of power and influence, and the importance of national interest in shaping, if not determining, international outcomes. All this is not to praise political scientists and disparage economists, but it is to say that those who designed the Alliance, while they had political and strategic goals in mind as the ultimate purpose of the Alliance, nonetheless ignored fundamental political realities in carrying out the program. They focused almost exclusively on the economic goals while ignoring the political factors or assuming that the economic accomplishments would render the political rivalries irrelevant. But that did not happen; that is also why the high-priority political and strategic goals of economic integration were never realized and why the several regional integration efforts, though not completely dead, continue today to limp along with only modest accomplishments to show for all the efforts.[30]

## Assumption 6: The "Democracy versus Dictatorship" Dichotomy

In the early 1960s the United States saw but three possibilities in Latin America. The first was a Castro-like regime, "another Cuba in the Caribbean," which had to be avoided at all costs. The second was a dictatorial or authoritarian regime. The third was a democratic regime, which was our first preference. But as John F. Kennedy reminded us, as quoted by Arthur F. Schlesinger, Jr., the United States could not renounce authoritarian regimes in favor of democracy unless it could first be assured that it could avoid a Castro-like regime.[31] In effect that gave the United States only two choices in Latin America: dictatorship or democracy.

I wish to submit here that this choice, as artfully and articulately put forth in numerous books on Latin America at the time, was and is a false choice, a misleading choice, even a choice that may wreak harm on Latin America and on our policy interests there. In fact there are many choices that lie between dictatorship and democracy: for example, a combined civil-military junta, gentlemanly understood alternations between civil and military rule, civilian rule where the military is the power behind the throne, military rule where civilians serve in many cabinet and other posts, parallel and coexistent power structures as in present-day Honduras, Guatemala, and Panama where civilian and military elements live uneasily together side by side, and where their precise relations with each other are a matter of almost everyday renegotiation. Not only is this image of numerous "half-way houses" between dictatorship and democracy a more realistic portrayal of Latin American politics than the dichotomous either-or scheme, but it is the ongoing genius of Latin American politics to continue fashioning such in-between solutions so as to avoid an often unrealistic choice between the one or the other.[32]

I am of the view that by posing the issue in such dichotomous terms, U.S. policy did a disservice to the creative genius of Latin American politics and politicians. By making the issue appear to be either dictatorship or democracy, we forced Latin American politics into a straitjacket and denied its creative capacity for ad hoc and combined solutions. The point is controversial but it needs to be made: By pressing so hard for democracy in the early 1960s, a democracy that I am not sure Latin America really wanted at the time, particularly in the pure U.S. form in which it came, and which many Latin American countries then lacked the institutional capacity to support, we and the Alliance undoubtedly paved the way for the wave of repressive military coups that followed in the mid- to late 1960s. Had we not pressed so hard and so precipitously, had we allowed more room for mixed or half-way solutions, or—heaven forbid—had we allowed the Latin Americans with our assistance to work out their own murky solutions to their own muddy problems, I do not think we would have seen the same kind of bloody, repressive regimes that emerged in the late 1960s and 1970s. Not only did the Alliance thus misread Latin America and its multiple developmental possibilities but it also, indirectly, by its misinterpretations of the area, sometimes brought downright harm, both to Latin America and to United States interests.

### Assumption 7: The "Reform or Revolution" Thesis

Not only was the choice of regime for Latin America—dictatorship or democracy—posed in dichotomous terms, but so was the ultimate goal or purpose of government and of public policy: either reform or revolution. That is the language and message that so many books, articles, and speeches of public officials used in describing the options open for Latin America: Either reform from within in quite radical ways, or else face the almost certain prospect of being overthrown by revolution, as in Cuba.[33]

The problems with this approach and the assumptions undergirding it were similar to those posed by the "one-minute-to-midnight" and "dictatorship-versus-democracy" approaches. Two comments especially need to be made. First, it was exceedingly arrogant, and downright unrealistic, for the United States to prescribe such a detailed agenda of reform proposals as we did for Latin America under the Alliance for Progress. The agenda included vast agrarian reform proposals, sweeping educational reform, an overhauling of the tax structure, new norms of bureaucratic and political behavior, vast changes affecting the family, legal reform, social policy reform, military reform, labor reform, economic reform, and so on. In countries like the Dominican Republic, for instance, we all but ran the major institutions in the country; in Brazil we had in the late 1960s over 2,000 U.S. personnel involved in one program or another. In short, in preferring and pursuing the "evolutionary" path over the revolutionary one, we were advocating a complete restructuring of all of Latin America's basic institutions, and we put in vast amounts of money and personnel to help bring that about. To put an unkind cut on it, Latin America was to be used as a laboratory for a vast range of social programs and experiments, quite a number of which we would not have been willing to carry out in the United States and would certainly not have passed muster in the U.S. Congress. The agenda was far too broad and all-encompassing to be accepted in Latin America—and certainly not all at once. In addition, Latin America often resented the paternalism involved and the implied conclusion that all its institutions were misguided, unworkable, and therefore required a thorough restructuring.

Quite apart from these important considerations, the either-or approach was also wrong and unhelpful. Latin America had not only a variety of regime types from which to choose but also a great variety of possible policy responses. Moreover, the Latin American polities, quite frankly—and the fact should have been recognized by Alliance planners—are like most other polities: They have problems, they cope, they seek to muddle through. Only North Americans seem to believe that problems are ever really finally solved or that political choices represent either-or propositions. The rest of the world faces problems by coping and muddling through, which in fact is what the United States in reality also does. Moreover, a good case can be made that it is precisely such muddling through, and the need for consultation and trial-and-error, that is at the heart of the democratic process. By forcing on Latin America too much too soon, we not only ran roughshod over the region's own, gradual, accommodative political processes,[34] but we also overloaded the system and ourselves, thereby contributing to the wave of military coups that swept the region from 1962 on.

## Assumption 8: The "We Know Best for Latin America" Thesis

There was a lot of arrogance and presumptuousness in the Alliance for Progress. The presumption was that we knew best for Latin America, that we could solve Latin America's problems. In part this attitude stemmed from the myth of Latin America's own incapacity to solve its own problems; in part it derived from the missionary, proselytizing tradition of the United States, the belief that we are a "city on a hill," a "new Jerusalem," the "last best hope of mankind". It also stemmed in part from the certainties imparted by the new literature on development, which seemed to provide universal social science legitimacy to the reformist impulses of American academics and policymakers.[35]

Surely the Alliance for Progress is a case *par excellence* of inappropriate U.S. meddling, usually with the best of intentions, into matters that we actually knew little about. It represented a modern-day expression of that larger missionary, Wilsonian, peculiarly American inclination to bring the benefits of democracy and social progress to our poor, benighted brethren in Latin America. The United States (or at least most of its officials) was certainly sincere in wanting to bring democracy and development to Latin America, while also serving our strategic interests there; but it sought to do so without really understanding the societies with which the U.S. was dealing, their dynamics or political processes. We used simplistic labels to describe the changes desired ("development," "modernization," the "revolution of rising expectations") but without really knowing how to work within the Latin American system to accomplish our purposes, and frequently riding roughshod over them (in the name of superseding "traditional" society) when they stood in the way or proved inconvenient. Only rarely did an occasional voice suggest that "they know how,"[36] that Latin America itself knew its own problems best and was probably best qualified to resolve them. No, the dominant orientation was that *we* knew best, coupled with the fact that the development literature suggested that the model we were pursuing was both universal and inevitable. That was a deadly combination: the arrogance attached to the idea that we knew best, together with the certainty that what we were doing was part of an inevitable march of historical processes. And eventually the commitment of change and progress itself in Latin America gave way to an overriding emphasis on stability.

## Assumption 9: The "American Model of Development"

Not only was the dominant presumption that we knew best for Latin America and that Latin America was incapable of solving its own problems, but further the models of development we used in Latin America were all U.S. models or derived from the U.S. experience.

These models grew out of what Louis Hartz called the liberal–Lockean principles of American democracy.[37] The question is whether these principles apply also in Latin America, or apply in the same way, and what happens when a fundamentally liberal polity in the Hartzian sense (the United States) runs up against a society and political culture whose values and experience were so much at odds with our own.

As applied to foreign policy and development issues, the liberal principles upon which the United States was founded and which undergirded our historical experience imply the following mistaken assumptions that we sought to apply in Latin America:[38]

1. Change and development are both possible and relatively easy, as they were in the U.S. with our vast frontiers and natural resources. But in Latin America, with its meager resources, change and development have never been easy.

2. All good things (social, economic, and political development) go together. But in Latin America they have not always gone together; frequently economic and social development has been disruptive of political development rather than contributing to it.

3. Stability must be maintained; instability is to be avoided at all costs. But in Latin America stability has often entrenched bloody dictators in power, and instability and even revolution have often been the means to achieve democracy and development.[39]

4. Distributing power is more important than concentrating on it. But in Latin America the problem is not necessarily in achieving checks and balances; rather, the problem is to gather up sufficient central power to get something done.

It is easy to see why these fundamental principles of the U.S. political and historical experience would often lead us astray in attempting to promote development in Latin America. But the problem went deeper than the grounding of the Alliance on the vague and sometimes fuzzy principles of American democracy. It also involved the use of very specific and concrete U.S. models and ways of doing things that had little relevance to the realities of Latin America. Since the author has written on these themes before,[40] only a brief summary will be provided here.

For example, the model of agrarian reform that we attempted to export to Latin America was based on a model of the American family farm—middle-sized, capitalistic, self-sufficient, using the most advanced technology, peopled by yeoman farmers who were participatory democrats with a high degree of civic consciousness. None of this applied in Latin America.[41] The model of labor relations we sought to impart was based on nonpolitical collective bargaining, when the tradition of Latin American labor had always been political bargaining.[42] The model of local government was that of a self-governing town meeting, while Latin America's experience was of a centralized, top-down, napoleonic tradition.[43] We sought to professionalize the Latin American military in our mold, which frequently—after the military had been thoroughly trained in modern management, administration, and national security doctrines—had the effect of promoting more, not fewer, military interventions.[44] The educational reform we brought was derived from the pragmatic, John Deweyish educational system of the United States; it had no firm grounding in the scholastic and deductive traditions of Latin America. And so on. In virtually every area (and, recall, the

Alliance sought reform in almost all areas of Latin American life) the model used derived from the United States and lacked firm foundations in the actual Latin American experience. That fitted our notion that Latin American institutions were wholly "traditional," incapable of reform, and therefore deserving to be swept away. But that of course was not an accurate reading, and it led us to press our institutions and programs onto a set of societies in which they could not possibly work. Had we been more cognizant of and sympathetic toward Latin America's own considerable capacity for change and reform—and toward the institutions and processes by which the region reaches new accommodations—we would likely not have gotten so deeply involved ourselves in everyday Latin American decision-making and the results would surely have been more impressive, particularly in long-range terms.

### Assumption 10: Internal Contradictions

This final criticism focuses not on any further wrong or mistaken assumptions of the Alliance but on its internal contradictions. In addition to the different views of the Alliance held by Latin Americans and by North Americans, or by different groups within Latin America and in the United States, the main contradictions include the following:

1. The Alliance sought to strengthen both democracy in Latin America and anti-communism. But the agency we chose to assist in order to ensure anti-communism, the Latin American armed forces, was also the agency that destroyed a whole gamut of democratic governments in the region.[45]

2. We sought to build up the Latin American middle class as a bastion of stability and democracy, but we also tried to mobilize peasants and workers to stave off *Fidelista* appeals and to increase societal pluralism. But the mobilization of the lower classes frightened the middle classes who then turned to the military, who repressed the lower classes, destroyed democracy, and snuffed out pluralism.[46]

3. We tried to create a trade unionism that was both nonpolitical and anti-communist, a strategy that was inherently contradictory and in a number of countries helped to divide, fragment, and weaken the labor movement.[47]

4. The United States often sought to stimulate Latin American local government and grassroots participation, but the vehicle of that was often another national organization, which had the effect of centralizing power still further.[48]

5. The U.S. sought to promote independence and self-sufficiency in Latin America, but the practical result of the Alliance was to increase Latin America's dependence on the United States. More radical critics of the Alliance would say that was the intention all along.

6. The Alliance had clear long-term development goals, but numerous short-term political and strategic expediencies kept getting in the way. Eventually the short-term expediencies all but overwhelmed the long-term goals, and the Alliance ended in disarray and with a sense of failure.

## CONCLUSIONS

The Alliance for Progress was formulated, designed, and administered by some of the country's ablest scholars and public officials. The Alliance brought together some of the nation's foremost economists, planners, lawyers, sociologists, economic historians, statesmen, and specialists in development. It truly incorporated the "best and the brightest."[49] Unfortunately, almost no one in this group had the detailed background or expertise in Latin America necessary to understand fully why the fundamental assumptions of the Alliance would not work there.

The failures of the Alliance are legendary. There were endless snafus and missteps. Enormous amounts of money and effort were wasted on a large number of misguided and misdirected programs. The policy measures we sought to implement produced a host of backfires, unanticipated consequences, and sheer disasters. The false assumptions on which the Alliance was based led us in numerous wrong directions. Moreover, a strong case can be made that there was a close connection between the Alliance and the wave of repressive military regimes that swept Latin America in the 1960s, wiping out earlier democratic gains and paving the way for some of the bloodiest practices ever seen in Latin America. Never resolving the internal contradictions of the Alliance, ultimately the strategic considerations (in the form of Latin American military regimes) prevailed over the democratizing and developmentalist ones. Indeed, one could say that it was the Alliance's very reforms (assistance to trade unions and peasant groups, mass mobilization and the like) that helped trigger the armed forces to intervene. Further, by disparaging and undermining Latin America's traditional institutions long before anything new or "modern" had been created to replace them, the Alliance may have left the hemisphere with the worst of all possible worlds: a complete vacuum.[50]

But the Alliance also produced major successes. New roads, highways, housing projects, water systems, electrical grids, hospitals, schools, and so on were all built under Alliance for Progress auspices and with Alliance funds. The health and educational levels of millions of Latin Americans were improved. The infrastructure, bureaucratic and administrative as well as physical, for future development was also put in place. Alliance capital provided for a great deal of economic pump-priming (and even some "trickle down") which helped the Latin American countries to take off. Latin American living standards and per capita income went up impressively. Most importantly, in the strategic sense it could be argued that the Alliance helped prevent, for over two decades, any other country from following the route of Castro's Cuba—which, after all, was the chief purpose of the Alliance to begin with. Between 1959 and 1979, not a single Latin American country went communist or became an ally of the Soviet Union. In short, even though its assumptions were all wrong, the Alliance could be considered successful in its primary purpose. In this sense the Alliance worked, but for almost all the wrong reasons. Therein may lie some lessons for the present.

The first lesson has to do with the Caribbean Basin Initiative and the Kissinger

Commission recommendations for Latin America, both of which bear a striking resemblance to the Alliance for Progress.[51] The CBI and the Kissinger Commission recommendations can be seen as a "warmed-over" version of the Alliance and are based on many of the same assumptions as the earlier program. Now, while the outside scholar in me suggests that these new programs and initiatives are likely to repeat the same mistakes as the past, the Washington person in me suggests that despite their faults the Alliance, the CBI, or the Kissinger Commission recommendations are—given our frequent and widespread lack of understanding of Latin America, our historical lack of attention to the area, our condescension, and our still powerful belief that we know best for the hemisphere—about as good as we can do. One comes to accept the Alliance and these other recent programs not as "pure" or "ideal" policy and not without their many flaws and problems (not the least of which is that we seem to have learned relatively little about Latin America since the 1960s) but prudently as a second-best solution. They are certainly better than no program at all or than the several alternatives put forth by the radical Left or the far Right that are far more wild-eyed than these. More than the Alliance, the CBI, or the Kissinger Commission recommendations we probably cannot reasonably or realistically expect. That is the first lesson.

The second lesson involves assessing which of the Alliance programs worked and which did not. The analysis here and elsewhere makes clear that the best and most successful programs were those aimed at building social infrastructure (roads, housing, schools, health) as well as economic development. The narrower and more technocratic the programs, the better they worked. What did not work well—indeed were dismal failures—were all the grandiose social and political engineering programs of the Alliance: all the efforts to refurbish Latin American society and politics and recast it in our own image. Virtually all of these programs were failures.[52] The moral for current policy, therefore, is: Don't get so deeply involved in Latin American social and political life except under special circumstances (e.g., El Salvador from 1980–84); for the most part let the Latin Americans handle their own political problems and processes in their own murky way. Concentrate on simple and straightforward social and economic aid, and largely forget about "reforming" and "restructuring" Latin America from top to bottom. We would, I have reluctantly concluded (and only half in jest), generally be better off simply dropping the assistance money randomly from helicopters than in getting so deeply involved in all the everyday issues of Latin American life as we did under the Alliance. These lessons of the Alliance have strong implications for current policy disputes.

The third lesson has to do with understanding what the Alliance actually did. Essentially, it bought us some time—20 years to be exact. Few of the grandiose designs worked well or as expected, we have seen, and the assumptions were often flawed, but in its fundamental strategic purpose the Alliance succeeded: It bought us time and it kept any additional Marxist-Leninist regimes from coming to power. That was not, one suspects, a result of the Alliance's more grandiose political designs but simply a by-product of the fact that we pumped so much assistance money into Latin America during this period that the countries of the area were bound to prosper and succeed. Only after the Alliance was abandoned and we returned in the 1970s to our traditional policy of benign neglect – and precious little assistance – did any new revolutionary regimes in Latin America come to power. Now, buying time is not a "great and glorious" dream as the Alliance was, but as former Secretary of State George Marshall once noted in an offhand response to an interview question, it is not a bad basis for American foreign policy. That lesson, and its broader implications for U.S. assistance programs, is as true now as it was when Marshall articulated it.

## NOTES

1. Jerome Levinson and Juan de Onis, *The Alliance that Lost Its Way: A Critical Report on the Alliance for Progress* (Chicago: Quadrangle Books for the Twentieth Century Fund, 1970).

2. Eduardo Frei Montalva, "The Alliance that Lost Its Way," *Foreign Affairs* 45 (April 1967): 437–48.

3. The better full-length critiques, in addition to Levinson and Onis, include Victor Alba, *Alliance Without Allies* (New York: Praeger, 1965); William Manger, ed., *The Alliance for Progress: A Critical Appraisal* (Washington, D.C.: Public Affairs Press, 1963); and Harvey S. Perloff, *Alliance for Progress: A Social Invention in the Making* (Baltimore: Johns Hopkins University Press, 1969).

4. Milton S. Eisenhower, *The Wine Is Bitter: The United States and Latin America* (New York: Doubleday, 1963).

5. See the discussion in Howard J. Wiarda, *Latin America at the Crossroads: Debt and Development Strategies for the 1990s – A Report Prepared for the Inter-American Development Bank* (Boulder, Col.: Westview Press, 1986).

6. Adolf A. Berle, *Latin America: Diplomacy and Reality* (New York: Harper and Row for the Council on Foreign Relations, 1962); DeLesseps S. Morrison, *Latin American Mission: An Adventure in Hemisphere Diplomacy* (New York: Simon and Schuster, 1965).

7. The main literature on the founding and assumptions of the Alliance include William Benton, "Latin Americans Must Do Their Part," *Challenge* 10 (January 1962): 9–13; Chester Bowles, "The Alliance for Progress: A Continuing Revolution," *Department of State Bulletin* 45 (November 6, 1961): 239–45; Joseph Grunwald, "The Alliance for Progress," *Proceedings of the Academy of Political Science* 27 (May 1964): 78–93; John C. Dreier, *The Alliance for Progress: Problems and Perspectives* (Baltimore: Johns Hopkins University Press, 1962); Lincoln Gordon, *A New Deal for Latin America: The Alliance for Progress* (Cambridge: Harvard University Press, 1963); Nathan A. Haverstock, "The Alliance for Progress," *Americas* 15 (August 1963): 3–9; Albert O. Hirschman, "Second Thoughts on the Alliance for Progress," *The Reporter* 24 (May 25, 1961): 20–23; John F. Kennedy, "Fulfilling the Pledges of the Alliance for Progress," *Department of State Bulletin* 46 (April 2, 1962): 539–42; Jerome I. Levinson, "After the Alliance for Progress: Implications for Inter-American Relations," *Proceedings of the Academy of Political Science* 3 (1972): 177–90; Alberto Lleras Camargo, "The Alliance for Progress: Aims, Distortions, Obstacles," *Foreign Affairs* 42 (October 1963): 25–37; Abraham F. Lowenthal, "Alliance Rhetoric versus Latin American Reality," *Foreign Affairs* 48 (April 1970): 494–508; Thomas C. Mann, "The

Alliance for Progress," *Department of State Bulletin* 50 (June 1, 1964): 857–63; Ernest R. May, "The Alliance for Progress in Historical Perspective," *Foreign Affairs* 41 (July 1963): 757–74; J. Warren Nystrom and Nathan A. Haverstock, *The Alliance for Progress: Key to Latin America's Development* (New York: Van Nostrand, 1966); John N. Plank, "The Alliance for Progress: Problems and Prospects," *Daedalus* 91 (Fall 1962): 800–11; Brandon Robinson, "The Alliance and a Divided Heritage," *Foreign Service Journal* 40 (January 1963): 38–41; W. W. Rostow, "The Alliance for Progress," *Department of State Bulletin* 50 (March 30, 1964): 496–500; Dean Rusk, "The Alliance for Progress in the Context of World Affairs," *Department of State Bulletin* 46 (May 14, 1962): 787–94; Arthur F. Schlesinger, Jr., "The Lowering Hemisphere," *The Atlantic* 225 (January 1970): 79–88; Robert M. Smetherman and Bobbie B. Smetherman, "The Alliance for Progress: Promises Unfulfilled," *American Journal of Economics and Sociology* 31 (January 1972): 79–85; Adlai E. Stevenson, "Problems Facing the Alliance for Progress in the Americas," *Department of State Bulletin* 45 (July 24, 1961): 139–44; Tad Szulc, "The First Year of the Alliance for Progress," *The World Today* 18 (October 1962): 407–15; Szulc, "The U.S. and the Alliance for Progress," *Congressional Digest* 42 (March 1963): 67–96; United States Senate, Committee on Foreign Relations, *Survey of the Alliance for Progress* (Washington, D.C.: Government Printing Office, 1969).

8. Based on interviews by the author with a number of the State Department persons involved in these changes.

9. Schlesinger, "Lowering Hemisphere."

10. For a full discussion see Howard J. Wiarda, "The Context of United States Policy Toward the Dominican Republic: Background to the Revolution of 1965." Paper presented at the Center for International Affairs, Harvard University, December 8, 1966.

11. Pat M. Holt, *Survey of the Alliance for Progress: The Political Aspects* (Washington, D.C.: Government Printing Office for the Committee on Foreign Relations, United States Senate, 1967).

12. For earlier, more extended treatments by the author see *Politics and Social Change in Latin America: The Distinct Tradition* (Amherst, Mass.: University of Massachusetts Press, 1982); *Corporatism and National Development in Latin America* (Boulder, Col.: Westview Press, 1981); and *Ethnocentrism in Foreign Policy: Can We Understand the Third World?* (Washington, D.C.: American Enterprise Institute for Public Policy Research, 1985).

13. The subtitle derives from Daniel Bell's essay on how to interpret the Soviet Union: "Ten Theories in Search of Reality: The Prediction of Soviet Behavior in the Social Sciences," *World Politics* 10 (April 1958): 327–65.

14. See especially Schlesinger's comments in "Lowering Hemisphere," p. 81; for a more general treatment of our lack of knowledge about Latin America see James W. Symington, "Learn Latin America's Culture," *New York Times* (September 23, 1983); and Howard J. Wiarda, *In Search of Policy: The United States and Latin America* (Washington, D.C.: American Enterprise Institute for Public Policy Research, 1984).

15. For a more detailed critique see Chapter 5 of Wiarda, *Corporatism and National Development*.

16. *One Minute to Midnight in Latin America* (Washington, D.C.: League of Women Voters, April 1963).

17. Luis Mercier Vega, *Roads to Power in Latin America* (New York: Praeger, 1969), Chapter 4.

18. Howard J. Wiarda, *Dictatorship, Development, and Disintegration: Politics and Social*

*Change in the Dominican Republic* (Ann Arbor, Mich.: University Microfilms Monograph Series, 1975).

19. See the discussion in Holt, *Survey*.

20. The main literature includes C. E. Black, *The Dynamics of Modernization* (New York: Harper and Row, 1966); Robert L. Heilbroner, *The Great Assent: The Struggle for Economic Development in Our Time* (New York: Harper and Row, 1963); and W. W. Rostow, *The Stages of Economic Growth* (Cambridge: Cambridge University Press, 1960).

21. Seymour M. Lipset, *Political Man: The Social Bases of Politics* (New York: Doubleday, 1960).

22. See the two volumes edited by Claudio Veliz, *The Politics of Conformity in Latin America* (London: Oxford University Press, 1967); and *Obstacles to Change in Latin America* (London: Oxford University Press, 1965).

23. See, for example, John Bartlow Martin, *Overtaken by Events* (New York: Doubleday, 1966).

24. Especially, Gabriel A. Almond and James S. Coleman, eds., *The Politics of the Developing Nations* (Princeton, N.J.: Princeton University Press, 1960).

25. Particularly in *Ethnocentrism in Foreign Policy*.

26. Lipset, *Political Man*; and Rostow, *Stages*.

27. John J. Johnson, *Political Change in Latin America: The Emergence of the Middle Sectors* (Stanford, Ca.: Stanford University Press, 1958).

28. See, among others, Richard N. Adams et al., *Social Change in Latin America Today* (New York: Vintage, 1960); and Charles Wagley, *The Latin American Tradition* (New York: Columbia University Press, 1968).

29. Mark Falcoff, "Arms and Politics Revisited: Latin America as a Military and Strategic Theater," in Howard J. Wiarda, ed., *The Crisis in Latin America* (Washington, D.C.: American Enterprise Institute for Public Policy Research, 1984), pp. 1–9.

30. Some balanced assessments include Miguel S. Wionczek, "The Rise and Decline of Latin American Economic Integration," *Journal of Common Market Studies* 6 (September 1970): 49–67; and Hermannn Sautter, "LAFTA's Successes and Failures," *Inter-Economics* 5 (May 1972): 149–52.

31. Arthur F. Schlesinger, Jr., *A Thousand Days: John F. Kennedy in the White House* (Boston: Houghton Mifflin, 1965) pp. 769–70.

32. Howard J. Wiarda, ed., *The Continuing Struggle for Democracy in Latin America* (Boulder, Col.: Westview Press, 1980); also Wiarda and Kline, *Latin American Politics and Development* (Boulder, Col.: Westview Press, 1985).

33. Within this genre, see Karl M. Schmitt and David D. Burks, *Evolution or Chaos: Dynamics of Latin American Government and Politics* (New York: Praeger, 1963); Mildred Adams, ed., *Latin America: Evolution or Explosion?* (New York: Dodd, Mead, 1963).

34. Charles W. Anderson, "Toward a Theory of Latin American Politics," Occasional Paper No. 2, Graduate Center for Latin American Studies, Vanderbilt University, Nashville, Tennessee.

35. Wiarda, *Ethnocentrism in Foreign Policy*.

36. After the title of the volume prepared by the Inter-American Foundation, *They Know How* (Washington, D.C.: Government Printing Office, 1977).

37. Louis Hartz, *The Liberal Tradition in America* (New York: Harcourt, Brace and World, 1955).

38. For a full elaboration see Robert Packenham, *Liberal America and the Third World:*

*Political Development Ideas in Foreign Aid and Social Science* (Princeton, N.J.: Princeton University Press, 1973).

39. Anderson, "Toward a Theory"; also Kalman H. Silvert, *The Conflict Society: Reaction and Revolution in Latin America* (New York: American Universities Field Staff, 1966).

40. Howard J. Wiarda, "The Problem of Ethnocentrism in the Study of Political Development: Implications for U.S. Foreign Assistance Programs," Paper presented at the 13th World Congress of the International Political Science Association, Paris, July 15–20, 1985; published in *Society* (1986).

41. Especially, T. Lynn Smith, *Agrarian Reform in Latin America* (New York: Knopf, 1965).

42. James L. Payne, *Labor and Politics in Peru: The System of Political Bargaining* (New Haven, Conn.: Yale University Press, 1965).

43. Carlos Mouchet, "Municipal Government," in Harold E. Davis, ed., *Government and Politics in Latin America* (New York: Ronald Press, 1958), pp. 368–92; also Arpad von Lazar and John C. Hammock, *The Agony of Existence: Studies of Community Development in the Dominican Republic* (Medford, Mass.: Fletcher School of Law and Diplomacy, 1970).

44. Alfred E. Stepan, *The Military in Politics: Changing Patterns in Brazil* (Princeton, N.J.: Princeton University Press, 1971).

45. Edwin Lieuwen, *Generals versus Presidents: Neo-Militarism in Latin America* (New York: Praeger, 1964).

46. Jose Nun, "The Middle Class Military Coup," in Veliz, ed., *Politics of Conformity*, pp. 66–118.

47. Wiarda, *Dictatorship, Development, and Disintegration*, Chapter 7.

48. See the exchange between the author and a U.S. community development official in *The Nation* 206 (February 19, 1968), and May 6, 1968.

49. After the title of the book by David Halberstam, *The Best and the Brightest* (New York: Random House, 1972).

50. Wiarda, *Ethnocentrism in Foreign Policy*.

51. Compare *The Report of the President's National Bipartisan Commission on Central America* (New York: Macmillan, 1984). The author of this paper served as a lead consultant to the Commission.

52. See, by the author, *Ethnocentrism in Foreign Policy*; "The Problem of Ethnocentrism"; and "At the Root of the Problem: Conceptual Failures in U.S.-Central American Relations," in Robert S. Leiken, ed., *Central America: Anatomy of Conflict* (New York: Pergamon Press for the Carnegie Endowment, 1984), pp. 259–78.

# II
## The Machinery

# 8

# Making the Alliance Work

## Carlos Sanz de Santamaría

The Inter-American System, the oldest regional organization ever to exist, will very soon reach its centennial. Important achievements have been made, mainly in the field of international law and, on a few occasions, protection of the continent against foreign imperialistic attempts.

For almost ten years I headed the Inter-American Committee on the Alliance for Progress (CIAP). We could probably say that inter-American relations at that time reached their highest peak of understanding as the countries of the hemisphere worked together in a multilateral development program of mutual interest.

Concepts and values have changed. Many events forced us to take a different path: the Vietnam war, the political situation in the Middle East, the cautious attitudes of some U.S. members of Congress, the reticent position of some Latin American governments that did not follow democratic principles, and so on. But if we take a retrospective view of that historic time, we could also state that, on the whole, the Alliance for Progress fulfilled an important role in the economic and social development of Latin America, despite its promoters' human mistakes. One point is important to remember: The agreements signed at Punta del Este had a genuine Ibero-American origin and spirit.

Publications dating back to the 1950s show that ideas first developed by Dr. Raúl Prebisch and the Economic Commission for Latin America (ECLA) came to influence profoundly the ideas of such statesmen as President Juscelino Kubitschek of Brazil, promoter of Operation Pan-America, Alberto Lleras Camargo and Carlos Lleras Restrepo of Colombia, Arturo Alessandri and Eduardo Frei of Chile, and Romulo Betancourt of Venezuela, among others. They were all critics of the disparity in income distribution, not only within Latin American countries, but also between Latin America and the technically advanced nations. They condemned the inequity between the prices of commodities and raw materials exported by developing nations and those of manufactured goods and machinery exported by the industrialized countries. They also condemned the inaccessibility of technology and patents in a world where the existence of "perfect competition" was, and is, utopian.

Multilateral policies toward Latin America were first attempted, and proved useful, during the administration of Franklin D. Roosevelt. When John F. Kennedy came to power, multilateralism as a concept and as an instrument of inter-American relations matured with the Alliance for Progress. Under different historical circumstances and for different reasons, the political interests of President Kennedy coincided with the economic and social aspirations of Latin America. The Alliance for Progress provided a new framework for the conduct of relations between industrialized nations and those that Raúl Prebisch called "the periphery nations."

I want to underline one point about the Alliance that is frequently ignored. The Alliance for Progress can be viewed as the sum total of U.S. foreign policy toward Latin America in the 1960s, a decade that includes the Bay of Pigs, counterinsurgency, the invasion of the Dominican Republic, and the Cuban missile crisis. Or it can be viewed and analyzed as the creation of an imperfect, but useful, multilateral mechanism by which to solve economic and social problems within and among Latin American nations. Too often, serious discussion of the Alliance for Progress has been lost in the polemics over the conduct of U.S. policy, while the importance of multilateral cooperation in the social and economic fields—policies based on the ideas of men like Prebisch, Betancourt and the other statesmen already mentioned—is not properly understood.

As an illustration of the latter—the "other" Alliance for Progress—I would like to discuss its principal tool, the Inter-American Committee on the Alliance for Progress, or CIAP.

CIAP's activities covered a wide scope. Its central instrument was the country review, in which each year the economic, planning, and development ministers from member Latin American nations presented their short- and medium-term development plans to the CIAP committee of experts. Plans and objectives were reviewed, modified, refined, and altered. The country reviews provided a forum to mobilize some of the best ideas and intellectual resources in the hemisphere to assist each nation in developing its economic and social agenda for the coming years, within the broad guidelines provided in the Carta de Punta del Este. We even convoked three country review studies of the United States!

CIAP had no coercive power. Implementation of the Alliance for Progress consisted of three main elements: planning, self-help, and external assistance. The ideas that emerged in the country review meetings could not be imposed against the will of any nation. Some advice was heeded; some was ignored or deemed politically unfeasible. But it must be remembered that in the early 1960s, the idea of national planning offices was novel, even radical, although it had been a central component of the ECLA development strategy. CIAP worked with most Latin

American nations to develop and strengthen their planning capacity. Today, all these countries have strong, central and regional planning offices capable of assimilating data and forecasting areas of economic changes, technological development, and population growth. This is one of the principal legacies of the Alliance for Progress.

Another area in which CIAP was active was commodity prices, which continue to be a central issue for Latin American nations. For example, the situation for sugar-exporting countries today is similar to that encountered at the time of the Alliance for Progress: Sugar prices are excessively low. The economies of several small countries depend essentially on sugar exports. Nevertheless, some industrialized countries—for good domestic political reasons, of course—continue to compete in the sugar market by producing beets. CIAP understood the interest of some European nations and the United States in producing these raw materials—beets or sugar cane—but on many occasions suggested an alternative. CIAP urged those countries, which were manufacturers of equipment and exporters of technology, to study the possibility of reducing sugar production and purchasing sugar from the Latin American nations. This would enable the latter to obtain the hard currency needed to purchase machinery, equipment, and even raw materials from the developed nations. At the same time, of course, this would boost economic development in Latin American and Caribbean sugar-producing countries.

Industrialized nations, however, still don't seem to realize that by competing with Latin American producers in the sugar market, they seriously affect the hard currency income of these countries, thereby losing potential sales of machinery and equipment.

The case of coffee is somewhat different. One of the first commodity agreements reached was the International Coffee Agreement, which effectively stabilized prices for both producing and consuming nations. The agreement has not been in effect for nearly 25 years. There are many critics of these commodity agreement systems in different parts of the world, but I have not heard or read of a satisfactory new alternative that could cope with this very serious problem for most of our countries in Latin America. Since the machinery needed for development is produced in industrialized countries that fix the price of the machinery, it would seem wise to continue to work toward reaching commodity and raw material agreements directed and handled by consumers and producers together.

With the experience already acquired, these agreements could be refined and modified, but they should not be abandoned altogether.

The initial call for a ten-year development effort through the Alliance for Progress aimed at alleviating pressing illnesses in the Latin American environment and at fostering education, health care, housing, and employment opportunities. One central measurement was to be expressed in terms of GNP. The Charter of Punta del Este mentioned a rise of 2.5 percent in per capita income per year, along with the provision of better sanitation and health care facilities. Specific goals were set in these areas. To attain them, new norms were established and implemented largely through fiscal policies throughout the hemisphere.

## EDUCATION

Latin American countries attained under the Alliance for Progress what one of the directors of the Inter-American Council for Education, Science and Culture (CIECC) called "the education explosion." Much progress was evident in this field, although students in various countries were sometimes not prepared to take full advantage of this type of help. In any case, the impetus given by the Alliance to educational programs was important. Unfortunately, these activities had been weakened considerably by 1976.

## AGRICULTURE

The CIAP put a great deal of effort into the exchange of agricultural experiences among the countries of Latin America through IICA, the institute devoted to agriculture and animal husbandry. With the cooperation of the UN Food and Agriculture Organization (FAO) and the Inter-American Institute of Agricultural Cooperation (IICA), it was hoped that Latin America would be in a position not only to provide food for its own population but also to export it to those countries experiencing severe hunger and poverty. The results here, too, have varied from country to country.

## HOUSING

Another area central to the Alliance was housing. Again, we learned by doing. The World Bank had established a Social Progress Trust Fund to invest $200 million from 1961 to 1965 in low-income housing for the urban poor. New *barrios* were created in Bogota, Mexico, Lima, Rio de Janeiro, and elsewhere. In Rio de Janeiro, for example, two new projects were constructed. Villa de la Alianza and Villa Kennedy. At the time, they were considered to be model programs for the relocation of slum (*favela*) inhabitants to new and sanitary communities. Yet the newly constructed communities encountered much resistance, and some of the relocation, unfortunately, was achieved through the use of force. Why? For most of these people, income was dependent on easy access to downtown areas. The new *barrios* were located far from the center of town, a problem which meant considerable additional expense for transport, which itself was inadequate. Later, we changed the focus of these projects toward providing essential services—sewerage, electricity, water, and transportation—to the existing *barrios*.

## POLITICAL CHANGE

In the political realm, the Alliance sought to foster democratic institutions in part through social and economic measures and in part through the application of the principles of self-determination by individual countries. This was the most problematic area, for no multilateral program can determine the political destiny of a participating country. During the period of the Alliance, some nations succumbed to military coups, while others became functioning democracies.

Many Latin Americans involved in the Alliance, including myself, continued to believe that democracy is rooted in more equitable social and economic structures and that these in turn would stimulate more rapid economic growth. The relationship between economic development and types of political systems was not properly understood, and the difficulties that were experienced by the Alliance for Progress on that score need to be further analyzed.

However, it must be noted that the trend today in Latin America is toward the return to democratic regimes, a fact that is most heartening for those of us who worked with the Alliance for Progress, and for most Americans, North and South.

## MULTILATERAL COOPERATION

Another area of multilateral cooperation within the Alliance for Progress must be underscored: the cooperation of Canada and some European nations. Although the Canadian government did not want to be an active member of the Organization of American States, it did not object to working with CIAP. Excellent cooperation efforts were undertaken with some countries, especially the Caribbean nations. This was also the case with European countries, Japan, and other nations of the East. This prompted me to suggest, when I resigned from the presidency of CIAP, the development of a different approach to the future of the inter-American system. This new approach should be based on the coordination of the principal intergovernmental agencies, CIES, CIAP, CEPCIEC, and CIECC, in a manner similar to the OECD in Europe. In such a system a forum similar to the country reviews could be undertaken with full cooperation from international financing agencies, including those of the United States, Canada and Europe, as was the case during the Alliance, to help the Ibero-American and Caribbean areas develop their national economic plans.

Such a system would be most valuable today in the handling of the international debt crisis, for example, one of the most serious problems facing Latin America. If a country cannot obtain hard currency through international trade, there is no possibility whatsoever that that country can pay its external debt. Recently Dr. Henry Kissinger suggested a Marshall Plan to help Latin America solve this problem. James Baker, the current U.S. Secretary of the Treasury, also suggested a new plan of investment opportunities to solve the debt crisis. Good ideas have also been provided by universities and economists in the United States, Latin America, and even Europe. It is essential to look for ways and means to solve this problem, as it affects the banking systems in all of the Western countries and Japan.

This situation demonstrates the need for an organization such as CIAP. It would have been the perfect forum to discuss and perhaps solve these matters.

Concerned about the situation even then, CIAP undertook a study 20 years ago to determine what new international monetary system could replace the

Bretton Woods agreement. This study was conducted by several of the leading economists of that time, including two Nobel prize winners.

There is a need today to reexamine some of the good ideas of the past and to create new ideas and programs for the future. Charles de Gaulle, when he was president of France, showed his deep concern and understanding of these pressing issues. He said:

In our time, our cause is man. It is man whom we must rescue, whom we must try to elevate and develop. . . . Why don't we make a cooperative contribution of a percentage of our raw materials, of our manufactures, of our scientists, technicians, economists, a part of our trucks, our shops, our planes, so that we can abolish misery, so that we can stabilize the prices of our natural resources to help the less-developed nations in their effort to grow? Let's do it. Not because they follow our ideology but just because we can give life and peace a better chance. How much more valuable that would be than territorial demands, ideological aims, imperialistic ambitions that would bring the universe death!

It seems to me that this should be a major item to be included in the agenda for an eventual conference between East and West.[1]

My suggestion today is simple: As a continent facing many common problems and situations that affect us all, we need an organization, a forum where we can take our problems—our common problems—for discussion and solution. Remember that while the Alliance existed, despite its failures, the inter-American system reached its best climate of understanding, good relations, and—why not say it—accomplishments.

## NOTES

1. French President Charles de Gaulle speaking at a press conference at the Palais de l'Elysee, March 25, 1960. Free translation.

# 9

# Overcoming the Inertia

*Antonio Ortiz Mena*

It is well that we celebrate the achievements of the Alliance for Progress because, preoccupied as we are with today's weighty problems, we tend to forget how much Latin America has accomplished, and how much it has changed during the past 25 years. To appreciate the scope and depth of those changes, we need to recall the evolution of our region's development strategy and its goals, from the establishment of the Organization of American States through Operation Pan-America, the Act of Bogota, and the Charter of Punta del Este, the Protocol of Buenos Aires, and the Consensus of Viña del Mar. Not to be forgotten in this chain of events, of course, was the establishment of the Inter-American Development Bank (IDB) and the specific role assigned to it.

As my contribution, I would like to recall a few events in which I had the privilege of participating and which had some impact on the course of the Alliance, our bank's contribution to its efforts, and the evolution of present-day Latin America.

The first of those events took place in Mexico City in 1962. This was the first annual meeting at a ministerial level of the Inter-American Economic and Social Council. As the secretary of finance of the host country, I had the honor of chairing that meeting.

One of the results of our deliberations consisted of enlisting the services of former presidents Juscelino Kubitschek of Brazil and Alberto Lleras of Colombia to review the Charter of Punta del Este and to help put in place a working mechanism of the Alliance for Progress. In time, that mechanism came to embrace a series of institutions and processes, including the Inter-American Committee on the Alliance for Progress. CIAP, as it was called, represented the first multilateral effort in our hemisphere to coordinate development assistance, to evaluate each country's progress in development, to promote self-help, and to make recommendations concerning regional policy matters.

CIAP's coordinating role also meant that our countries voluntarily committed themselves to discussing the progress they were making and the obstacles they faced in meeting the objectives of the Charter of Punta del Este. These involved the adoption of certain policies and measures, including steps to introduce land reform, increase agricultural and industrial production, improve social conditions, encourage exports, promote investment, control and reduce inflation, maintain realistic exchange rates, and reform tax systems.

While CIAP's important role lasted only about a decade, this grandchild of the first ministerial meeting of the Alliance for Progress in large measure embodied the visionary spirit of our countries and their governments in attempting the most profound transformation of an entire continent. Change and progress were not to be left in the hands of fate: Free men, working through democratic institutions, cooperating and pooling their resources and experience, would attempt to raise the living conditions of the vast majority of our people. And they would make the first giant step in that direction before the decade of the 1960s came to an end.

Ten years later, as we began to assess the results of the Alliance, some analysts concluded that the best efforts of our countries, supported with tremendous generosity by the United States, fell considerably short of the goals of the Alliance.

I remember participating in some of those assessments as a newly elected president of the Inter-American Development Bank. A meeting of the governors of the bank in Buenos Aires, in the spring of 1971, comes particularly to mind. We were wrestling at that meeting with the future role of our bank. Having survived the 1960s, what would we try to achieve during the 1970s? To find an answer to that question we first had to review the condition of our member countries, evaluate the success and the shortcomings of their development efforts, and arrive at some conclusions regarding the financial and technological requirements of the next stage of progress.

The IDB, I would like to point out, had by then already achieved some renown for its contribution to the Alliance. Admittedly, in dollar terms, the volume of its lending could not compare with other sources of official development financing. Our strength and impact – then as now – came primarily from the project orientation of our institution and our readiness to innovate. Our governors and the management realized early, for example, that social development had to accompany economic growth. To this end, our bank began to enter fields that were new to international banking; financing water supply and sewerage projects, farm settlement and improved land uses, low-cost housing, credit for small- and medium-size industries and farms, expansion of universities and technical schools, as well as projects designed to stimulate regional economic integration – that is, to provide new links among the Latin American countries.

It became obvious to us in the course of our assessment that in spite of the broad-based support that it received from our bank and from other public and multilateral organizations, the Alliance was not meeting its objectives. Admittedly, rates of economic growth in the region were impressive. Levels of investment were high. Changes were taking place in the economies, in the institutional structure, and in the social sectors of virtually all of the countries. Yet those changes were neither as extensive nor as pervasive as our people and their leaders had hoped for. The condition of life was improving for many, but the disparities in the distribution of incomes and in access to the amenities of life were in some cases even more pronounced than when the Alliance was launched.

We realized also that the problems confronting our region on the threshold of the 1970s were quite different from those we had faced ten years earlier. Economic and social development in Latin America was being profoundly affected by massive changes taking place outside our continent. "The winds of change were blowing," I told our governors, "stirred by the widespread search for greater economic and social justice . . . but those winds know no boundaries." The whole world appeared to be in turmoil as Latin America and other developing regions began their hesitant entrance into the world economy. The problems of one region communicated themselves quickly to other parts of the globe. Pluralism and interdependence became the new catchwords.

Three examples serve to underline what was happening. For these, I have arbitrarily selected foreign trade, technology transfer, and capital flows.

In the field of trade, a distressing trend became evident: While the Latin American economies grew and modernized, and while the volume and value of world trade continued to climb, our region's share of world exports declined from 13.4 percent in 1950 to 5 percent in 1969. This suggested three things: first, the terms of trade were turning against our region with a decline in the price of our chief exports; second, that together with other developing regions, we were losing markets to man-made raw materials; and third, we were making all too little progress in the one area of world trade that was expanding most rapidly – the trade in manufactures.

The situation was somewhat similar in the field of technology. We had been devoting the lion's share of our imports to capital goods designed and produced in the industrialized countries, but to what effect? That technology was not helping us either to gain an advantage in trade or to make the best use of our resources. In addition to the relatively lackluster performance of our exports, unemployment in the region continued to grow, and with it, social and political tensions.

Financial flows also presented a paradox. Never before had any region benefitted from such a large-scale infusion of financing – a good part of it on very liberal terms – as did Latin America during the 1960s. Most of those transfers financed new productive capacity and infrastructure, creating the means for their repayment. Nevertheless, our region's external indebtedness was rising at an alarming pace. Some of us began to view with unease this potential source of difficulty – fully ten years before the current debt problem captured the world's attention.

We wrestled with those problems and paradoxes during the 1970s, while even bigger challenges came to assail the world economy. Certainly, aside from the Great Depression, nothing compared to the blows delivered by the successive increases in the price of energy, especially of petroleum. We coped with those also, but the vulnerability they engendered and the excesses they invited produced very serious consequences. We have seen them reflected in the tragic reversals of the past four years.

This brief survey brings me back to the questions that continue to haunt occasions such as this: Was the Alliance for Progress a success? Was the effort—and the sacrifice—worth it? Did this noble enterprise achieve its aims?

I believe that, on balance, we will all agree that the vast majority of Latin American people have experienced real improvement in their living conditions, and that Latin America emerged from relative isolation and entered the mainstream of the world's economy. In specific terms, life expectancy increased on the average by six years. Birth rates declined in four-fifths of our countries. Infant mortality dropped. The extent of illiteracy was reduced and educational opportunities were opened for millions of our people. While total population rose by 70 percent, primary school enrollment went up by nearly 200 percent, secondary school enrollment by 350 percent, and higher education by an amazing 800 percent.

Since the beginning of the Alliance, the regional gross domestic product (GDP) tripled in size and by 1981, our region's per capita GDP had doubled. An impressive physical infrastructure came into being. For example, the paved road network expanded by some 300 percent while total road mileage increased 250 percent. Installed capacity of electricity increased 350 percent on a per capita basis, with commercial energy consumption trailing closely behind. The number of people living in cities skyrocketed from 100 to 250 million, but by the beginning of this decade, 170 million of those—as compared to 40 million in 1960—were served by potable water supply systems.

We could continue this recitation, but you may ask: Are you begging the question? Could those changes have occurred without the Alliance for Progress?

I, for one, do not believe so.

The changes that have taken place in Latin America since 1961 are nothing short of revolutionary. They have transformed our societies, profoundly altered both the capacity and the orientation of our governments, created a whole new texture of intra-regional relationships, and opened up our region to the world economy. Changes of this scale find no parallel in the history of western civilization—except when they were brought about by widespread violence. In our case, this transformation came peacefully, through a unique and continuing interaction and collaboration between our people and their governments. This, to me, is the real essence of the Alliance for Progress, and the true measure of its success to date.

I do not want to leave the impression that I consider the goals of the Alliance to have been attained or invalidated by the passage of time. The basic purpose of the Alliance, summarized by the late President John F. Kennedy as the quest for *techo, trabajo y tierra, salud y escuela*, remains as valid today as it was 25 years ago. That quest will not be over until all of the people of our region are assured of the enjoyment, in peace and freedom, of these basic rights.

*10*

# The Assumptions of the Alliance

## Jack Heller and Miguel S. Wionczek

### THE ASSUMPTIONS OF THE CONTRACT
### OF PUNTA DEL ESTE

#### Jack Heller

My contribution to this examination of the Alliance for Progress will be to focus on some of the assumptions that undergirded its designs and implementation. I shall focus on these assumptions whose reexamination might inform our contemporary discussion about the role and limits of foreign economic assistance.

Let us first look at the nature of the bargain that was struck in the Charter of Punta del Este. It is instructive to begin by asking: Whose assumptions are we talking about? The question is a useful one, because different parties to the bargain made very different assumptions about the nature of the commitments that had been undertaken. These differences had important consequences for the way in which the Alliance was implemented and what it achieved.

There probably would have been little disagreement in the early 1960s with the following formulation about the significance of the Charter of Punta del Este.

The Charter was ratified by the OAS member countries as a collective commitment to national and regional development goals and as a commitment by each country to take national actions necessary for achieving these goals. Underlying these commitments was the bargain struck between the United States and the remainder of the Charter signatories. The United States agreed to provide externally required resources commensurate with each country's development efforts. In return, the countries of the hemisphere agreed that they would undertake sweeping reforms required for achieving needed political, social, and economic progress.

It seemed clear when the Charter was adopted that the commitments to development change that it embodied were understood throughout the hemisphere, including the United States, as signifying a sweeping redefinition of the ground rules of the hemispheric system. In effect, the Charter was perceived as a fundamental redefinition or rewriting of the "constitutional" ground rules of the inter-American system. With its ratification, the constitutional center of gravity of the inter-American system appeared to shift away from the region's historic preoccupation with collective security and peacekeeping. Collective responsibility for economic and social progress, it seemed, had displaced these traditional concerns as the new center of the region's collective or cooperative purpose.

The Charter, in constitutional terms, declared social and economic underdevelopment "unconstitutional," and legitimized sweeping prescriptions for change.

Americans in the United States and those in the rest of the hemisphere, however, tend to view the force of their national constitutions through very different political and jurisprudential lenses. It is not surprising, therefore, that they also had very different understandings about the nature of the hemispheric, or international constitutional, bargain struck at Punta del Este.

As seen from the United States, constitutional standards carry the weight of law. They are contractual and give rise to enforceable rights and obligations. Implicit in this jurisprudential outlook is that departures from constitutional standards are unlawful, intolerable and hence, are to be speedily remedied. Consistent with this outlook, the Charter tended to be regarded in the United States as constitutionally rescinding the legitimacy of underdevelopment and therefore, as requiring extraordinary national and international governmental efforts to achieve speedy change.

Constitutions and constitutional law tend to be viewed more elastically in Latin America. Hence, while the constitutions of many of the American republics are generous in the inclusivity and scope of the rights, benefits, and protections that they copiously confer, these norms are usually not rigorously adhered to or attained. Seldom perceived as carrying the force of law, constitutional norms, instead, tend to be viewed in pragmatic terms. Although not conferring enforceable rights, they are important as expressions of idealized societal goals. As compilations of standards by which the imperfections of the political order can be measured, constitutional norms tend to be regarded as ideals to be striven toward rather than as expressions of enforceable rights and obligations.

The ratification of the Charter, as Harvey Perloff used to say, was a singular international "political and economic experiment." No comparably broad hemispheric consensus about common political and economic goals or cooperation is likely to be replicated soon. Indeed, this consensus could not have been achieved if the parties to the bargain on which it rested had viewed the Charter from a shared constitutional tradition; that is, if they had a common understanding of the bargain or commitments entered into. Because each side interpreted the Charter through its own jurisprudential lens, both were able to maintain their mutually inconsistent developmental and reformist expectations, goals, timetables, and priorities essentially intact. In this sense, the Alliance may have been a ten billion dollar misunderstanding.

The early years' strong political appeal and support of the Alliance in the United States derived in large measure from the assumption that the bargain struck in the Charter involved a strong—constitutional—Latin American commitment to immediate and sweeping development reform and change. It was only because of this assumption that the Alliance bargain seemed sensible, prudent, and attractive to the United States public and Congress.

Consistent with this assumption, for example, the Administration's annual proposals to Congress for Alliance funds were cast essentially in scorecard form. The Administration welcomed congressional insistence upon monitoring Latin American performance in meeting the Charter's goals and, at least initially, shared with the public and the Congress the view that country assistance allocations could and should be precisely linked to that performance.

Unfortunately, this halcyon view of the bargain also had disadvantageous long-run consequences. For example, it no doubt contributed to unrealistic public and congressional expectations about how rapidly the goals of the Charter would be achieved. The price of these unrealistic expectations—as Latin American governments failed to embrace sweeping reforms enthusiastically and far-reaching progress did not materialize rapidly—was a disenchanted cooling of the Alliance's initially broad political support.

The United States' view of the bargain also seemed to preclude the development and application of intellectually coherent, politically sustainable, and publicly understandable criteria for determining to which countries and on what conditions the United States would provide development assistance. The assumption that U.S. assistance would in some way be directly proportionate to country reform and self-help was effective on the rhetorical level, but was conceptually meaningless. As a general and vague test of assistance worthiness, it masked the subtlety, complexity, and intricacy of the development and assistance process. Hence, while sold to the public and the Congress as a meaningful standard for dispensing assistance, the broad self-help formulation actually furnished little concrete guidance for the day-to-day negotiation and implementation of foreign assistance programs.

As was inevitable, the inconsistency between rhetoric and practice soon became apparent. Discrepancies between country reform performance and the levels of assistance conferred became increasingly difficult to square with the bargain that the United States public and Congress thought had been made at Punta del Este. For example, the principle that assistance was reserved to governments committed to preserving or expanding democratic institutions was more often ignored than honored. The priority given to reform that achieved a more just distribution of income was subordinated to policies that promised to preserve the status quo through stable growth. Assistance was often furnished for political purposes that seemed unrelated to the recipient's development achievements or policies.

The price paid for the dissonance between the Alliance rhetoric and the realities of program implementation was, of course, that political support for the Alliance soon dwindled. One indication of the political and intellectual disarray of the Alliance was that many early supporters of the program became indifferent or hostile, while many former adversaries reversed their positions and came to its support. The Alliance, in short, became all things to all people who had overseas interests that foreign assistance might conceivably serve. Hence, the Alliance gradually lost policy coherence and clarity of purpose.

In contrast to its inception, the demise of the Alliance some years later went wholly unnoticed and unlamented. There was no press, academic, or government comment made when the U.S. government one day abruptly removed the Alliance logo from Agency for International Development stationery and did away with the office of the Coordinator of the Alliance for Progress.

The Alliance had become politically uninteresting. Once the United States' view of the constitutional nature of the Charter bargain was jettisoned and the Latin American perception in effect adopted, it also became politically unsustainable.

Oddly, and lamentably, the lessons of this intellectual and political failure have not been learned. Much of the conceptual underpinnings of today's foreign assistance programs, both bilateral and multilateral, seem to resonate eerily in the frozen rhetoric of the early 1960s. The concepts of self-help and reform, still the central conditions used to justify assistance programs, remain as substantively empty and useless for guiding policy today as they were then.

Most disheartening is that the nature and purpose of the bargain between assistance donors and recipients remain essentially undefined, and no politically supportable, conceptually developed rationale for these programs has been hammered out.

As in the final years of the Alliance, it is often observed today that in most donor countries assistance programs have no political constituency. Less often understood is that they obviously will not and cannot be expected to attract one unless and until their rationale is more convincingly and coherently articulated and their rhetoric is congruent with their actualities. Unfortunately, so long as the donor-recipient bargain is unclear, this clarity of purpose is unlikely to materialize. The dilemma, of course, is that if donors and recipients were to perceive the terms of the bargain in the same way, it might be nearly impossible to negotiate a mutually acceptable assistance program.

There is another packet of closely related Alliance assumptions to which I would like briefly to turn because of the related lessons they may hold for contemporary assistance policies and practices. While these assumptions are more often clung to by assistance donors than recipients, they have adherents on both sides of the equation, and they clearly figured in the calculations of both in the establishment of the Alliance.

It was assumed that the combination of an appropriate diagnosis of development problems (or, as was fashionable in the 1960s, development "bottlenecks") coupled with sufficient resources to pay for the prescribed solutions, would yield dramatic breakthroughs in the hemisphere's fundamental problems – including the problems of politically repressive, undemocratic government.

The Alliance experience seems to have imprinted on the collective awareness of the development profession some appreciation of the fact that many of the problems whose effects are observable as manifestations of underdevelopment are too complex or obscurely rooted to defy accurate diagnosis or effective prescription. The many inadvertent failures, effects, and achievements of the Alliance left a healthy residue of skepticism and caution in place of the heady hubris of the early years.

Nonetheless, the Alliance assumption that the offer of external assistance can provide an effective inducement for a country to adopt basic policy changes and reform still appears to retain considerable vitality in U.S. assistance strategies and negotiations. Since the Alliance experience can be interpreted as an overwhelming repudiation of the general efficacy of this assumption, its continued vitality is striking.

The problem with this simplistic assumption is that it started from a politically silly view of the nature of change and power in any country. It bypassed and ignored the fact that the fundamental development problems of the hemisphere's countries reflect complex, often bloodily attained, political balances and deadlocks over how power is held, competed for, and used, and about who gets what, how they get it, and how they intend to hold onto it. Problems such as grossly skewed distributions of income, opportunity, wealth, and land, or economically unsound and unjust wage, health, banking, housing, and educational policies, have usually evolved over centuries of political and cultural turmoil and accommodation. Contrary to the Alliance assumptions, they were more often than not impervious to outside influence and the essentially politically irrelevant enticements of foreign resources.

The implications of these conclusions for the self-help rhetoric of the Alliance were, of course, devastating. The Latin American "constitutional" view of the nature of the Alliance bargain was not unrealistic. There were then, and remain today, powerful reformist political currents in the hemisphere. It was no less true in the Alliance days than today, however, that the fundamental changes that they are achieving or energizing are occurring, and by their nature will continue to occur, essentially independently of (often despite) the functioning of foreign assistance programs. Certainly, no responsible Latin American politician could or would realistically subscribe, either during the Alliance or today, to a set of national commitments incorporating the United States' constitutional view of the Alliance bargain.

This conclusion raises even more difficult questions about the nature of the assistance bargain, and indeed, whether there is any bargain left to be made at all. These questions need to be addressed and answered if economic assistance programs are ever to achieve more coherence of purpose.

Finally, the failure of these Alliance assumptions also points to basic lessons for the future of foreign assistance, its limitations, and its purposes. Judging from such recent assistance events as the Caribbean Basin Initiative and the spectacular failures of recent Central American assistance efforts, it does not appear that these lessons have been thought through or learned. The unrealistic political notions that undergird these recent unsuccessful assistance adventures are very much akin to those of the Alliance.

## THE REALITIES OF HEMISPHERIC RELATIONS

### Miguel S. Wionczek

Since the promulgation of the Monroe Doctrine in the 1820s, the presence of the United States in Latin America has been increasing steadily, not diminishing as some will state. Looked at from Latin America's point of view, the region continues to be considered by the U.S. as its backyard which presumably, in the interest of all parties concerned, must be defended against external threats as defined in Washington. The Monroe Doctrine is still very much alive, not in words but in practice. The difference between its original version and the present one is that while at its birth the Monroe Doctrine was meant to keep Europeans out of the hemisphere, today it is addressed to a competing superpower. In this regard, U.S. attitudes on international issues with regard to Latin America are very parochial indeed.

The serious U.S. failure in its present hemispheric relations is in part due to a sort of intellectual and mental block to accepting some common-sense propositions at the highest levels of policymaking. The key proposition is that economic growth and related social change under any model, particularly in the underdeveloped world, evade any sort of outside control, since economic growth and social change encounter a wide range of conflicts within those countries themselves independent of outside forces. The assumption that the intervention of an external invisible hand in the development process can influence the intensity of social change conflict is at best a liberal and naive dream.

There is another important element to be taken into account in considering the potential for economic growth in Latin America. Carlos Manuel Castillo, former vice-president of Costa Rica and former president of the central bank of that country, was in the Alliance years directly involved in the design and implementation of the Central American economic integration scheme. He has insisted that "the present crisis in Central America is not a crisis of debt, but a crisis of political and economic viability."[1] The same is true of Latin America as a whole. I share Castillo's diagnosis, and I am not particularly impressed by the statistics on Latin American economic performance during the golden days of the Alliance for Progress.

At the highest official level all over the western hemisphere—with the obvious exception of Cuba—both the Declaration of Peoples of America and the Punta del Este Charter were considered at that time as proof of a new era in continental relations, based upon democratic cooperation between the governments and the governed of the hemisphere. This enthusiastic appraisal of the results of the Punta del Este Conference was far from unanimous at other levels. I was one of the skeptics in this respect, as can be judged by the contents of a rather long essay on the Punta del Este results, published in Mexico City in October 1961.[2]

The reasons for my immediate criticisms of the Alliance for Progress promises were rather simple. After having studied closely the proceedings of the Punta del Este hemispheric summit, I realized that, to put it bluntly, in the best tradition of most hemispheric and Latin American gatherings, that "historical meetings of minds" were long on words but short on commitments of all the parties involved. Latin American participants—again with the exception of Cuba—were in agreement in principle that it was necessary "to make great cooperative efforts aimed at accelerating social economic development in Latin American countries so that they could achieve an optimal degree of welfare with equal opportunities for all democratic societies."[3]

On its part, the United States committed itself also in principle to providing the region with a considerable volume of economic aid and technical assistance. The U.S. commitments, however, were as vague with respect to the future implementation of the lofty Alliance for Progress goals as those of Latin America. The unbridgeable gap between rhetoric and commitment became clear shortly after the Punta del Este Conference had adjourned. In its 1961 session the U.S. Congress limited itself to confirming only the aid commitment already promised for that year and in part already disbursed. Latin Americans began immediately to dedicate a lot of time and attention to devising the subtle ways to water down their commitments. The bargaining process that characterized U.S.-Latin American political and economic relations in the past, a hemispheric club with minor members and "the majority of one," came back to life. Latin Americans started sending signals that perhaps they might consider the possibility of some reforms if they would get additional aid; the U.S. intimated that it might perhaps give more money to the region if Latin Americans were to do what they promised at Punta del Este. In spite of the pressure of time and growing social conflict in the region, nobody, however, became engaged in the task of clarifying the commitments. There is at least no evidence in that respect in the official documents of the Punta del Este meeting. The more closely one looked at their real, rather than rhetorical, content, the deeper was the feeling of deception.

It is true that the ambitious objectives of the founding fathers of the Alliance for Progress were spelled out in some detail. But who could have declared himself against a "substantial and sustained economic growth," "better income distribution," "more equilibrated diversification of domestic economies," "rational industrialization," "agrarian reforms," "regional economic integration" and many other badly needed reforms? One could have easily concluded that once all these objectives were reached, the western hemisphere could live in a paradise. Unfortunately, the Punta del Este documents did not adequately spell out how such a paradise would be reached.

Every time the Alliance for Progress founding fathers went from general proposals to particular solutions and from declarations to recommendations, both solutions and recommendations were written in a language not only difficult to understand but impossible to be analyzed with rational and coherent criteria. The Punta del Este Charter was full of terms such as "just prices," "equitable treatment," "well-conceived programs," "necessary flexibility," "as far as possible," and so on. What did this language mean? While God in his infinite wisdom may know, many human beings found it impossible to answer this simple question, raised by careful study of the 14 unanimously approved resolutions annexed to the Punta del Este Charter. Such was my immediate reaction to the birth of the Alliance for Progress and not only my reflections a quarter century later.

## NOTES

1. Carlos M. Castillo, *Growth and Integration in Central America* (New York: Praeger, 1966).

2. Miguel S. Wionczek, "El nacimiento de la Alianza para el Progreso," *La Gaceta del Fondo de Cultura Economica* 3(8), (August 1961).

3. Ibid.

# 11

# The Early Days of the IDB:
# A Personal Reminiscence

## T. Graydon Upton

As most observers of Latin America are aware, efforts to create an inter-American financial institution began some six decades ago and represented a profound aspiration of Latin Americans. These attempts received the support of the U.S. administrations in earlier days, but were twice rejected by the U.S. Congress. However, since the creation of the World Bank in 1944, successive administrations declined to support an inter-American financial institution.

It is ironic, then, that the final decision to support the creation of such a bank was made practically overnight in Washington, for purely diplomatic reasons. At a meeting on August 11, 1958 with President Eisenhower and Secretary of State Christian Herter, Treasury Secretary Robert Anderson learned that the U.S. planned to submit a proposal for the creation of a Middle Eastern development bank to the UN two days later. Anderson immediately sensed that a new crisis in inter-American relations could only be averted by a prior announcement of U.S. support for a development bank for Latin America, and so persuaded the President.

A telephone call to Assistant Secretary Richard Rubottom prompted the drafting of a declaration, which was cleared immediately, paving the way for the historic statement by Douglas Dillon the next day, August 12. At a hastily called meeting of the Inter-American Economic and Social Council, Dillon announced that the U.S. was prepared to support the formation of an inter-American financial institution.

President Eisenhower's decision to back the creation of the bank was the last unilateral U.S. decision on the matter. Henceforth, Washington had to defend its views at the negotiating table, where on a unitary country-basis Latin American delegates outnumbered the U.S. by 20 to 1. Many of the Latin negotiators had already participated in numerous debates on the subject, while the U.S. side had not. Since economic disputes pitting Latin America against the U.S. were normally won or lost in negotiation, the Latin American team were experienced negotiators. Indeed, it is not far-fetched to say that Hispanic culture, with its emphasis on intellectualism, has produced a large number of good negotiators.

Early discussions were led on the U.S. side by the State Department, which had good bilingual personnel. But when the discussions reached the stage of the Specialized Committee for Negotiating and Drafting the Charter of the Inter-American Development Bank, the Treasury Department led the interdepartmental team. Treasury personnel had done most of the drafting for the Bretton Woods institutions, and the team had done its new preparatory work well, but the Treasury staff had less experience in Latin American affairs. Most of the group were disciples of Secretary George Humphrey, whose chief concern in prior Latin American negotiations had been to keep the draw from the U.S. Treasury to a minimum, and who strongly supported the philosophy that the private sector should play the key role in development.

The Latin American viewpoint, put forward by the Brazilian delegate Cleantho Paiva Leite, was just the opposite. It favored substantially greater public funds, with Latin American contributions to be made in local currencies. While not opposed to the private sector per se, the Latin American delegates felt that any contribution it made to development would be inadequate. Thus the stage was set for a stimulating confrontation at the inter-American negotiating table!

The Specialized Committee began its work on January 9, 1959, in the Columbus Room of the Pan American Union building. The 21 countries were represented by some 86 delegates, alternates, and advisors. It is interesting to note that 15 of the Latin American delegates, three of the participants from the Organization of American States, and five members of the U.S. delegation eventually came to play key management roles at the IDB; indeed, Felipe Herrera, head of one of the two subcommittees that were formed, became the bank's first president.[1]

The first skirmish, after the formation of all the necessary committees, was the struggle over whether or not observers would be admitted to the meetings – a fairly common practice at international meetings. The U.S. took the view that the negotiation of a bank was not an ordinary meeting and that the presence of observers was not appropriate. The Latin Americans felt otherwise. Actually, only one observer was at issue, and his name was never mentioned. He was Raúl Prebisch, the head of the UN Economic and Social Committee on Latin America (ECLA), who had been an influential personality at earlier meetings where the concept of the bank had been debated and was a figure of towering intellect and great oratorical capacity, greatly admired throughout Latin America.

The Treasury staff feared Prebisch as a left-wing economist with ideas about Latin American development that would be very costly to the U.S. They were apprehensive that even as an observer, Prebisch would dominate the negotiations and considerably increase the U.S. ante to the bank. Eventually Treasury won the skirmish and no observers were invited.

On the first working day of the conference, the U.S. presented a complete draft of a charter as well as a substantive memorandum outlining what the still unnamed bank should be and do. It was, from the negotiating standpoint, a master stroke. It is far easier to defend one's own draft from attack than to create a document from scratch. It also probably reduced the negotiating period by several months.

The document was based on the charter of the World Bank. The U.S. team could point out, off the record, that the Congress would be far more likely to approve a charter based on an institution that it knew and respected than one that broke completely new ground. After some minor objection, the U.S. draft became the basis of negotiations—and no other working document was presented.

Nonetheless, the draft charter was worked over extensively. The Latin American negotiators were sensitive to wording per se, as well as to the question of future interpretation of the document. The purpose finally agreed, after many hours of discussion, was "to contribute to the acceleration of the process of economic development of the member countries, individually and collectively." The U.S. opposed the use of the word "collectively," ostensibly for its Marxist connotations but really because it was a catchword to commit the bank to financing integration projects with significant financial implications. The U.S. document had originally suggested the phrase "promote Latin American development." Changing this to read "accelerate the promotion of Latin American development" might appear to be a minor semantic matter, but as a Latin American writer later noted, the Latin American countries, in achieving the use of the word "accelerate," put into evidence the dynamic scope that was to be one of the attributes of the future functioning of the bank.

Of more immediate import was the question of the bank's financial resources, the amount of each country's contribution, the relationship between capital in dollars and other national (but frequently nonconvertible) currencies, and a host of other complex financial issues. What portion would be available for "hard" loans (repayable in the currency lent) and what portion for "soft" loans (repayable in local currency)? How much of the funds would be available as paid-in capital and how much would be guarantee capital, to be called on only to meet a potential default in the bank's bonds? How was the value of local currency capital to be maintained?

The discussion over capital lasted many weeks. One of the thornier issues was the amount that the U.S. would contribute. The initial U.S. proposal was for a total capitalization of $850 million, including dollars and local currencies, paid-in and guarantee capital. Of this total, the U.S. would contribute $400 million. This was countered by a Brazilian proposal for $5 billion, a Chilean proposal for $1.25 billion and a Cuban proposal for a total capitalization of $200 million (one of the few suggestions made by Cuba—probably an indicator that the country did not intend to join the bank).

In the end, the U.S. agreed to a total capitalization of $1 billion (an increase of $150 million in guarantee capital), plus a pledge to support a $500 million increase in guarantee capital when the original resources had been exhausted. Of the $1 billion, $150 million was allocated to a newly named Fund for Special Operations (FSO) with low interest rates and principal repayable in local currency.

It was Brazil, through its able negotiator Cleantho Paiva Leite, that astounded other delegates by suggesting that industrialized countries outside the hemisphere should be eligible for membership. This idea was supported by Chile and one or two other countries, despite its novelty. The U.S. and most Latin countries, however, wished to maintain the traditional hemispheric character of future negotiations and the proposal was rejected. It is too bad that Paiva Leite was not still at the bank when, some 14 years later the U.S., tired of being backed into a solitary corner, agreed to participation by countries outside the hemisphere, making the IDB a sort of World Bank for Latin America.

The question of where the bank would be located was both a practical and emotional issue, and one about which the U.S. had strong feelings. Since the bank had been conceived from the beginning as a predominantly Latin American institution, there was much to be said for having its headquarters in Latin America. If nothing else, it would distance the bank from day-to-day U.S. influence and a possibly hostile press. On the other hand, a Latin American site—if one could be agreed upon—would subject the bank to local factors such as revolutions and earthquakes, and communications with other countries would be less efficient. A location in the U.S. would facilitate coordination with other multilateral institutions, as well as with Latin American embassies, the OAS, and AID. There would also be easy contact with the U.S. administration and, for better or for worse, with the major source of fund approval—the U.S. Congress. Perhaps most importantly, it would facilitate contact with the capital markets of the world.

As discussion proceeded, it became evident that only two countries were offering to provide a site: Venezuela and the United States. A preliminary straw vote was taken, which came out 10–8 in favor of Washington, with three countries abstaining. At the next session, the ambassadors from Ecuador and Nicaragua put in an unexpected appearance as heads of their respective delegations. The Ecuadorian ambassador made an eloquent speech praising both Venezuela and the United States, and then requested a second round of voting to decide whether the site should be "in the United States or in Latin America." This subtle diplomatic maneuver permitted a number of Latin American countries to vote for the United States without voting for Washington against Caracas. The vote was 15 to 6 in favor of the United States, and after brief discussions of New York, Los Angeles, and Miami, Washington was chosen as the site for the new bank.

The next, and perhaps most difficult, problem facing the negotiating committee was to establish a procedure for choosing the bank's directors. The U.S. proposal recommended six directors, each with an alternate, to be elected for two-year terms. Since the preponderance of their weighted voting power entitled the U.S., Brazil, and Argentina each to appoint a director, only three director positions were left to be divided among the remaining countries. This formula sparked an intense debate over the philosophy of weighted voting based on capital contribution versus the accepted Latin American custom of unitary voting—one country, one vote.

After many suggestions were raised, debated, and rejected, it was finally decided to increase the number of directors to seven, have alternates representing other countries (except for the U.S.), and increase the term in office to three years. Four of the directors would be chosen through a vote equalling the total of the weighted votes cast by the largest and smallest "stockholder," and the others would be chosen by a majority of the unitary vote. The U.S. delegation prudently left this matter entirely to the Latin American members, having long since learned that when dealing with issues that concerned only Latin America, a U.S. presence was less desirable than its absence.

By the time this decision was reached, three months had elapsed, all the important issues except the name of the institution and the selection of its president had been agreed, and everybody was tired. The decision on who was to become president was left to the Latin Americans. With respect to the name, some amusing exchanges took place. One suggestion was Banco Interamericano de Fomento, but the word "fomento" had unpleasant connotations in the banking community, where a number of bad loans had been made to institutions using that word in their name. So "desarrollo" was substituted for "fomento" and the word "economico" was added: the Inter-American Bank for Economic Development. This was generally accepted among the delegates until the Haitian representative pointed out that since institutions are usually known by their acronym, francophone countries were unlikely to take an organization called BIDE very seriously. So the "E" was dropped, and the bank became known as the BID in Latin America.

Looking back, it can be said that this lengthy period of negotiation produced something very important besides the formation of the bank. The North American and Latin American negotiators came to know one another very well; indeed, became fast friends, and a number of them subsequently worked together for many years in the BID in good fellowship—a good omen for inter-American relations in years to come.

The nomination of Robert Cutler to be the U.S. director of the BID was sent to the Senate in October 1959. Bobby, as everyone called him, had a long and distinguished career as a lawyer, corporation counsel, U.S. Army general, banker, and head of the planning board of the National Security Council. At first blush, he seemed an odd choice for the new bank: He spoke no Spanish and was only slightly acquainted with Latin America. But as it turned out, the choice could not have been a better one.

Cutler was a close personal friend of President Eisenhower's and had a great capacity for human warmth. He was not a man in a gray flannel suit, nor a man of measured merriment. He could, and did, lose his temper on occasion in board meetings. Afterwards, he could, and once did, execute a *paso doble* with a table cloth and a walking stick, surrounded by startled and admiring Latin American directors. He was everything that Latin America could hope for in a representative of the U.S. government: He had prestige, he was politically well-connected, he was a scholar and a gentleman, and he loved to be with his new Latin American friends. He was also an extraordinarily hard worker—60 hours a week was his norm—and an outstanding administrator. The choice of Cutler as U.S. director was the greatest compliment that the U.S. could have given the bank.

Cutler's role, however, came under question in the early period of the Alliance for Progress, which saw the BID as a key part of its financial strategy. When a substantial part of the $500 million of the Social Progress Trust Fund was assigned to the BID for administration, following the Act of Bogota in September 1961, headlines appeared such as: "Use of bank for Latin aid assailed—Cutler criticized as conservative" and "Some liberals object: Cutler's role in Latin aid under White House study." Columnist Rowland Evans wrote that a conservative banker might not be best suited to the kind of imaginative risk-taking that the foreign aid people believe is necessary to promote land and social reform. The fear was that bankers such as Cutler, by nature conservative, would not get behind real efforts toward social reform and change.

Subsequent events showed these liberal concerns to be unjustified. Indeed, Cutler noted in his memoirs that his fellow directors rejoiced to find a Norteamericano filled with urgency to get the bank's money out to work in Latin America as soon as possible. Jim Lynn recalls that on one occasion Bobby brought every pressure to bear on him to move forward a housing loan to Brazil in anticipation of a visit by President Kennedy. There was no project, no borrower, no agreement. But, "By #@$&," said Bobby, "you're going to get that loan out!" So against the better judgment of the U.S. staff, the loan went forward. A short time later, President Kennedy cancelled his trip.

As the meetings of the Negotiating Committee drew to a close, it was recognized that a number of matters required attention in preparation for the first meeting of the board of governors. A Preparatory Committee was created with a mandate to convene in September and remain in session until the governors' meeting began. Among the issues to be worked on were determining a procedure for electing the bank's president, choosing a site for the governors' meeting, preparing draft resolutions for the meeting, and determining procedures for electing new members. The committee was also asked to begin looking for a site for the Washington headquarters and to review certain administrative and operating procedures of the World Bank.

Most important, the committee was given the responsibility of ensuring that all future members of the bank would formally join before December 31, 1959. The Charter called for 85 percent of the countries, by voting power, to have deposited their instruments of ratification before that date and to have made a small payment on capital account. If this were not done, the whole operation would be null and void.

By November, the outlook was poor. Cutler wrote: "I am deeply concerned that we are not going to have a bank in force after all. The lethargy of the Latin

American countries is definitely not understandable. . . . I must say, to a prudent man the outlook seems mighty grim."

But Bobby underestimated the determination of the members of the Preparatory Committee. The fanned out through the capital cities of the laggard countries, paying their own expenses, and nagged the governments for congressional action; sometimes they even helped draft the necessary legislation. Cuba was a special case. Its delegates had participated in the Negotiating Committee and Foreign Minister Raul Roa had signed the agreement. But when Jorge Hazera visited Havana to obtain the ratification documents, it was another story. Felipe Pasos had been replaced as president of the central bank by Che Guevara, and when Jorge met with Che at 7:00 one morning, Che denounced the bank, said the U.S. was getting off too easily, the capital was inadequate, and that Cuba would not join. Despite this rebuff, the diligent work of the Preparatory Committee paid off, and by December 31, some 87 percent of the countries, by voting power, had officially ratified their membership.

There was never any question that the president of the new bank would be a Latin American. The formal election was to take place at the first meeting of the governors in El Salvador, scheduled for February 1960. It had been previously agreed that to be elected, a candidate would need a majority of the weighted votes and also a majority of the individual country votes. The U.S. had stated it would stand aside and support whatever candidate was chosen by Latin America.

As months went by, it became evident that three candidates were in the running: Felipe Herrera, a former Chilean finance minister, manager of Chile's central bank, and a director of the IMF. A second candidate was Ignacio Copete of Colombia. He, too, had been manager of the central bank, and was a well-known private banker and former president of one of Colombia's largest and most prestigious commercial banks. The third candidate was Fernando Berckmeyer, the Peruvian ambassador to the U.S., who was highly esteemed in diplomatic circles in Washington, but had played no role in the formation of the bank.

The jockeying for votes took place through personal communication in Latin America. According to the recollection of those involved in the process (formal records were not kept), no agreement had been reached up to the eve of the governors' meeting. Ignacio Copete had the support of some of the "coffee countries," with the particular exception of Brazil and El Salvador. Felipe Herrera was backed by the larger countries but did not have a majority of the country votes, and Berckmeyer had one or two key votes. Diplomatic cables from the field indicated that an impasse had been reached and that a dark horse candidate might be elected at the last minute.

This presented a dilemma for the U.S. Both Herrera and Copete were acceptable to Washington, but a dark horse, in those days of turbulent inter-American relations, was something else again. Should the U.S. take a position or shouldn't it? To do so might cause lasting resentment. Not to do so opened up the risk of a new, and possibly unacceptable, candidate.

Senior members of the U.S. delegation recall that the matter was brought to the attention of Secretary Anderson, who decided to back Felipe Herrera, making his election certain. However, Rafael Glower Valdivieso of El Salvador recalls that on the eve of the election Herrera had only ten sure votes. At that point Valdivieso, representing a country that strongly supported Herrera, contacted the Haitian delegate, Hibbert, and urged him to change his vote from Copete to Herrera, in return for which the smaller countries would support Hibbert's election to the board. Hibbert changed his vote, Felipe Herrera received the necessary majority, and Hibbert became a member of the first board of directors, which would have been unlikely without special circumstances. Copete, a gallant loser, played an important role in the future development of the bank.

Opening ceremonies for the first meeting of the board of governors were set for February 4, 1960. The meeting took place in San Salvador, where the delegates were entertained lavishly by the "Fourteen Families" whose haciendas the bank would soon have a responsibility to break up as part of land reform efforts. When the delegations arrived, however, the meetings could not begin because Venezuela and Uruguay had not yet deposited their instruments of ratification. The meeting adjourned. The finance and economy ministers flew off to visit neighboring countries while the Secretariat worked desperately to overcome the legalities, and when everyone returned the roster was complete except for Cuba.

The tone of the meeting was set by Secretary Anderson, who after the first round of speeches invited the governors to a private meeting at which he emphasized the need for subdued rhetoric and a clear focus on the bank's future operations. He pointed out that the international press corps was waiting avidly to report on the traditional and frequently acrimonious debate between Latin America and the U.S. Avoiding this pitfall, Anderson stressed, would help show the seriousness of the new institution, which in turn would help gain the confidence of the capital markets. Secretary Anderson, with his sensitivity to Latin American feelings, was probably one of the few North Americans who could have said this without giving offense. His appeal was effective; a few days later the press drifted away, bored by the lack of fireworks.

The work of the Preparatory and Negotiating Committees had been effective, leaving only a few organizational matters to be attended to. Felipe Herrera was elected president for a five-year term, and responded with unusually brief remarks, in which he said: "I am convinced that only one attitude and standard of values is possible—total dedication of all our efforts, dreams, loyalties, and future to consolidation of the bank and fulfillment of its promise in terms of the progress of our countries."

The BID formally opened its doors for business eight months later, with over 200 loan requests to be processed. In its first year, which corresponded approximately to the first year of the Alliance for Progress, the bank committed almost $300 million in some 73 different operations—a volume of loans not equalled during the next decade. The bank was thrown into the vortex of conflict between supporters of peaceful revolution through the Alliance and conservative resistance to social change; between proponents of the private versus the public sector; between conservative insistence on a careful, prudent banking operation and liberal urgings to get the funds flowing to Latin America. It was also caught in the middle of each country's feelings of national sovereignty (and its share of the loans) and U.S. arm-twisting against loans to a country whose political action or philosophy it opposed.

The bank had staff from 21 countries who worked in three and sometimes four different languages, and among its staff could be found wide differences in cultural background and administrative philosophy. But above all, it was an institution that evoked great loyalties and support. The "chemistry" between Latin American and North American staff, between Felipe Herrera, Jack Kennedy, and Douglas Dillon (who became governor of the bank in early 1961), between Bobby Cutler, "the Hill," and the convoluted bureaucracy administering the U.S. end of the Alliance was all excellent. In those early days, everyone wanted to protect the lusty infant; everyone wanted the bank to succeed. Felipe Herrera was himself the personal embodiment of the aspirations of the Alliance for Progress, and nowhere did its flames burn more brightly than in the Inter-American Development Bank.

## NOTES

1. Mario Mendivil, Cleantho Paiva Leite, Julio Heurtematte, Federico Intriago, and Ignacio Copete all became directors. Jorge Hazera became head of administration and later secretary of the bank. Pedro Irañeta became the bank's first secretary. On the U.S. side, Elting Arnold, Alex Rosenson, Jim Lynn, and Bob Menapace all eventually served in top positions at the IDB.

# 12

# The Alliance and Institutional Development in Latin America

*José Luís Restrepo*

No definitive assessment of the Alliance for Progress has yet been made. In fact, it is doubtful whether there will ever be a final appraisal of the Alliance. The nature of the program itself prevents an objective judgment being made on its relative success or failure until the passage of time has tempered the emotional responses the Alliance still provokes.

The Alliance, like all other development programs, was essentially political. It was based on the belief that progress can be more fully achieved through the cooperative efforts of people from different nations, within genuinely democratic societies, and by the joint action of the public and private sectors. The Alliance also recognized that development is primarily the task of the people of developing nations, a task to which outsiders can contribute, but which cannot be achieved from the outside. The Charter of Punta del Este, which embodied the basic principles of the Alliance for Progress, attached equal importance to economic and social development, identified popular participation as the key factor contributing toward improved living conditions for the people of the hemisphere, acknowledged the leading influence of government and its responsibility for fostering constructive change and building more equitable and wealthier societies, and accepted the mutually supportive role of both developed and developing American countries in the pursuit of their common goals.

Prevailing current opinion in the United States on both development and inter-American relations runs counter to the spirit of the Alliance. Incentives for free enterprise and insistence on the virtues of the marketplace are at the core of every recent U.S. initiative for cooperation with Latin America and the Caribbean.

The views presented in this paper reflect the author's personal opinions, not the official position of the Organization of American States or its General Secretariat.

These tenets are also an integral part of every United States-sponsored bilateral or multilateral program for hemispheric development. Prevailing doctrine states that the "excessive" size of governments in Latin America poses the main obstacle to development of the region, and privatization has been recommended as the most important goal to be achieved. Economic objectives supersede social targets. Development cooperation schemes are offered to the developing world, not devised with their input.

Without passing judgment on the relative merit of their approach, I suggest that the sponsors of the current philosophy on development cooperation—and their numerous followers in political, academic, business, and civic circles—may not be able to look with impartiality at the accomplishments and shortcomings of the Alliance for Progress, which was based on premises contradictory to the doctrine now in vogue.

Latin American scholars and politicians, as well as the common person, tend to think that the Alliance for Progress was just another political program whose basic objective responded primarily to the United States' national interests in Latin America. They seem to forget that the original seeds of the Alliance were Latin American. The ideas that gave birth to the program were first expressed by Presidents Juscelino Kubitschek of Brazil and Alberto Lleras of Colombia. It took the vision and wisdom of President John F. Kennedy to engage the United States in the cooperative adventure of developing Latin America. However, President Kennedy's sponsorship of the Alliance was in response to a Latin American initiative, which was presented by Latin American leaders in line with the region's own perception of its interests.

In their frequent leanings toward ideological positions and their excessive zeal for regional autonomy, Latin American analysts seem also at a loss to assess objectively the results of the Alliance. Their conclusions are often tainted by their innate mistrust of the United States and their failure to recognize that international cooperation, when based on autonomous decisions, is not incompatible with self-determination.

There are finally those of us who were directly involved with the Alliance for Progress, at different levels of responsibility. We are not yet free of the almost mystical inspiration of those enlightened times. It would be unfair to ask from us an unbiased evaluation of the Alliance. A salient feature of the Alliance for Progress and those who led it was the capacity to enlist people from all walks of life in a task in which they believed with an eagerness that many of us miss in today's endeavors. Our objectivity is impaired by our undying faith in the validity of those basic principles that inspired the Alliance.

Enough for the emotional reactions of the Alliance for Progress. There are other, more concrete obstacles that hinder an appraisal of its results. The most important relates to the difficulty of measuring social changes. The development process comprises the interaction of many social forces; development itself is the transformation of society deriving from such processes. Unlike physical change, which can easily be quantified, social mutations defy attempts at measurement.

There are, admittedly, many social and economic phenomena that can be directly measured, or at least assessed through adequate proxies. The system of national accounts has been developed, for instance, as a way to quantify changes in global production, trace its origin, and illustrate its structure. Some aspects of social welfare can also be statistically described by, for example, employment rates, literacy levels, school attendance, child and general mortality, and life expectancy. In some relatively more sophisticated nations, income and wealth distribution statistics are available. Furthermore, the depth and scope of change itself can be gauged through data on per capita income, industrialization, urban growth, and population expansion.

The development path has frequently been understood as the gradual approach of developing nations to those key economic and social indicators characteristic of the industrial world. If this were a correct understanding of development, it would be possible to measure advances in achieving it, within limitations imposed by the quality of available statistical data and the difficulties in weighting the relative importance of different indicators. Development, however, is not just imitation of alien patterns, which is at best only one dimension of development. Development is also the enhancement of indigenous cultural, technological, political, and social values, and most importantly it is affording people choices for living their lives in ways that ensure the full realization of their potential. These intangible features of development, while intellectually verifiable, are not suitable to measurement.

Some goals of the Alliance for Progress—per capita economic growth, levels of adult literacy and access to primary education, years of life expectancy at birth, provision of drinkable water and sewage disposal to urban and rural populations, transfer of real and financial resources to Latin America—were expressed as concrete numerical targets. Others—higher agricultural productivity and output, a more equitable distribution of national income, export diversification, accelerated industrialization, eradication and control of endemic and epidemic diseases, maintenance of stable price levels—lent themselves to quantification.

One salient example of measurement of the results of the Alliance for Progress is reported in the 1973 OAS Inter-American Economic and Social Council (CIES) publication, *Latin American Development and the Alliance for Progress.* This is probably the most accomplished attempt at researching and presenting in an analytical context the effects of the Alliance on the variables it was intended to modify. The study featured numerous references and summary interpretations of several non-quantifiable features of the Alliance, but it failed to capture the spirit of the hemispheric program because its authors were eager to remain within the limits of an objective and numerical interpretation of history. It was also unsuccessful in trying to isolate the effects of the Alliance from those of many other factors at play during the 1960s.

The ideological aspects of the Alliance for Progress have also been the subject of much scrutiny and appraisal. The interest in the doctrine from which the Alliance originated is reflected, for instance, in most of the contributions of this volume. No matter how thorough these presentations are, their scholarly quality cannot overcome the fact that they contradict each other in some cases and, as a set, are inconclusive as an evaluation of Latin America's development during the decade of the 1960s.

There is another, more mundane aspect of the Alliance for Progress which has not received the attention it deserves. One important, long-lasting contribution of the Alliance was the improvement of what could be described as the tools for development: The Alliance sought to have an impact on Latin America's institutional framework for development, and to encourage a pragmatic inter-American approach to cooperation for development.

The most important direct effect on institutional build-up was the enhancement of planning as a tool for progress. The Charter of Punta del Este linked transfer of resources to Latin American nations to the preparation of long-term development plans by those nations. The plans were to comprise both economic and social goals, including maximization of domestic efforts, rationalization of the external sector, and the establishment of objectives for the public and private sectors. The Committee of Nine, a group of distinguished persons from the hemisphere, was established within the OAS to evaluate those development plans, discuss with governments ways to improve policies for achieving nationally adopted goals, and present recommendations to international financial agencies and cooperating governments on the amount and quality of external cooperation required to adequately implement the plans. The Committee of Nine later gave way to the Inter-American Committee on the Alliance for Progress (CIAP), an intergovernmental body that was most influential in the implementation of the Alliance.

Although development planning had taken place in Latin America before the beginning of the Alliance for Progress, mainly through pioneer efforts by the United Nations Economic Commission for Latin America (CEPAL), planning was at a very incipient stage in 1961. Lured by the prospect offered by the Alliance for Progress of access to badly needed external resources, Latin American governments seriously undertook the task of strengthening their planning mechanisms and improving their planning skills.

By the end of the 1960s, planning had become a widely accepted development tool in Latin America. Comprehensive long-term development plans were prepared and presented for evaluation by the Committee of Nine with increasing degrees of sophistication and professional authority. The expertise of the members of the Committee of Nine and the very professional way in which they approached their task made an important contribution to the improvement of planning in Latin America during the early 1960s. Government officials in the region respected the Committee's assessments and held its recommendations in high regard.

In many cases, the operational aspects of the general development plans were strengthened through the preparation of public investment programs and sectoral development plans. Planning agencies were endowed with ministerial authority, and on occasion they reported directly to the presidents of their countries. Planning boards, frequently chaired by the president of the nation, gradually became the center for decision-making on economic and social policy. The consolidation of the national planning agencies and the fundamental importance of development plans in guiding policy contributed to a very large extent to improving the process of decision-making in Latin America.

There were, however, several shortcomings to planning as practiced in Latin America during the Alliance years. The emergence of planning agencies as strong governmental units was not always welcomed by the public servants who had traditionally been in charge of some key aspects of the economic process: ministers of finance and economics, chairmen of central banks, or those at whose discretion the management of the bulk of fiscal resources had historically been left, such as ministers of public works and agriculture. It was not enough to include the traditional centers of power on planning boards or to attempt to persuade them that planning was not a threat to their authority. In many instances, planning agencies became isolated from the executing institutions, and plans came to be exercises in futility, lacking support from those who, not directly involved in their preparation, were nonetheless essential for their implementation.

During the decade of the Alliance, national development plans were supposed to cover both the public and the private sectors, as should be the case in the mixed economies that are characteristic of Latin America. However, in only a few exceptional cases was the private sector really involved in the preparation of the national plan. As a result, even when the plans had governmental support and were used as guidelines for public policy and practice, they were not supported by private entrepreneurs, who were the dominant force in most Latin American economies.

A very significant weakness of most Latin American development plans during the period was the lack of concrete projects to achieve the broad guidelines of the plans themselves. Planning became increasingly sophisticated in the areas of macroanalysis and projections, but due regard was not given to the preparation of individual projects that would provide the solid backdrop necessary for effective implementation. Availability of projects acceptable to the international financial institutions and governmental development agencies became just as important as socioeconomic performance under the goals of the Charter of Punta del Este to ensure access to external funds. The importance of projects was a powerful incentive for improving the techniques of project identification, preparation, evaluation, and implementation. However, the lack of high quality projects remained a serious constraint for most Latin American countries under the Alliance for Progress.

Starting in 1964, following a resolution adopted by the ministerial meeting of CIES in Sao Paulo, Brazil, the yearly cycle of country reviews afforded an additional incentive for the improvement of planning in Latin America. The remarkable, but somewhat academic, approach to evaluation of development plans by the Committee of Nine gave way to a more pragmatic practice of annual assessments of the relative accomplishments of each member state and its need for external cooperation.

CIES gave the Inter-American Committee on the Alliance for Progress (CIAP) the mandate to estimate periodically the needs and availability of external resources for each developing country in the system. Given the intrinsic limitation of financial resources available from external sources, such estimates implied a recommendation on the distribution of resources among participating countries. Each participating country in Latin America voluntarily decided to take part in annual country review meetings conducted by CIAP subcommittees. They presented their development goals, evaluated the advances made in achieving them, assayed the scope of the domestic effort, and quantified the amount of external financing needed to complement national saving in the context of the nation's social and economic targets. Starting in 1972, the annual country review of the United States was held, analyzing the effects of that country's economic and cooperation policy on Latin America.

Documents independently prepared by the CIAP Secretariat, after gathering information and consulting with the authorities in the country under review, were presented to the subcommittee members as background papers. High-level government officials submitted formal presentations on the main aspects of their nation's development process, and participants in the reviews—representatives of major donor countries and agencies—discussed in detail the available information over a three to five day period. During the initial country review cycles, attention was centered on financial needs and flows, but later the availability and requirements of technical cooperation received equal scrutiny.

Final reports of each meeting, including statements by representatives of cooperating governments and agencies, were prepared by the chairmen of the subcommittees. The final report was a summary assessment of the salient features of the country's performance and outlook as viewed by the participants in the meeting. The report also included a record of the goals to be achieved during the subsequent period and recommendations both to the government—regarding issues of development policy—and to donor governments and institutions, regarding the amount and kind of cooperation needed.

The country review mechanism was refined during the period it was in place, and ways were established to monitor the implementation of the subcommittee's recommendations. Most effective among the monitoring devices were the so-called interagency meetings, held at the request of the developing country, usually in the country itself, and dealing with the implementation of ongoing projects, availability of internal and external resources to implement new projects, and advances in putting into effect policy recommendations of the CIAP subcommittees.

The country reviews had three basic positive characteristics. First, they afforded an opportunity to those responsible for development policy in each nation to focus their attention on fundamental issues rather than remain preoccupied with the daily emergencies that usually demanded most of their time. Latin American governments attached great importance to the annual reviews during the decade of the Alliance, and they viewed the annual meetings as occasions to argue their case for their fair share of available external resources. The attention directed to the reviews resulted in increased awareness of the need to carefully appraise the current situation, to program in detail the policies needed to overcome bottle-necks in development, and to improve project preparation as a means of ensuring the possibility of access to external financing through bankable undertakings. The country review mechanism thus strengthened planning in Latin America and provided a broader perspective for designing and implementing economic policy.

Second, the country reviews were instrumental in improving Latin American leaders' skills in international negotiation. Latin American government officials had considerable experience in international negotiations before the Alliance for Progress. One case in point is the fact that debt rescheduling in the Paris Club was first conducted in 1955 for three Latin American nations. Many Latin American officials were subsequently parties to that forum. However, there is no doubt that the regular periodic meetings of the CIAP subcommittees afforded an important opportunity for a select group of Latin American civil servants to develop their skills at the international negotiating craft. A number of those who were members of their countries' delegations to the country review meetings today hold positions of responsibility in the ongoing exercise of debt rescheduling and renegotiation, the most delicate current issue for many Latin American nations. The lessons learned during the Alliance are probably significant in the present emergency.

Third, the country reviews significantly strengthened the practice of multila-teralism as the preferred way to channel international cooperation for develop-ment. Bilateral cooperation programs are, by their very nature, biased by the political interest of the donor party. Multilateral arrangements were an attempt to overcome the political content of development cooperation programs by ensuring that only technical issues affect the allocation of resources. The creation of the Inter-American Development Bank, preceding the Alliance for Progress but close-ly linked to the Alliance's origin, was the first and most important example of multilateralism in inter-American cooperation. The Alliance for Progress was in essence a multilateral program. Even if the United States was the main provider of external resources for Latin American development through the Alliance, the continued flow of resources was linked to the developing countries' attainment of definite, predetermined goals, and it was not subject to the whims of U.S. political interests. Furthermore, both in theory and in practice, resources were increasingly channeled through multilateral institutions. The country reviews were a multilat-eral exercise. The country under review participated actively, as did CIAP mem-bers representing different countries or groups of countries in the hemisphere and high-level functionaries of donor governments and multilateral financial institu-tions.

The subcommittees were adamant in their defense of the principle that develop-ment cooperation resources should be allocated on strictly technical grounds, without the interference of ideological or political biases. The multilateral, profes-sional standing of CIAP on issues relating to development cooperation was partic-ularly clear when it dealt with the cases of Peru, during the initial stage of the military government in that country from the late 1960s to the early 1970s, and Chile, during the socialist government of Salvador Allende in the early 1970s. In both instances, CIAP subcommittees recommended on several different occasions that resources in substantial amounts should be made available to support the development efforts of those countries, regardless of the fact that their policies were not within traditional molds.

Another important contribution to multilateralism was the establishment in 1970 of the Special Committee for Consultation and Negotiation (CECON), which was an offspring of the spirit of dialogue at the core of the Alliance for Progress, and which had been the basis of the country reviews. Intended as a forum for consultation and negotiation in both trade and financial matters, CECON has limited its role to the trade area. Whatever its limitations, CECON is the best legacy of the Alliance for Progress within the international institutional framework for cooperation in the Americas.

The Fulbright Amendment to the Foreign Assistance Act, enacted by the United States Congress in 1966, established one of CIAP's recommendations as a requirement for authorizing loans to individual countries under the Alliance for Progress. However, implementation of CIAP's recommendations was largely left to the discretion of donor governments and agencies, and the subcommittees' conclusions did not have the effect that would have been desirable. Disenchantment with the relative weight of CIAP's recommendations led to the gradual decline of the country review mechanism, as governments started to disengage from the process in the early 1970s. After 1976, country reviews were held only sporadically, and for all practical purposes their importance ended.

Other institutional innovations developed during the Alliance for Progress years were closely linked to the broader perspective brought about by the emphasis on planning. Thus, for instance, although the public sector had traditionally been an instrumental factor in Latin American development, conceptual limitations and lack of reliable statistics prior to the Alliance had generally restricted the scope of analysis of public sector activities to central government operations. In several countries, public enterprises and regional and local governments contributed a much larger share of the public sector than the fiscal sector, and in every country entities different from the national government were significant. Recognition of the importance of the public sector as one key element in the development process, and also of the relative importance of agencies other than the national government, led to the implementation of techniques for assessing the economic effects of the consolidated public sector and to detailed analysis of its major components.

# III
## Implementation

*13*

# The Alliance for Progress: Reflections for Our Time

*Rodrigo Botero*

It is altogether fitting that we commemorate the twenty-fifth anniversary of the Alliance for Progress. We are still close enough in time to that spring of 1961 to regard it as a relevant part of our lives. Yet the chronological distance is sufficient to provide historical perspective and a certain degree of detachment from the controversy of the moment. Thanks to the relative distance, we can look back at this event, keeping in mind the enormous changes that have occurred in the hemispheric context. At the same time, the relative proximity suggests that there are still meaningful lessons to be learned from that endeavor. While one must resist the temptation of nostalgia for a period when life appeared simpler—if for no other reason than that we were then much younger—one must also be wary of the counsel of cynicism that would dismiss that initiative as a futile anachronism.

Several words of caution appear to be in order. On the question of definition, the expression "Alliance for Progress" has been applied simultaneously to a concept and to a process. While the two are closely related, they are different. The concept refers to a hemispheric commitment to economic modernization and social justice within a democratic framework. The process refers to the pragmatic and administrative procedures that were set in motion in order to carry out that commitment.

The above differentiation becomes meaningful when discussing the lifespan of the Alliance for Progress. Understood as an intergovernmental program, or as a description of the administrative apparatus established to implement it, it can be said that the Alliance lasted almost a decade. Understood as a major hemispheric initiative undertaken with the enthusiastic and unmistakable support of the United States government, the life of the Alliance was much shorter—not quite three years.

*159*

President John F. Kennedy played a decisive role both in formulating the concept and in setting in motion the process that was to give it a concrete expression. He was the indispensable link between the word and the deed. This proved to be the great strength as well as the fatal weakness of the Alliance for Progress. After 1963 the machinery of the Alliance continued to operate, but the mood had changed. If a specific event could be pointed to as a clear sign that a new idea in hemispheric relations had been discarded, it would be the Dominican Crisis of 1965. By then, official Washington had started to turn its attention away from the western hemisphere in response to a distant drummer calling from a strange land. The opening scenes of a colossal tragedy were being acted out. When the American chiefs of state gathered at Punta del Este in 1967, hemispheric matters, from President Johnson's viewpoint, had already become a distraction from the serious business at hand, which was the war in Southeast Asia.

Finally, we should try to avoid the pitfalls of trying to pinpoint precisely the relations of causality between the objectives of the Alliance and the long-term trends of social and economic change in the hemisphere. It is helpful in this context to think in terms of a symbiotic relationship between the two, rather than in terms of cause and effect. In certain instances the Alliance for Progress initiated changes, in others it reinforced emerging trends, and in still others its main contribution was to have incorporated and given legitimacy to previously unrecognized aspirations. But in each of these instances the role of the Alliance was unambiguously positive, and that is a remarkable achievement by itself.

The case in favor of the Alliance for Progress is weakened rather than strengthened if it is forced to shoulder an unreasonable historical burden. Yet even if we accept that the grand hemispheric undertaking proclaimed in March 1961 lasted for only a few years, and we also recognize that it cannot be given credit for all or for most of the subsequent economic and social change that has taken place, the fact remains that the Alliance for Progress is unique in the history of inter-American relations. It was without precedent when it came into being. There has been nothing comparable since it passed away. Any present or future initiatives for cooperation and understanding in the Americas will find a logical reference point in the experience of the Alliance for Progress.

In a period of unrelieved economic hardship throughout Latin America and the Caribbean, and in the midst of ominous disarray in hemispheric relations, it seems therefore appropriate to study the not-so-distant past.

President Kennedy announced the beginning of "a vast new ten-year plan for the Americas, a plan to transform the 1960s into an historic decade" at a reception in the White House for Latin American diplomats and members of Congress. He asked the people of the hemisphere to join in a cooperative effort "unparalleled in magnitude and nobility of purpose, to satisfy the basic needs of the American people for homes, work and land, health and schools." The challenge, as he understood it, was to demonstrate to the entire world that the aspiration for economic progress and social justice could best be achieved by free people working within a framework of democratic institutions. The hemisphere was confronting a threat from "the alien forces which once again seek to impose the despotisms of the Old World on the people of the New."

Within Latin America the immediate problem was described as follows:

Population growth is outpacing economic growth, low living standards are even further endangered, and discontent – the discontent of a people who know that abundance and the tools of progress are at last within their reach – that discontent is growing.

The suggested response was an affirmation of progress and a rejection of tyranny. A ten-point plan of action was outlined, which included the commitment of resources from the United States and a request for initial funds from Congress; a calling of a ministerial meeting of the Inter-American Economic and Social Council to "begin the massive planning effort which will be at the heart of the Alliance for Progress"; support for economic integration in Latin America; the offer to examine commodity market problems; a food-for-peace emergency program; scientific cooperation, technical training, Peace Corps programs and cultural exchanges; a pledge to come to the defense of any American nation whose independence was endangered; and an invitation to the region's military to participate in the task of nation-building. The speech ended with words of inspiration and optimism:

Let us once again transform the American continent into a vast crucible of revolutionary ideas and efforts, a tribute to the power of the creative energies of free men and women, an example to all the world that liberty and progress walk hand in hand. Let us once again awaken our American Revolution until it guides the struggles of people everywhere – not with an imperialism of force or fear but the rule of courage and freedom and hope for the future of man.

President Kennedy's proposal for hemispheric cooperation has withstood the test of time. With minor alterations in style and in content, his 1961 speech can be read as a document with a message that remains valid to this day. From a Latin American viewpoint, the following features provide continuity between the perspective of the 1960s and present realities:

- The recognition that responsibility for the failures and misunderstandings of the past is bilateral demonstrated a willingness to accept parts of our mutual history that shape present-day attitudes.
- The suggestion that the specific proposals for the implementation of the Alliance were to be drawn up jointly by experts from the United States and Latin America reflected a new hemispheric sensitivity.
- The central role assigned to social change in the process of hemispheric modernization was a crucial innovation, as was the understanding of the sustained effort required to bring about significant results. The provision of more and better jobs, housing, health and educational services to the community have become central issues of governance throughout the hemisphere.

These questions have been incorporated into the contemporary political process, and to a large degree they determine the success and failure of a modern government. But the articulation of these priorities by a North American president in 1961 was a welcome innovation in inter-American discourse.

From today's perspective, it is precisely in the area of social change that one can identify long-term trends that are consistent with the objectives of the Alliance for Progress. It is now evident that the period of ten years proved to be too short for the fulfillment of the social goals of the Alliance. Nevertheless, more rapid social progress has been achieved in the hemisphere from 1960 to 1985 than in any previous comparable period of time. For Latin America and the Caribbean, adult literacy rates increased from 66 to 81 percent. Infant mortality rates decreased from 107 deaths per 21,000 live births to 60. Average life expectancy at birth increased from 56 to 65 years.

We are certainly not close to satisfying the basic needs of the people of the Americas. But the steady advance that has been made to date provides evidence that the eradication of absolute poverty in the hemisphere within the next decade is a realistic goal, given the political commitment to do so.

An important by-product of the Alliance for Progress was the institutional development that took place at both the national and hemispheric levels to formulate and execute the various programs. Of the regional bodies, the Inter-American Development Bank deserves special mention because of the role it has played in building up the social infrastructure throughout the region through the Social Progress Trust Fund, the Fund for Special Operations, and other lending activities.

The International Coffee Agreement, a multilateral initiative bringing together the principal producers and consumers of coffee to ensure orderly market conditions, came into being with the decisive support of the United States government in 1962, during the Alliance for Progress. Millions of farmers throughout Latin America continue to benefit from this agreement, which has become the most successful of all international commodity stabilization schemes.

Between 1961 and 1981, overall economic growth in the region was satisfactory, in comparison with previous performance. In retrospect, the growth rates achieved during the past two decades proved to be as good, if not better, than had been expected at the beginning of the Alliance for Progress.

It is perhaps in the economic sphere that the most unexpected changes have taken place. Over the past 15 years, Latin American and Caribbean countries have suffered the impact of sudden and severe oscillations in the world economy. Sharp fluctuations in the price of petroleum have proven to be disruptive, in an upward direction as in 1973 and 1979 as well as downward, as has been the case in recent months. Unprecedented flows of commercial bank lending into the region took place between 1975 and 1981. After August 1982, the private banks abruptly stopped lending region-wide. The earlier eagerness to extend bank credit was followed by a sudden reversal of policy. More prudent behavior on the part of both borrowers and lenders would have spared the hemisphere the disruptions brought about by an unnecessary financial crisis.

At great sacrifice, and with varying degrees of success, the countries of Latin America and the Caribbean have been adjusting to economic adversity. In early 1986 the presidents of Brazil, Mexico, and Venezuela addressed their respective nations to discuss economic problems. In the case of Brazil, a bold new program to combat inflation was announced, which included a currency reform and temporary wage and price freezes. The heads of state of Mexico and Venezuela focused their attention on the loss of revenue that would result from the fall in petroleum prices and on the consequent difficulties their respective countries would face in servicing external debt.

The substantial changes that have taken place in recent years in world petroleum markets and in international capital markets have brought about a reformulation of development strategies throughout the region.

The combined effect of the oil shocks, the turmoil in the financial markets, and the recession in the industrialized countries brought region-wide growth to a halt. Since 1982, the countries of Latin America and the Caribbean have been coping with the most serious economic crisis since the Great Depression. Stagnation, retrenchment, and the burden of foreign debt are threatening to overwhelm the administrative capacity of several governments in the region.

Unless a solution is found to the economic crisis, the social and political progress that has been achieved since the 1960s will be jeopardized. Economic hardship is becoming an issue that threatens domestic stability in several countries of the region and could eventually endanger hemispheric security. Because it is a real and present danger, the economic crisis could also become the driving force for a joint endeavor in the Americas.

If it is to be successful, a new hemispheric program will have to address the urgent problem of debt and renewed financial flows into the region. But beyond the immediate financial issue, the truly important task is the restoration of vigorous economic growth in the Americas. With a context of stagnation or retrogression, it will become increasingly difficult for the countries of the region to advance toward greater social justice or to strengthen the democratic process. It is perhaps on this issue that the differences in perception between the United States and Latin America are more clearly defined. United States officials have assigned the highest priority—in strategic and military terms—to the Central American conflict, while hemispheric economic and social issues receive sporadic and secondary attention. For the democratic governments in most of Latin America, security is viewed in economic and social terms. Those matters are assigned the highest priority, while the tensions in the Central American isthmus are viewed as a localized, subregional conflict. These differences will have to be resolved if a consensus on the meaning of hemispheric security is to be reached. A first step in that direction would be to recognize that the permanent basis for hemispheric unity is the existence of the shared spiritual and political values inherent in western civilization, rather than strategic considerations or military alliances.

The record of the past 20 years shows how difficult it is to obtain the proper conditions, in the United States as well as in Latin America and the Caribbean, for launching major new hemispheric initiatives. The cultural gap between the two sides leads to different perceptions of our shared reality. Yet another lesson of the recent past is the need to make ample allowance for the role of the unexpected in human affairs. A realistic assessment of prevailing attitudes in the hemisphere— North and South—would probably lead to the conclusion that a multilateral solution to the region's economic crisis, in a spirit of mutual cooperation and pursuit of common values, is seen as unlikely, if not far-fetched, by most people. Yet such an outcome should not be discarded altogether, even if it is easier to imagine more colorful scenarios. On previous occasions the hemisphere has come forth with constructive responses to situations of adversity and common danger. Such was the case 25 years ago.

In different times and altered circumstances, the spirit of the Alliance for Progress remains current, as a message of hope and a guide towards common goals in our hemisphere.

*14*

# The Alliance for Progress:
# The Learning Experience

*Enrique Lerdau[1]*

> The tendency to achieve our foreign policy objectives by inducing other
> governments to sign up to professions of high moral and legal principle
> appears to have a great and enduring vitality in our diplomatic practice.
> — George F. Kennan
> *American Diplomacy 1900-1950*

When the Alliance for Progress came into being, many of its promises—as well as
its future implications—had not been given critical study. Perhaps this was inevitable since, as far as I can see, there was no well-articulated approach to Latin
America and its problems, let alone to the role of the U.S. in the region. The
"Good Neighbor" policy may have signified a notable advance in putting an
official end to military intervention, but once this principle was generally accepted
by the end of the second world war, it had lost most of its political impact. And it
was not, in itself, a guide to positive action. In the 1950s some important events
had taken place: the Guatemalan episode was one; the acceptance, in principle,
that the U.S. would participate in an International Coffee Agreement was another; and the creation, first of the Inter-American Development Bank (IDB) and
later, in 1960, of a US$500 million Social Progress Trust Fund, still another. But
by and large, these were all fairly belated responses to events and to pressures
emanating from the region. The proposal for Operation Pan-America—primarily
a call for an ambitious U.S. foreign aid program in Latin America—in 1958 by
President Kubitschek might have been the most significant event of the decade,
had there been any positive response from the U.S. government. But by the end of
the decade one major new development occurred in Latin America: the advent of
the Castro government in Cuba and the ensuing rapid deterioration of relations
with the United States. It was against this backdrop that the Kennedy Administra-

tion took office, and in line with its general activist approach to problems, it proposed the Alliance.

I do not want to be misunderstood; it is too easy to assert—and it may not be true—that without Castro no such initiative would have been taken. All one can safely say—and Schlesinger's account makes this abundantly clear—is that the magnitude of the program and the speed with which it was mounted and accepted by the country, can best be understood in this context.

One further point about the 1950s is relevant: It was then that for the first time Latin America attempted to formulate a theory of the Latin American development process that claimed to arise from its own experience. This effort carried with it a diagnosis and a set of prescriptions drastically different from those of the neoclassical market economics of the Anglo-Saxon world. I refer, of course, to the pioneering work of Raúl Prebisch and the United Nation's Economic Commission for Latin America (ECLA).

I need not go into the conceptual framework that was developed in Santiago; the literature in the last 20 years has explored its analytic merits and shortcomings quite extensively. It is probably fair to classify much of the Santiago approach as "historicism" in Popper's sense.[2] The mere stress of Latin America's similarities and underemphasis of its differences point to a nonempirical, nonpragmatic approach. Some of its limitations were once described rather fancifully by a sympathetic critic:

ECLA's detailed projections, where all economic sectors are made to mesh harmoniously, are in a sense the 20th century equivalent of Latin America's 19th century constitutions—and are as far removed from the real world. They are a protest, both pathetic and subtle, against a reality where politicians relying on brilliant or disastrous improvisation hold sway, where decisions are taken under multiple pressures rather than in advance of crisis and emergency situations, and where conflicts are resolved on the basis of personal considerations after the contending parties have revealed their strength in more or less open battle rather than in accordance with the objective principles and scientific criteria.[3]

My own conclusion regarding the general character of this work is that its most serious shortcomings are a result not so much of bad theory but of too much theory too soon. The root of the trouble lies in the absence of a serious concern in Latin America with economic history over the past 100 years. Relevant theory arises from a simplification and systematization of observed reality, but only a painstaking and scholarly concern with facts and with how economic processes really work can give theorists the material on which they can impose an orderly and logical pattern. The work of the Institutionalists in the United States, of the Webbs in Britain, and of the German Historical School on the continent—none of this really has a counterpart in the Latin American intellectual tradition. It is easy to list many crucially relevant questions on which until only 20 years ago virtually nothing except impressionistic knowledge existed, and the situation is only marginally better today. Land tenure shifts over time, income distribution changes, the development, character, and impact of trade unions, the economic and social role of the military, changes in the geographic and economic composition of public expenditures and the determinants of these changes, the determinants and the history of foreign investments – the list could go on. Obviously, any global development theory would be hard put to serve as an adequate guide for action, or even an adequate explanation of events, if the basic facts about such items as those listed above – and practically everything else – had not been accumulated during previous decades, or even centuries.

But whatever the shortcomings of the model developed in Santiago, it had one enormous attraction: It was there. And its influence on the North American intellectuals who were called upon to formulate an action program in early 1961 was profound for just that reason. It was the only new doctrine that they could draw on. Moreover, it offered just what they were looking for: a global and homogeneous interpretation of hemispheric problems that would lend itself to a global and homogeneous set of remedies. One crucial consequence flowed from this: The Alliance's rhetoric as well as its institutional framework was cast – like ECLA's doctrines – into a single mold, with the implicit assumption that it would fit all member countries reasonably well.

The following words of Mr. Prebisch should dispel any doubts about the intellectual origin of the Alliance ideology:

Indeed, the basic ideas underlying this document were conceived and gradually developed over a period of years in Latin America. In times that are not yet far behind, some of these ideas encountered very strong resistance, which was frequently couched in tractable and dogmatic terms. Now they are recognized as sound and valid and largely embodied in the Charter of Punta del Este. However, there has developed a rather peculiar tendency to present these ideas as having been conceived in the United States, or as constituting a ready-made blueprint to be applied in Latin America. I am really concerned about this trend, for not only is it contrary to the facts but its political implications are highly detrimental to the Alliance itself and to the broad popular support it requires in Latin America.[4]

## THE FRAMEWORK

Three main themes ran through the early Alliance rhetoric, were enshrined in the Charter of Punta del Este, and lingered on in subsequent years in about the same way as the grin of the Cheshire cat. They were the three roads to salvation, which had to be trodden simultaneously if development was to come to Latin America: long-term economic planning; land reform and tax reform; and foreign capital on concessional terms.[5]

The Alliance was basically to be a mutual commitment to act meaningfully in these areas: Latin American governments in the first two and the United States in the last. In order to monitor progress under this reciprocal plighting of troth, an independent technical body of nine economists – soon to be known as the Nine Wise Men – was established to assess the long-term plans that the Latin American governments were to prepare and from which, *inter alia*, each country's foreign aid requirements were to be determined.

These prescriptions obviously implied that the domestic bottlenecks to development lay in the property and power relations within each country and in the form in which the dominant classes were using their power to govern. The external bottleneck here is the least controversial one; it was not internally contradictory for the United States to pledge substantial amounts of foreign assistance, even though later problems did develop about making good on these pledges. But could the same be said about the domestic component? In other words, was there a basic inconsistency between diagnosis and prescription? If the diagnosis was correct—and it certainly had been expounded with considerable brilliance by ECLA's economists—was it not illogical to expect governments to pledge themselves to do away with their own power base and to follow through on such a pledge? Did the diagnosis, which treated governments as the representatives of the dominant classes whose position allegedly was the basic obstacle to development, not imply that such commitments could not, by definition, be meaningful?

Personally, I do not accept an unqualified affirmative answer to these questions because I do not believe that all Latin American governments are simply the passive spokesmen for such simplified social groups as "landlords," "industrialists," "labor," and so on.[6] But the point I wish to stress here is that the basic question was not even asked at the time, or, when it was asked, it was only in the naive terms of whether a particular government was "sincere" in its commitment to structural reforms.

I suggest that many of the later disappointments in the Alliance can be traced to the elements sketched out so far:

- The lack of a tradition of serious and creative concern in U.S. government circles with long-term policy issues in Latin America;
- The consequent need to improvise when events made a major reorientation of policy clearly desirable.
- Such improvisation consisted in adopting an intellectual framework with certain attractions but which, given the lack of a tradition of empirical economic research in Latin America, was based on unexamined premises, and which was flawed by overemphasis on a uniform approach to vastly different countries.[7]
- Moreover, the prescription was inconsistent with the diagnosis to the extent that it relied on commitments by Latin American governments to repair ills which, under the terms of the diagnosis, these governments could not possibly repair.

It may thus be less paradoxical than it sounds to assert that such successes as were achieved in Latin America during the Alliance years were largely a proof that the diagnosis was mistaken, while the failures were at least in part the result of the inconsistency between the prescription and the diagnosis.

## THE RECORD

It would be impossible in the confines of this brief chapter to summarize the economic developments that took place in 19 Latin American countries under the Alliance. Nor would it be useful or necessary: They have been documented in innumerable reports of national and international agencies. Some of these I have read; some I have even written. I doubt that any one person in the world has read them all, and if such a person existed he probably would have even greater difficulties in deriving valid generalizations than do the rest of us. The only generalization that I would venture to make here is that the developments of the 1960s have increasingly demonstrated that neither economic theory nor the art of applying it through economic policymaking has been directed to Latin America's most perplexing development problem: that of building up an efficient industrial structure. The textbook paradigm of primary versus secondary activities, with its implied initial *tabula rasa*, may have been solved neatly enough; however, in reality we start with installed equipment, employed labor, existing levels of protection, distorted price structures, and a whole gamut of vested interests willing and able to argue that their particular shares in these distortions cannot be dispensed with. The problem seems to me to become increasingly complex in theory and acute in practice. To my knowledge, there is no country in Latin America in which even an approximate measure of the impact of these distortions exists,[8] but neither are there many countries in which questions of industrial efficiency do not seem to be the main constraint on the prospects for economic growth.

No serious concern with this problem can be reported in the Alliance for Progress framework. Hence, I will not pursue it further in this chapter. Rather, I want to concentrate on the experience with respect to the three central articles of faith that I listed above as the cornerstones of the Alliance: namely planning, redistribution of property and income, and capital aid.

## Planning

It is in the area of planning that the air of initial unrealism was greatest and, I think, where the inferences about the future are clearest. The initial scheme, under which each country would submit long-term economic development plans to the technical scrutiny of the Committee of Nine, who would then determine the justified level of external assistance, was to be discredited and abandoned in less than three years. It was ill-conceived on almost every count, in spite of the high intellectual caliber of many of the members of the panel.

The distinguished Cuban economist Felipe Pazos, who was one of the original members of the panel, once observed that there were three types of planning in the world: the Soviet type, or imperative planning; the French type, or indicative planning; and the Latin American type, or subjunctive planning. The elegance of the formulation should not obscure its serious content, which is that what has been done in the way of medium- and long-term national economic planning in Latin America has been, almost without exception, nonoperational. It has not, in other words, done much to influence the course of events, be it with respect to public sector investment decisions or economic policy measures. When one considers that some of the finest Latin American economists spent much of their time during the Alliance period formulating such plans, and that in this they were assisted by a glittering array of imported talent financed by the proliferating technical assistance programs of national and international agencies, it is indeed astounding that the above observation can be made without fear of serious contradiction.[9] Equally astounding is the wide agreement, among planners and non-planners alike, that Mexico, the country with the most impressive develop-ment record in Latin America at that time, was among the very few that had not participated in the formal ritual of drawing up a long-term national development plan.

While there is not much dispute about the facts described above, the same cannot be said about explanations for them. These include simplistic views, such as the one that, while the economists have done their job when they have made a "good" plan, if "bad" politicians will not carry it out, this is a fortuitous and unforeseeable misfortune that has no bearing on whether the plan was "good" in the first place. Other explanations stress technical imperfections in the data; still others suppose that the fault lies in the insufficient sophistication of the mathe-matical techniques used.[10] Still other explanations stress—correctly, I think—the technical impossibility of planning under inflation, the lack of political continuity in Latin American governments, and the difficulties inherent in drawing up realis-tic multiyear plans in which an important component is external financing provid-ed by a donor whose foreign aid allocation is subject to annual legislative determi-nation.

While the set of causes listed above has some bearing on the failure of particular countries' planning efforts, I don't think that it goes to the heart of the matter. Albert Waterston's common-sense conclusion that

the system of national planning should therefore be permitted to evolve gradually, firstly, as soon as possible, from the project-by-project approach to a second stage in which the country learns to prepare and implement a coordinated public investment plan preferably accompanied by sectoral surveys and programs, and ultimately, when improvements in information, administration and experience permit, to full-scale comprehensive planning[11]

may seem obvious once it is reached, but it was not applied in Latin America's planning except, as Waterston shows, in Mexico. It should be added that the nature of the stages described by Waterston implies that they normally cannot be compressed into a period as short as a decade.

While no one can give a timetable in advance for the kind of changes that they require, one should mistrust any program that supposes that a country currently in Waterston's first stage will be ready for the second in five or ten years. The superimposition of planning organizations on the existing administrative structure in many Latin American countries was bound to fail as an economic policy-making tool as long as its main motivation was to improve a government's public relations image *vis-à-vis* either the domestic intelligentsia or the external aid-giving agencies. In very few cases did the decision-making machinery of the public sector absorb the impact of the work of the planning office, and in those cases it happened more often because of good personal relations between the director of planning and the president than because of a permanent change in the decision-making process.

In short, it takes more than a planning office to plan. It takes competent spending agencies capable of generating well-conceived investment projects; it takes financial authorities willing and able to make their decisions with longer time horizons than those customary in a treasury ministry or a central bank; and finally, it takes a constellation of political relations within the public sector whereby these various agencies are willing to subordinate their decisions to the central authority of a president or the collegiate authority of a cabinet when scrutiny by the planning office reveals inconsistencies among the programs of different agencies or between the sum of these programs and financial resources. The paradoxical experience here is that the better one of these preconditions is fulfilled, the more difficult becomes the achievement of another. The greater the technical capability of spending agencies to generate and execute projects, the more difficult it is for the central authority to influence the decisions of these agencies. In any event, the failure to distinguish between the subjunctive (quantitative projections by technicians) and the indicative articulations of policy decisions by authorities capable of carrying out these decisions, strikes me as one of the most serious original misconceptions in the Alliance. It helps account not only for the virtual absence of influence of the plans on the course of domestic events, but also for the relative insulation of the panel of experts from the foreign aid-giving decisions, and thus from the frustrations that this insulation necessarily produced. These frustrations are brought out clearly by the account of the distinguished former chairman of the panel, Mr. Raúl Saez:

In vain the Committee of Nine's Coordinator requested that the recommendations of the *ad hoc* committees for Chile and Colombia be put into effect as tangible evidence of the validity of the spirit of the Alliance. This would be, he said, 'the most effective means of convincing the peoples of Latin America that the conditions governing assistance are limited to those contained in the [panel's] reports, which are the result of technical and impartial studies, and are not the result of other requirements which would deprive the Alliance of its character as a cooperative and multilateral effort'.[12]

If the aid-allocating process did not become multilateral, the frustrations did. They can be attributed largely to the formalistic conception of planning described above, and already in 1965 Waterston could report that "the emphasis in the Alliance for Progress has not shifted from long-term comprehensive planning to short-term public investment planning."[13] While this in itself was not the full answer to the problem, if the above diagnosis is correct, it nevertheless showed movement in an encouraging direction.

## Structural Reforms

The notion that domestic reforms are an indispensable prerequisite to economic development was not a new one, nor did it seem much more than a tautology.[14] It was present, for instance, in the 1960 Act of Bogota that created the US$500 million Social Progress Trust Fund, to be administered by the IDB. At that time the member governments of the OAS pledged themselves to programs of reform in taxation, land tenure, housing, sanitation, and education. Few observers of the Latin American scene in the years preceding Bogota and Punta del Este had failed to notice the shortcomings in some or all of the aspects mentioned.

However, differences of opinion became important in two related respects once the Alliance for Progress purported to establish a viable program through which development would be achieved by deliberate government action in these fields. The differences centered on the emphasis to be placed on domestic reforms versus foreign aid, and the relative importance of actions altering the distribution of income and wealth *vis-à-vis* an approach concentrating primarily on the provision of more adequate facilities.

Since I am trying, *inter alia*, to offer some suggestions regarding the intellectual background of the Alliance, I should like to note at this point that the second area of disagreement has a rather curious history. Few observers of Latin America have failed to notice the explosive growth of the major cities in the past 30 years and equally few have failed to express concern about the visible misery that accompanied this process. Santiago, Lima, Rio, Caracas, Mexico City—each has received its share of attention as populations doubled in 15 to 20 years (or even less), while shantytowns sprang up in the outskirts to accommodate hundreds of thousands of new arrivals. Naturally, the provision of basic services and facilities, inadequate to begin with, did not keep up with the growing needs. And our modern humanitarian instincts are prone to rebel against conditions in which our neighbors are inadequately housed, drink polluted water, and discharge their waste products into the streets, especially when these things are happening in such proximity that their physical reality can be neither ignored nor denied. In addition, many observers doubtless recognized that large masses of men, women, and children, living under conditions that by modern urban standards were intolerable, would eventually become a menace to the rest—hygienically, socially, politically. The stress on more and better social services thus clearly responded to a perception of a need and a danger. Whether it was a true perception, and whether the prescription was valid, is less clear.

It is interesting to ask why so much more attention had been paid to the effects of the urban explosion than to its causes. In virtually all of Latin America north of Argentina, Chile and Uruguay, the annual rate of population growth then was in excess of 3 percent and in spite of exceedingly weak demographic statistics, there was a reasonable consensus that this rate had been rising in the past two or three decades. Nevertheless, neither the Santiago school (until quite recently), nor the social meliorists responsible for the Act of Bogota, nor the writers of the Charter of Punta del Este, raised the question of population growth rates and their relevance to Latin American development. In one sense the explanation for this almost universal silence is obvious, as one statesman who did raise the issue reports:

Rarely have I seen a debate so beset by pervasive irrationalism and demagogic romanticism. . . . Some think that the use of the pill is a North American conspiracy to keep the

Amazon basin underpopulated; others believe that it is a Protestant or Masonic conspiracy to undermine the Catholic faith of our people; some believe that by limiting the formation of mass armies or of mass markets in the underdeveloped countries, the industrial nations are seeking to perpetuate their predominant position; still others see in the present intensive research into the negative effects of the population explosion on economic growth nothing but a conspiracy of the pharmaceutical trusts, eager to amass profits through the sale of the pill.[15]

There is no doubt that the issue is sensitive, and perhaps it was inevitable that in the design of the Alliance for Progress it was omitted from either diagnosis or prescription. But this did involve a certain intellectual confusion in that it appeared as if the provision of more and better social infrastructure was an adequate way of dealing with the problem.

But in practice, real problems of priorities in the allocation of scarce investment resources could not thereby be avoided. Housing is a case in point. The objective of the Alliance was to provide, by 1970,

adequate potable water supply and sewage disposal to no less than 70 percent of the urban and 50 percent of the rural population . . . to reduce the present mortality rate of children less than five years of age by at least one-half . . . to increase the construction of low-cost housing for low-income families in order to replace inadequate and deficient housing and to reduce housing shortages; and to provide necessary public services to both urban and rural centers of population.[16]

This was simply inconsistent with the claims on available savings and foreign funds, if a sufficient amount was to be left for public investments in economic infrastructure, private investments in industry, agriculture, and all the other activities that had to expand if the economic growth targets of the Alliance were to be achieved.

Moreover, developed countries had already discovered that if very poor people are to be "adequately" (by rich countries' standards) housed they need public subsidies, and this need could not be met in Latin America. The implication was that the larger the truly low-cost housing programs were, the greater would be the future claims on government expenditures. This, by the way, is an experience that in Latin America antecedes the Alliance. Some of the most impressive blocks of low-income apartments were put up in the 1950s by some governments for tenants who, being only sporadically employed, failed to pay the rents that were needed to provide for minimum upkeep. The results have been either new slum properties—this time government-owned—or rising budgetary transfers on current account, or both.[17] This experience is beginning to influence the attitudes of governments and external lenders, and the enthusiasm for programs of this type is waning. At the same time there are, of course, urban projects that can meet any test of economic feasibility and in which the beneficiaries are perfectly capable of paying for the cost of the services provided. In these cases the above strictures do not apply and the positive impact of such investments on the social and economic progress of countries may be great.

The question of social services and of viable levels of investment in socially desirable but nonproductive fields is one issue that has bedevilled governments and aid-giving agencies. Another, even more serious issue is land and tax reforms. I do not feel qualified to address the land reform issue in depth, but I think that the conclusion is warranted that the impetus to a meaningful land reform cannot come from an international agreement but must emerge from the right constellation of political forces at home. In evidence I would adduce that the few Latin American countries in which land reform has meant massive transfers of rural property—Mexico, Bolivia, Venezuela, and Cuba—all took the basic steps before the Alliance came into being. In other countries, land reform has so far mostly meant more or less selective, and more or less successful, colonization programs on publicly owned land or, in some cases, the mere creation of a new bureaucratic institution whose employees may be a multiple of the number of beneficiaries. This is not necessarily a reflection of an improper response by the countries in question to their development problems; it may just as easily reflect an improper diagnosis of what these problems were. Certainly the problems of countries in which new, arable land is one of the scarcest factors of production—that is, in which the cost of bringing additional acreage under cultivation is far higher than in other countries—are qualitatively different from those in which reasonably fertile land is still to be had without heavy investments. And the best tenure arrangements for reasonably efficient pastoral producers, such as the River Plate countries, have very little to do with those of the heavy concentrations of Indian populations on infertile land in Central Mexico or in the Andean Altiplano. In practice, this, as well as the different degrees of political readiness of countries to do anything about the distribution of agricultural property, was reflected by the fact that Alliance for Progress financing—mostly through the IDB—was awarded in a few places to support ongoing programs, but that it never became a centerpiece of the foreign aid associated with the Alliance. In something as closely connected with the very nerve center of social relations as land tenure, each country will necessarily have to come to terms with its own tensions and conflicts in its own way. Fortunate indeed are the countries in which this process takes place both peacefully and systematically, with a minimum of suffering and losses! But given the fierce passions associated with land ownership, it should surprise no one that the spirit of the Alliance—revolution without violence, rapid change carefully planned and carried out by capable technicians, more social justice *and* more economic efficiency—did not find much application and expression in this area.

Tax reform is almost simple, but only by comparison. In fact the issues are similar, but the possibilities for accommodation and compromise—or even obfuscation—are greater and the emotive content of the subject is correspondingly lower. Moreover, here, too, short-run realities—the need to raise revenues quickly—have often clashed with the long-run objective of a less regressive tax system. By and large, I suggest that not very much has been done to change the fundamental structure—as distinguished from the level—of the revenue systems of Latin

America, which would tend to confirm the view of those who hold that tax systems too are part of an intricate sociopolitical matrix that cannot be altered lightly or by mere executive decision. This is not to say that some improvements have not been made in some countries, but they are national improvements arising out of particular national experiences. In some cases, the improvements consist much more of increasing awareness of the inequities of the traditional system of tax administration than in replacing indirect taxes by direct ones, which is some of the more simple-minded Alliance rhetoric was virtually the only test of grace.

If the Alliance has had much of an impact in this area it is, I think, a more subtle political one than one of directly induced action. If one examines the traditional literature of the left in Latin America, it is notable how little emphasis was placed on tax reforms as a key plank in their programs for political action. Marx and Engels may have put a progressive graduated income tax into *The Communist Manifesto*, but neither their Latin American followers nor these followers' competitors have paid much attention to this or other "meliorative" measures. There are, of course, exceptions, but by and large the emphasis has been on other things. One important explanation is the different historical experience of Latin America. For the most part, protest movements against the vested interest have been closely linked to reactions against the perceived abuses of foreign economic groups. It was only very gradually, as the importance of these groups either clearly waned or as some accommodation with them was found that was clearly profitable to the national economy, that the attention of domestic reformers turned to purely domestic injustices. The Alliance rhetoric, on balance, may have contributed to this to some extent, even though at times the opposite seemed to be the case, as when domestic interests were able to discredit particular reform measures as foreign impositions, offensive to the nationalists of the left as well as to the right.

Increasing attention is also gradually being paid to an issue closely related to that of greater equity in the tax system, but virtually ignored by the Alliance ideologists. I refer to the redistributive aspects of public expenditures. A consideration of these aspects may at times cast quite different light on the incidences of the fiscal operations than does the mere analysis of the sources of revenues. Thus, in Brazil a system of tax-sharing arrangements came into being—a sort of gigantic Heller Plan—that transferred large sums from the relatively affluent Center-South to the much poorer Northeast. A much less impressive, but more widely spread redistributive practice is that of making cheap credit available through publicly owned agricultural banks to peasants and small farmers with extremely high default rates; while hardly a rational way to improve the lot of the "beneficiaries"—and in the long run a counterproductive one—there is no doubt that in the short run the system serves an important sociopolitical function. All this is not to say that the net impact of public expenditure necessarily redresses the inequities of the revenue system. Often the benefits of public investments go to small groups of affluent entrepreneurs in agriculture or industry.

### External Assistance

The deficiency of national savings *vis-à-vis* the investments required for a high growth rate are an article of faith in virtually all post-World War II development economics. The difficulties of effectively raising these savings rates in countries whose export products face a world demand that is cyclically unstable and has low income and price elasticities, have also become part of the conventional wisdom in this field. Add to this the constraints imposed on the capacity to import by the need to service large and growing external debts, and the need for external assistance on noncommercial terms seemed clear for many countries. I include in this category of assistance so-called "hard" loans from the World Bank and the ordinary capital of the IDB; it is clear that countries borrowing from them, almost without exception, would have had to pay higher interest rates and would have received shorter maturities and grace periods if they had had to go to the private capital market for the same amounts. Neither would direct private investment alone provide the answer, not only because the required amounts may simply be too large, but also because the continuation of substantial net inflows would require such high reinvestment ratios that the political strains of a rapid rise in the foreign-owned share of a country's capital stock might become intolerable.

In the Preamble to the Charter of Punta del Este it was stated that

The United States, for its part, pledges its efforts to supply financial and technical cooperation in order to achieve the aims of the Alliance for Progress. To this end, the United States will provide a major part of the minimum of $20 billion, principally in public funds, which Latin America will require over the next ten years from all external sources, in order to supplement its own efforts.

While the estimate of total requirements could not be more than a notional number, and the U.S. commitment was far from precise, it is well to recollect that by any standard the declaration presaged a major increase in public external assistance. And this did in fact take place (see Table 14.1).

Whatever reservations one may have about the inclusion or exclusion of particular items—such as compensatory loans and some PL480 sales—and whatever one's views about the relevance of commitment as against disbursement figures, there can be little question about the massive nature of the change in the years after Punta del Este. Moreover, the numbers in one important respect understate the shift, inasmuch as the share of funds made available on concessional terms rose greatly.

The following figures bear this out, but they also cast some doubt on the role of the Alliance, since the average terms of new debt in the rest of the less-developed countries seems to have improved even more (see Table 14.2). Moreover, the increase in official aid to Latin America came at a time when the payments for service of past and new borrowing were rising rapidly (see Table 14.3).

Nevertheless, if frustrations and complaints beset the foreign aid machinery in Latin America, it cannot be attributed primarily to defrauded expectations regard-

Table 14.1
Annual Average Loan and Grant Commitments (US$ million)

|  | | 1957–mid–1961 | 1961–1968 |
|---|---|---|---|
| U.S. Government a/ | | 572 | 1104 |
| World Bank Group b/ | | 127 | 318 |
| IDB c/ | | 20 | 359 |
| | Total | 719 | 1781 |

a/ Eximbank (including compensatory loans, U.S. Treasury compensatory loans, DLF, AID and PL.480.

b/ IBRD, IDA and IFC.

c/ All funds.

Source: OAS/ECLA Estudio Economico y Social de America Latina 1961, Vol. I, p. 185 and OAS External Financing for Latin American Development (OEA/Ser.H/X. 14, CIES/1382) p. I-2.

ing overall volumes or terms. There was, however, built into the conceptual and institutional framework of the Alliance a feature that could well have been expected to be a future source of difficulties. I refer to its multilateral character, which clearly meant different things to all parties right from the beginning. To the U.S., it did not mean an abrogation of the donor's right to decide where to put his money. To the large Latin American countries, it did not mean a change in their traditional bilateral relations with the United States. To the smaller countries, it

Table 14.2
Weighted Average Terms of External Public Debt

|  | 1960 | | 1966 | |
|---|---|---|---|---|
|  | L.A. | All LDC's | L.A. | All LDC's |
| Interest rate % | 6.17 | 5.66 | 4.83 | 3.39 |
| Grace Period (years) | 2.40 | 3.10 | 4.90 | 6.40 |
| Term to Maturity (years) | 10.70 | 13.30 | 20.90 | 26.30 |

Table 14.3
External Debt Service Ratios, 1960 and 1967

|  | Payments on External Public Debt | Commodity Exports | Debt Service Ratio |
|---|---|---|---|
|  | (U.S. $ billion) | | |
| 1960 | 1.4 | 8.4 | 16.7 |
| 1967 | 2.0 | 11.8 | 16.9 |

Source: World Bank Annual Reports 1965-66 (Tables 3 and 7) 1967-68 (Tables 6 and 11); IMF, International Financial Statistics, July 1969, (p. 32), adjusted for IBRD debt data country coverage.

meant the hope of an OEEC-like arrangement under which they expected to fare better than if their share in the Alliance funds were to be determined by undiluted bargaining strengths. Arnold Toynbee may have greatly exaggerated when, in his account of the Punta del Este Conference, he said:

It was therefore natural and proper that the structure and power of the proposed Committee [the Nine Wise Men] should have been the main focus of the discussion. . . . It is perhaps also ominous that this was the point on which the U.S. delegation met with opposition . . . and . . . the wills of the larger Latin American countries prevailed.[18]

But he is quite right in describing the conflict as one between the larger and the smaller countries. The OEEC-Marshall Plan analogy was not fully relevant in any event, not only because neither the U.S. Executive nor the Congress were as disposed to accord parity of treatment to Latin American governments in 1961 as they had been *vis-à-vis* Europe in 1948. One source of the ambiguity was that the Charter was a commitment of national governments. The IDB, being originally the product of a decision emanating from the same regional association of governments, could, of course, be expected to be responsive in some way to the decisions taken. But it was also a bank, with its own charter, terms of reference, decision-making machinery and autonomy, none of which it had either a right or an inclination to give up. So how was the new multilateral review procedure to influence the IDB's lending decisions? The World Bank had even less of a juridical link with the new machinery and was equally bound to keep intact the autonomy of its own board of directors in all lending decisions. But these two institutions were expected to provide 30–40 percent of the external official capital requirements of the region.

Moreover, they were, by statute, project lenders and even AID did not at any time abandon project lending as an important instrument for channelling aid. While a small body of technicians could conceivably make meaningful recommendations on the amounts and terms of program loans required to finance a particular country's development plan, how could this be done in a world of project lending? It is thus difficult to escape the conclusion that the multilateralization of aid decisions could not have been achieved in any case, regardless of what the panel might have done. The most that could have been achieved in this direction is probably what was, in fact, done later through the Inter-American Committee for the Alliance for Progress. CIAP provided a forum at which annual discussions took place that at least could be described as multilateralloid.

## SOME OTHER ISSUES AND IMPLICATIONS

In the preceding section, reference was made to the OEEC model. I cannot help feeling that the whole Marshall Plan analogy has been one of the worst sources of intellectual confusion and ultimate frustration in the Alliance for Progress experience. The analogy was unfortunate not only because the expectation of equally rapid and dramatic results was bound to be disappointed and therefore should never have been raised,[19] but also because of the different nature of the fundamental relation between the aid donor and the aid recipients.

It seems to me that the Marshall Plan could either not have worked at all, or at least would not have functioned nearly as efficiently as it did, if the West European governments had not shared with each other and with the United States a vital set of common values, premises, and goals. This may not be immediately apparent when one compares Attlee's Britain with Adenauer's Germany, Italy under De Gasperi and the Fourth French Republic. Nevertheless, it is probably true that the common ground was immensely important. It included basic attitudes on property rights, the welfare role of the state, foreign affairs (except for issues of colonialism), representative government and major civil liberties; it included all of that and a fairly simple common aim, namely to restore and develop a socioeconomic structure that had already existed in the past. It is not too difficult to understand why the relation with the United States was a workable one. The Congress, as well as the Executive, never had to go through agonizing questions regarding the fundamental political aims of the program or its consistency with the basic preconceptions of United States foreign policy.

This favorable constellation of circumstances never existed in Latin America, and neither side ever fully came to terms with the implications of this difference. The most familiar illustration of this is the uncertainties of U.S. policy regarding coups and military regimes. In its simplest and most abstract form the dilemma can be summarized as follows:

• The decision to extend foreign aid may be motivated by a desire to help countries, but its implementation works through governments. Specific acts of extending aid thus imply specific decisions to support particular governments at particular times.

- No Latin American country has ever had a government that corresponded both in form and substance to the form of government that has evolved in the United States (which has broad similarities with those of most of Western Europe); but the range of character and orientation of Latin American governments was itself an extremely wide one.

- In view of this, what were the concepts of national interest and national purpose that should guide the decision regarding who was to receive aid?

When the Charter of Punta del Este was written, it was hoped that the problem could be exorcized by an act of solemn incantation, entitled *Declaration to the Peoples of America*:

This Alliance is established on the basic principle that free men working through the institutions of representative democracy can best satisfy man's aspirations. . . . No system can guarantee true progress unless it affirms the dignity of the individual which is the foundation of our civilization. . . . Therefore the countries signing . . . have agreed . . . to improve and strengthen democratic institutions through application of the principle of self-determination by the people.

In the words of Brecht's Mr. Peachum, "But circumstance, it seems, won't have it so." The problem did not go away. Neither would any sober analyst at the time have been so fatuous as to maintain that this particular statement of intent was taken seriously by all signatories of the Charter. Rather, two types of answers were given at the time whenever this particular issue was raised, and both have since been proven wrong. One answer was that the economic development that would be engendered by the Alliance would eventually bring about political democracy; that is, that while some governments might plainly be signing in bad faith, they would eventually be the deceived rather than the deceivers. For did not everyone know that development means the rise of a middle class and strong middle class means democracy?[20] The other type of answer, on the face of it more pragmatic but in practice no less illusory, was that while the ideology was valuable for public relations purposes, in fact the sheep would be separated from the goats and governments that evidently did not share the basic value premises of the Alliance would neither want to, nor be allowed to be closely associated with it. They would be ruled out from receiving much aid because they were not living up to their Alliance commitments.

This did not happen, nor could it have happened given, on the one hand, the multiple purposes of bilateral foreign assistance and, on the other, the extreme complexity of the political judgments that such a policy would have required. Regarding the first point, Roberto Campos has drawn attention to the fact that the Congress, in the 1961 Act for International Development, committed the U.S. government to five principles in the allocation of aid:

- strengthening the economies of the underdeveloped friendly nations;

- encouraging the flow of private investment capital;

- making assistance available on the basis of an environment in which the energies of the peoples of the world can be devoted to constructive purposes, free of pressures and erosion by the adversaries of freedom;

• serving as an instrument in the cold war; and

• stimulating growth and favor the equilibrium of the economy of the United States.[21]

Clearly, the application of these principles was fraught with problems of internal consistency as well as with difficulties regarding their compatibility with the Charter of Punta del Este. But the second point is more fundamental. Does any government have the knowledge, the insight, and the wisdom required to make valid judgments regarding which foreign governments deserve support and which do not? It might be argued that such judgments are the essence of all foreign policy decisions, but this would ignore the vital distinction between the foreign aid relation and the conventional relations between governments. Conventional foreign policy does not have to go beyond the question of whether a particular country's form of government enables it to maintain long-term relations with other nations, based on a broad and statesmanlike interpretation of the national self-interest. But the aid relation is a far more intimate one, and it is here that the question posed above cannot but receive an uneasy reply. It should be noted that such institutions as the World Bank and the Inter-American Development Bank are, in this particular respect, fundamentally different from the U.S. government's aid-giving machinery; while the latter by statute must make such political judgments, the former are, also by statute, forbidden from making them. Or rather, as financial intermediaries who depend on the confidence of the capital market in their loan analysis and creditworthiness judgments, they are obliged to ask their debtors whether particular policies are suitable to foster economic development in a particular country. If the answer is clearly negative, they can try by persuasion or – ultimately – by withholding new loans, to induce more constructive policies. This is not easy, but experience shows that it can be done and that it is possible to do it in such a way that the basic propriety of such a posture is not called into question. Even though in particular cases the borderline between economic policies and economic politics may be debatable, the difference in the main thrust of the judgments that the two types of institutions are required to make is, in my understanding, a basic one. However one views the future of the region, the rising trend of a state-centered nationalism cannot be overlooked.[22] Any viable external assistance effort will have to include a continuing dialogue on innumerable economic policy issues. But to be and remain viable, an approach and a style will have to be developed that is sensitive to the underlying environment and to the limitations of external influence. A program that goes beyond this and that, in addition to attempting to influence particular actions, tries to impose from abroad a judgment–enforceable through the withholding of aid – on what kind of government is best suited to a particular people at a particular time, may be expected, at best, to be plagued by the most serious and persistent kinds of frictions. Or it may fail, as is especially likely when the peoples involved are as varied, as complex, and as alien as those of Latin America and the United States.

In support of this view, let me conclude by citing once more the author who gave me my initial theme for this chapter. Ten years before Punta del Este, he spelled out his vision of a proper approach to foreign relations:

It will mean the emergence of a new attitude among us to many things outside our borders that are irritating and unpleasant today . . . an attitude of detachment and soberness and readiness to reserve judgment. It will mean that we will have the modesty to admit that our own national self-understanding—and the courage to recognize that if our purposes and undertakings here at home are decent ones, unsullied by arrogance or hostility toward other people or delusions of superiority, then the pursuit of our national interest can never fail to be conducive to a better world. This prospect is less ambitious and less inviting in its immediate prospects than those to which we have often inclined, and less pleasing to our image of ourselves. To many it may smack of cynicism and reaction. I cannot share these doubts. Whatever is realistic in concept, and founded in an endeavour to see ourselves and others as we really are, cannot be illiberal.[23]

## NOTES

1. Since the Alliance was originally conceived as a 10-year effort, 1969, when the first version of this essay was written, seemed an appropriate time to attempt an evaluation. My opinions have changed only in some minor respects since then. I have not tried to update the story: the oil shocks, the debt crisis and the developments in Central America all deserve treatment of greater depth than would be possible within the confines of this chapter. I have shortened the original, modified a few tenses and added some footnotes where this seemed appropriate.

The views expressed do not necessarily reflect those of either the World Bank or the OAS. In preparing the original paper I received helpful comments from Gerald Louis Walinsky, Albert Waterston, and Mervyn Weiner who, however, must all be held blameless for any errors or misjudgments. I also benefitted from discussions with Ernesto Betancourt.

2. See Karl Popper, *The Open Society and its Enemies* (London: Routledge & Kegan Paul, 1945).

3. Albert O. Hirschman, "Ideologies of Economic Development," in *Latin American Issues*, ed. A. O. Hirschman (New York: Twentieth Century Fund, 1961).

4. Raúl Prebisch, "Economic Aspects of the Alliance," in *The Alliance for Progress*, ed. John C. Dreier (Baltimore, Md.: Johns Hopkins Press, 1962).

5. A fourth one—improvements of the position of primary commodities in international trade—was also there but vanished so fast that it will not be dealt with in this chapter. Ever since the creation of UNCTAD, this is the forum in which Latin America has sought multilateral action on commodities and only perfunctory lip-service is now paid to the possibility of inter-American action in this field.

6. Nathaniel Leff has made a quite convincing case for the relative independence of successive Brazilian governments from the pressures of such social groups. See his *Economic Policy Making and Development in Brazil 1947-1964* (New York: John Wiley & Sons, 1968). The truth, I think, is that political processes in Latin America are far more complex than the simple class schemes assumed. These are, at best, useful points of departure for detailed analysis.

7. Without developing it, Roberto Campos has suggested the same point. In "The Alliance as a Diagnosis" he wrote:

An analysis of this diagnosis would reveal an excessive generalization of the characteristic traits of economic and social development. If it is possible and desirable to establish the general outlines of the crisis, without which it would be impossible to prescribe the therapeutics for its solution, it is necessary, on the other hand, to keep always in view the diversity of the national and regional conditions of Latin America. The danger of generalization lurks behind its usefulness. It suffices to think of the differences in culture and mentality that exist between Spanish America and Brazil . . . to perceive the complexities which an abstract conception of the Latin American problem can bring to the task of its solution (Roberto de Oliveira Campos, *Reflections on Latin American Development*, Austin: University of Texas Press, 1967).

To the cultural and intellectual differences I would add the enormous differences in resource endowment and locational advantages or obstacles as well as the diversity in the evolution of social institutions—such as land tenure systems—which in part may be subsumed under cultural factors but which in part also responded to extraneous political events—such as the war of the Triple Alliance in Paraguay or the Mexican Revolution—and in part were themselves a consequence of factor endowment.

8. I refer, of course, primarily to their dynamic effects, that is, to the impediments that they create to future growth. Their static effects are at least roughly measurable, but that exercise is of more limited interest.

9. Thus a symposium, in trying to evaluate the planning experience of Latin America, concluded:

Although in principle there are many advantages to planning with a time horizon from ten to, say, twenty years, in practice usually a shorter horizon will have to be adopted. An annual plan related, perhaps, to a medium-term plan *may prove to be workable* [emphasis added].

See *Planning and Improvement of Planning in Latin America*, Report of Study Group No. 3, Ifigenia de Navarrete and K. B. Griffin, secretaries. Report published by the Conference on Crisis in Planning, held under the auspices of the Institute for Development Studies at the University of Sussex, Brighton, U.K. in July 1969. From the underlined phrase the inference is unmistakable that (i) other methods had not worked, and (ii) the proposed one had not been tried.

10. I once had it explained to me that a particular "plan" was going to be far superior to the preceding one because instead of an input-output matrix with constant coefficients, a model based on curvilinear inter-sectoral relations was to be used. The country in question, at that time, did not yet have an index of industrial production, and still does not.

11. Albert Waterston, *Development Planning: Lessons of Experience* (Baltimore: Johns Hopkins Press, 1965), p. 101.

12. Raúl Saez, "The Nine Wise Men and the Alliance for Progress," in *The Global Partnership*, eds. Richard N. Gardner and Max F. Millikan (New York: Praeger, 1968), p. 260.

13. Waterston, *Development Planning*, p. 100.

14. For a dissenting view, see Claudio Veliz in his Introduction to *The Politics of Conformity in Latin America* (London: Oxford University Press, 1967), p. 12:

Conversely, the reforms—agrarian, fiscal and administrative in the Alliance for Progress version—which were considered absolutely essential if economic growth was to take place, have not been implemented but this has not prevented industry from effectively taking root in a number of countries. Of course from every conceivable point of view, these reforms are most desirable . . . but they are not absolutely essential to ensure a moderate rate of economic growth.

15. Roberto de Oliveira Campos, *Do Outro Lado da Cerca* (APEC, Rio de Janeiro, 1967), p. 55–6 (my translation).

16. Charter of Punta del Este, Title I, paras. 8–9.

17. It should be noted that by now (1987) a far more pragmatic approach to truly low-cost housing has been developed and is beginning to be adopted by many of the World Bank's borrowers.

18. Arnold Toynbee, *America and the World Revolution and Other Lectures* (New York: Oxford University Press, 1962), p. 229. See also Raúl Saez, *Global Partnership*, p. 257.

19. It is odd that Kennan feels that, "seen historically, from the perspective of the decades, this distinction between Europe's needs and that of other areas seems too obvious to be challenged. This was, however, not the case at the time." See George F. Kennan, *Memoirs 1925–1950* (Boston: Little Brown & Co., 1967), p. 353. I can see little evidence that the distinction is widely perceived even now.

20. This point is stressed by Veliz:

These wrong models have inevitably been based on the successful industrial experience of some western nations only, less attention naturally being paid to the experience of those with less impressive industrial records. Thus the countries of the Mediterranean make little or no contribution to the construction of these models of growth. For equally obvious reasons the vague identification of political and economic liberalism with the growth of industry and the reform of pre-industrial institutions has been accepted, together with the notion that the central government is at best the passive instrument in the hands of one or other of the modernizing industrializing groupings (Veliz, *Politics of Conformity*, p. 9).

21. Roberto de Oliveira Campos, *Reflections on Latin American Development* (Austin: University of Texas Press, 1967), p. 129.

22. For a strong, but probably not exaggerated, statement to this effect, see Claudio Veliz, "Centralism and Nationalism in Latin America," *Foreign Affairs* 47 (October 1968): 68–83.

23. George F. Kennan, *American Diplomacy 1900–1950*, (New York: Mentor, 1951), p. 88.

# 15
# The Private Sector and the Alliance

*Daniel Sharp*

It is useful to reflect on the Alliance for Progress from the two seemingly opposite perspectives from which I had the opportunity to observe it: the U.S. Peace Corps and the U.S. private sector.

Although the Peace Corps was part of the Alliance, many in the Peace Corps saw the U.S. government not only as the major driving force behind change, but also as one of the chief obstacles—along with local governments and the private sectors of both the United States and Latin America—in its path.

During the first seven years of the Alliance, I worked with the Peace Corps, primarily in Latin America. Nine years later—a little older and, I hope, a little wiser—I moved into the private sector because I believed it had greater potential to achieve the goals of the Alliance. I felt it was a more effective source of needed technology, management skills, access to foreign markets, and capital. I had come to realize, for example, that government efforts to preserve jobs could not work efficiently in the absence of an energized private sector. Thus my contribution to this retrospective of the Alliance for Progress lies in the fact that I am one of the very few people who served with both the public and private sectors.

The Alliance for Progress was a government-to-government program, focusing more on political and social objectives than on economic goals. No specific role was ever carved out for the private sector to play. There were from the outset, and still are, many obstacles preventing the private sector from making its essential contribution—a contribution without which the Alliance's goals were not and could not be met. Latin America is facing increased world-wide competition for this private sector contribution of technology, capital, management, and market access. Only by forging what I call a "partnership in development" with its own private sector and the foreign private sector can Latin America achieve the full potential of the Alliance for Progress.

## THE VIEW FROM THE PEACE CORPS

In preparing these remarks, I consulted with at least a dozen of my colleagues and friends from the Alliance days. When I asked Jack Vaughan, who was the regional director for Latin America when I went overseas with the Peace Corps and who later succeeded Sargeant Shriver as director, he told me of an incident in which he participated that characterizes the views we held in the Peace Corps. Jack had been asked to translate a letter sent to President Kennedy by President Romulo Betancourt of Venezuela, which read: "Not since the first Texas Roustabouts came to drill our oil in Venezuela has there been such arrogance as that shown by the AID and State Department representatives of the Alliance for Progress who have come here to tell us what to do." President Kennedy turned to Shriver and Vaughan and asked: "How can we fix the fudge factory?" Shriver and Kennedy agreed that perhaps the Peace Corps was the antidote to this attitudinal problem.

In general, the leadership of the Peace Corps shared Betancourt's notion that U.S. government officials were more a part of the problem than of the solution. Nonetheless, we saw Kennedy leading the U.S. government toward idealism and action. In contrast, we clearly saw the U.S. private sector as the enemy, because we thought it was exploiting the poor in the less developed countries.

The Peace Corps also saw local governments as entrenched bureaucracies, but ones through which we had to work. In those days we preferred to go around the local government, directly to the people, whenever possible. As for the local private sector, we thought that it was at least as bad as its counterpart in the United States and in some ways worse, because it exploited its own poor people.

For the Peace Corps, local communities were the key. The volunteers worked to help create and/or strengthen local institutions and to help them demand their fair share from the bureaucracy and the exploitative local private sector. The Peace Corps viewed itself as a people-to-people program that would have a direct impact on the real future of Latin America.

## THE PRIVATE SECTOR ROLE IN THE ALLIANCE

Most of the people tied to the Alliance with whom I have spoken over the years believe that the private sector, like the AID and State Department bureaucracies, was more a part of the problem than of the solution. This feeling applied both to big U.S. investors and to the local private sector. For this reason, among others, the private sector role in the Alliance for Progress was largely an afterthought and, in fact, the private sector was pleased not to be part of the Alliance.

There were a few key Alliance leaders, such as William D. Rogers (the program's second U.S. administrator), who told me that it was not so much that the private sector was an afterthought; rather, he said, the focus was primarily on what governments could do to counter Fidel Castro. Most creators of the Alliance believed that it was governments that could win the hearts and minds of the Latin

American population and save them from Castro. It was their assumption that the private sector would follow, but these assumptions were never developed in explicit detail.

Everyone agreed that a major problem in Latin America was the weakness of its infrastructure. Their thought was that governments would improve and strengthen the roads, communication and transportation systems, schools, and so on, which in turn was supposed to motivate the private sector to create jobs, increase production, and make the economy grow, hand-in-hand with the Alliance. However, no real effort was made to ensure a key role for the private sector. Even more important, perhaps, there was little thought given to the question of how to motivate local investors to invest in their own countries rather than send their profits out of the country. The overall approach was one of statist, government-led development.

In the U.S., there was more appreciation for the private sector than was evident in Latin America. President Kennedy and others frequently referred in their speeches to the essential role of the private sector, although this generally was not translated into concrete means by which it could participate in the Alliance for Progress. However, JFK did invite Peter Grace to head a Commerce Committee for the Alliance.

The Alliance's limited success in achieving its specific economic goals was partially due to the fact that the private sector was not motivated, was not energized, and did not become a partner. In fact, the local private sector protected its own interests, which were often in conflict with the goals of the Alliance.

Local governments stifled entrepreneurial risk-taking and U.S. governments advanced the interests of a few U.S. investors in Latin America without making them a real part of the Alliance. U.S. government support of the International Petroleum Company against nationalization by Peru provides one example of this phenomenon.

As a result of this approach, capital flight from Latin America has sometimes approached and even exceeded capital inflows.

## OBSTACLES TO A PARTNERSHIP IN DEVELOPMENT

Among the many obstacles to the effective integration of the private sector into the Alliance for Progress were the following:

1. The Alliance represented a statist approach through institutions and regulations. The bureaucratic disincentives in Latin America were considerable. For example, in a recent two-year study in one Latin American country, it was found that it took 289 working days to create a small factory. It only took four hours in Miami, Florida, to create the same business. The Latin American effort involved offering 28 bribes, compared with none in Miami.

This expanded government role acted as a deterrent to the private sector rather than motivating it to participate. The statist approach led government to take an adversarial attitude toward business. In fact, most Latin American governments at the time had come to power with an anti-business bias and a program of social reforms.

2. During the Alliance period, there was a substantial increase in the number of state-owned enterprises, which often became enormous and wildly inefficient. State-owned enterprises devoured available capital, contributed to high debt/interest payments, and monopolized the field in various economic sectors, thereby discouraging the private sector and leading to noncompetitiveness in those industries and in the economy overall. The net result was the discouragement of foreign investment, with its potential for technology transfer, capital inflow, job creation, and the development of local infrastructure.

3. Tax laws tended to discourage private sector investment, as compared with other countries where tax laws represent incentives.

4. Corruption.

5. Rigidities in the labor market.

6. Delays in the resolution of disputes. It was much harder to get speedy justice in local courts in Latin America than in most other places.

7. Economic policies that led to high inflation, high capital costs, and unpredictability. These policies were also characterized by unrealistic exchange rates, price controls, and performance requirements. Latin American governments had limited contact with the private sector, and there were few institutions to facilitate exchange or consultation between the two. Finally, government policy generally followed an import-substitution approach rather than one of stimulating exports. These policies led to an overall business environment that was neither competitive for attracting foreign investment nor for exporting at competitive prices.

8. The local private sector had no interest in becoming competitive in the world-wide market. Local businessmen were protectionist; they opposed the competition that foreign investment would represent, and they supported the statist bureaucratic obstacles.

9. The U.S. government supported its multinationals in disputes against the Latin American governments, but did not enlist them as part of the Alliance for Progress.

10. National government leadership did not always define its real long-term national interests. For example, the educational system did not turn out people prepared to manage efficiently and innovate, and there was little government support for research and development. Governments did little to improve the climate for risk capital; instead, governmental attitudes tended to favor politics over pragmatism and ideology over reality.

## PARTNERS IN DEVELOPMENT: WHAT IS NEEDED
## TO CREATE A COMPETITIVE
## BUSINESS ENVIRONMENT

No longer is each Latin American country competing only against its neighbors for potential foreign investment. Rather, each nation in the region is increasingly competing against all developing countries, especially those in Asia, as well as the developed countries of Europe and North America. Even communist countries are increasingly using free-market principles. As a result, foreign capital is shifting from Latin America to other regions of the world.

Latin America needs a growth strategy based on becoming competitive within the world-wide marketplace. Such a strategy must include the private sector as an equal partner, not as an afterthought.

While most Latin American governments in the 1960s came to power with an anti-business bias, there is a new, positive trend toward shifting the emphasis away from government and excessive government controls and toward the private sector. This trend, though not so pronounced as in the U.S., Japan, and Western Europe, is still an important beginning and it needs strong reinforcement. The recently expressed attitude regarding privatization should be converted into action.

Moreover, governments appear to be limiting some of the excesses of their state-owned enterprises. There is also a growing awareness of the need to improve tax laws. Latin American presidents are realizing that to earn money to pay off their debts and fund necessary growth, they must sell and export goods and services on a competitive basis in the world marketplace, not only in their own protected local markets. This means that they must attract foreign investment, not just more loans, in order to become competitive. They are discovering that it may be easier to control investment than to deal with debt service. This is a healthy reversal of the earlier conventional wisdom.

Latin American governments are realizing as well that there is world-wide competition for foreign investment funds. They also have come to see that, ironically, it is often their own private sector that is resisting foreign investment in order to retain its own protected markets. It is a positive development that increasing numbers of Latin American countries are joining GATT and openly encouraging foreign investment and a more open, free-market economy.

Thus, there is a movement toward a competitive strategy for growth in partnership with the local and foreign private sectors. This should be developed in a balanced partnership in which governments and private sectors make more of an effort to understand each other and what is necessary to create a competitive business environment. This will require more open discussions and the development of institutions facilitating regular consultation. It will also mean the elimination of the red tape that required nearly one calendar year to create one small business in Latin America. Governments will have to foster competitive attitudes and procedures and continue to revise their tax laws and develop improved methods for resolving disputes.

Multinationals that seek to participate in a partnership with government must understand and accept the legitimacy of the host country's goals, laws, and values. They must propose to governments business plans that directly support these goals while ensuring profitability, so that both sides will be motivated to continue the partnership.

Multinationals must conspicuously practice model corporate citizenship in all of its aspects. This means paying all taxes, competitive salaries, wages, and benefits; contributing to the community; ensuring reasonable job security; and in all ways respecting the law and practices of the host country.

It is in the interest of U.S. multinational firms to build on the more than 100 years of U.S. experience in Latin America. As compared with investors from Europe and Asia, Americans know the region, its culture, language, and business environment relatively well. We should recognize that for a variety of reasons, "we are in this leaky rowboat together." If Latin America cannot grow and develop a strong, competitive economy, the U.S. will suffer not only through its banking system, but also in terms of its own world-wide competitiveness.

Multinationals can help countries where debate has evolved from the old argument of growth versus equity (redistribution of income) to the current conventional wisdom of striving equally for both, to see that perhaps the next step is to achieve equity as a precondition of growth. Unless we can promise our workers increased job security and a sense of fairness and participation to motivate their full commitment to productivity, we will not be able to remain competitive.

Finally, multinationals must ensure that communications are kept open between business and government to avoid future misunderstandings and to ensure an ongoing, attractive base for our developing partnership. These days, relationships are not forever unless they continue to serve the interests of both parties.

## CONCLUSION

To sustain the current positive trend toward democracy in Latin America requires an effective strategy for competitive growth. This strategy needs to be based on a new Alliance for Progress—one that builds on the successes of the old Alliance.

Perhaps my own transition from public to private sector parallels that necessary and emerging trend toward an Alliance for Progress that is an alliance not just of governments, but of the public and private sectors within each country. Perhaps through such a balanced partnership for development lies the road to achieving the visionary, 25-year-old goals of the original Alliance for Progress.

# 16
# *Labor and the Alliance*

*William C. Doherty, Jr.*

The AFL-CIO's American Institute for Free Labor Development (AIFLD) is probably the sole existing trade union organization that played an active role in the Alliance for Progress. A discussion of the Alliance by the AIFLD, naturally, will be restricted to labor's input and accomplishments.

First and foremost, the Alliance—not necessarily as it was conducted, but certainly as it was conceived—acknowledged that economic growth could not be relied upon, in and of itself, to develop democratic societies. These were not new thoughts, of course, but it was a new recognition of the need to develop aid programs that would be supportive of democratic institutions and forces in what was then still an area of the world dominated by authoritarian governments. The government of the United States, working through the Alliance for Progress, was supportive of the AIFLD because there had been an awakening to the fact that societies could not be or become democratic in the absence of a method of expressing worker opinion and discontent and, at times, support. The U.S. government recognized that only the AFL-CIO could successfully work with democratic labor in Latin America. AIFLD, for its part, became an immediate and willing partner in the Alliance. AIFLD also recognized the enormity of the task of providing education and social projects through which union movements could be integrated into the fabric of their societies and ultimately obtain the political power required for democratic change.

It must be recalled that 25 years ago the hemisphere was experiencing—or only recently emerging from—the dictatorships of Rojas Pinilla in Colombia, Perez Jimenez in Venezuela, Odria in Peru, Trujillo in the Dominican Republic, and one of the Somozas in Nicaragua. It would be easy, in 1986, to minimize the difficulty entailed in providing aid to democratic institutions such as trade unions that were opposed to this rogue's gallery. The traditional aid programs—well-intentioned in terms of improving health services, education, or sanitation – were good in and of themselves. There was, however, no guarantee that they would improve the status of the average citizen of Latin America unless one accepted the now discredited "trickle-down" theory. Moreover, democratic organizations that could be counted on to oppose the dictators could, under the pre-Alliance aid programs, be supported only marginally and in an indirect manner. Growth, therefore, while ultimately a necessary ingredient for social progress, was not a guarantee of it. Strong union organizations, which could be instrumental in better distributing increased wealth, were accepted by the planners of the Alliance not only as desirable but indispensable. In fact, the importance of labor to the development of Latin America received its first official recognition in the Foreign Assistance Act of 1961, which stated that it was in the interest of the United States to foster democratic institutions, particularly unions, overseas.

This congressional recognition of the role of labor in developing countries dovetailed quite nicely with the policies and principles of the AFL-CIO. The AFL-CIO had long argued that development programs must have the support of labor if they were to be successful. Furthermore, labor support for a country's development programs could be better assured if two things were taken into consideration: first, that labor had a voice in determining development priorities; and second, that labor could be expected to benefit from the programs. Development, therefore, had to be a national issue – not just a matter for consideration by the elites of business groups and political parties.

These principles, accepted by the AFL-CIO and the directors of the Alliance for Progress, were nonetheless frequently avoided in the practice and implementation of programs. They represented, in essence, an attempt to change historical political attitudes toward labor, and if change did not occur as rapidly as we would have liked, that is understandable. However, the education programs of the AIFLD all contained a component on the basic rights of labor and the need for labor's voice in the development process. The social programs of the Institute, such as workers' housing, credit unions, school rehabilitation, producers' cooperative formation and the like, were all directed toward improving not only the image of unionism but also the standard of living of workers. Gradually, the change occurred – imperfectly, grudgingly, and unevenly. Unions came to be accepted as necessary factors in democratic societies, the ultimate end of development policies.

Although it is by no means certain that the planners of the Alliance had this in mind, the attempt to elevate the political position of labor overseas certainly enhanced the role of U.S. labor in the formation of U.S. foreign policy. In so doing it made our own foreign policy more democratic. George Meany found it necessary in those early days to defend this foreign policy role of labor by telling Senator Fulbright of the Foreign Relations Committee that foreign policy was much too important an issue to be left solely to the State Department. While this was obviously not terribly complimentary of our foreign service, it did serve to forcefully state that the type of pluralism that the Alliance was encouraging for Latin America might equally well be adapted by the U.S. in the creation and execution of foreign policy. U.S. foreign policy would be better as a result of input by labor in other democratic institutions.

Historians will have to decide whether or not the Alliance lasted for a full decade or whether it terminated with the death of President Kennedy. Nevertheless, the ideals and the goals of the Alliance acted as a bridge from the previous policy of benign neglect toward Latin America to a more mature policy based on mutual respect. It is doubtful that many years later President Carter could have successfully initiated a policy based on the abolition of human rights violations unless there had been the previous emphasis on the development of democratic institutions.

It would be an error to give the impression that ideals such as the political participation of labor in pluralistic Latin societies or of labor's participation in the democratic process were immediately acceptable philosophies in Latin America. Indeed, even today, there are sectors within Latin America that equate the words "trade unionism" with communism. It can be forcefully argued, however, that this is significantly less so than it was 25 years ago. And it can be further argued that the diminution of extreme right-wing philosophy is, at least in part, a result of the work of the Alliance and of the efforts of many of the people who are today helping to celebrate the 25th anniversary of the Alliance for Progress.

There is a saying that "imitation is the sincerest form of flattery." Many of the goals of the Alliance were included in the recommendations of the 1984 Kissinger Commission Report on Central America; most important of these was the stipulation that economic progress must be accompanied in equal measure by social and political progress. Today, 90 percent of the people of Latin America live under a democratic form of government, not always perfect, most often struggling, but a far cry from the misery and political repression that existed 25 years ago. And whereas we have no guarantee of future democratic success, we have every reason to believe that many of the institutions, many of the trade unions, and perhaps most importantly, the vast majority of the people of Latin America will continue to strive for the types of pluralistic and democratic societies envisioned by the Alliance for Progress.

The Alliance, while not perfect by any means, did put this nation's aid-granting mechanisms on the right track. Latin America is better off for it.

*17*

*Reflections*

---

*Ernesto Betancourt, Arturo Morales Carrión,*
*Jorge Sol Castellanos, Miguel Urrutia, and Victor Urquidi*

## AN ALLIANCE BY ANY OTHER NAME

### Ernesto Betancourt

In the fall of 1960 I received a phone call at home on a Saturday evening from Karl E. Meyer—at that time an editorial staff writer at the Washington Post—asking if I had any suggestions for a name for a program of economic cooperation in the Americas. Meyer explained that the request came from his friend Richard Goodwin, at that time a member of Senator Kennedy's campaign staff. The phrase was to be used in a speech to be given in October, possibly in Tampa, I was told, and it needed to be similar in English and Spanish.

I had a fairly good idea of the essential elements involved, since at the time I was the coordinator of the Department of Economic and Social Affairs of the OAS, and in 1960 I had attended the Bogota Conference at which the issue of economic cooperation in the hemisphere had been discussed.

The idea was to reflect the twofold nature of Latin America's aspirations at the time in a brief phrase. On the one hand, the phrase had to reflect a partnership, or joint effort, rather than a paternalistic approach. On the other, the phrase had to reflect that the goal was for Latin America to enjoy an era of economic expansion similar to Europe under the Marshall Plan.

We rejected the terms "partners" and "neighbors," since they had been used for earlier hemispheric programs. Finally we agreed that "alliance," or *alianza*, was the best word to express the joint nature of the effort to be undertaken.

The second part of the phrase was a little more complicated. Development, or *desarrollo* in Spanish, was a concept much in vogue at the time. However, although development had already outgrown the narrow definition that restricts it to economic growth, and was increasingly understood to have a social dimension, the term did not seem adequate. In particular, the concept of development does not specifically address the issue of democracy.

The U.S. believed that its assistance program had to offer freedom and democracy as an alternative to the totalitarian model being advanced by Fidel Castro's Cuba. In so doing, it was going to be necessary to prod the existing dictatorships in Latin America to open the way to democratic reforms. The lesson of Cuba was that an unyielding conservative dictatorship was one of the best ways to facilitate a takeover by the totalitarian left.

So we decided that "progress" was the best word to reflect the goals to be pursued. The concept is broader than that of economic development. Progress conveys the notion of a better life, and a better life is impossible without freedom. In addition, progress in Spanish is *progreso*. A further reason for the selection of the word "progress" was that it was easier for Senator Kennedy to pronounce than *desarrollo*.

This, in sum, is the origin of the phrase Alliance for Progress. It reflected properly the meaning of what was intended. The people of Latin America responded and understood what was meant. It is for this reason that to this day, the name of President Kennedy evokes a reaction of sympathy among Latin Americans.

## A SPECIAL RELATIONSHIP

### Arturo Morales Carrión

From the very beginning, misconceptions were rife about the Alliance for Progress and disparagement was widespread. Shortly after it was established in 1961, the prominent Brazilian ecclesiastic Dom Helder Camara pronounced the Alliance dead. I don't recall if he actually gave it the last rites. The death-wish was not limited to the eminent Brazilian. From the Marxist left, it was denounced as a U.S. capitalist plot; from the right, as dangerous reform-mongering.

But now, 25 years later, the concepts that formed the basis of the Alliance for Progress are still very much alive. They refuse to die because many of the original aims stated at Punta del Este are just as valid today as they were when the Charter was signed. There is clearly a democratic resurgence in Latin America; a demand for land, housing, education, and economic opportunity exists—in varying degrees—in countries as different as Haiti and Argentina; and there is a growing insistence that the U.S. and other industrial democracies do their share to provide markets and ensure a solution to the crucial debt problem.

The Alliance was based on an intuition that the U.S. and Latin America had, despite many profound differences, a unique and special relationship. I was a witness not only to its creation, but during its incubation. Teodoro Moscoso and I were invited to join the task force that recommended the Alliance because President Kennedy wanted to bring the views of Puerto Rico, and particularly those of

Luís Muñoz Marín, into the picture. Muñoz, who brought a peaceful revolution to Puerto Rico, was also a spokesman for what came to be known as the "democratic left," a loose association of progressive Latin Americans. His prestige greatly helped the common effort and particularly impressed young Senator John F. Kennedy who was then campaigning for the presidency. Kennedy was interested not only in our thoughts on economic development, but also in our concern for functional democracies and the need for an empathetic understanding of Latin America by the United States.

Looking back, it can be said that from the standpoint of economic investment, the Alliance was a success. In the early 1970s, the targets set at Punta del Este were surpassed. The Alliance record in social development was mixed. Great advances took place in the areas of health and education. The Alliance provided international credits to universities engaged in modernization – a crucial element in Latin American development. Improvement in human resources was another key achievement, but the Alliance failed to secure a more just distribution of income. Many social inequities persisted; furthermore, the improvements wrought by the Alliance could not keep pace with the population explosion. The Alliance faced not only the oligarch's displeasure, but also Malthus and his rigid laws.

But it was in the political field that the failure of the Alliance was most evident. Few political leaders really understood what it was about – in contrast with the Marshall Plan in Europe. Perhaps it was a mistake that the Alliance was born at an economic and social meeting. It should have begun at a presidential summit. When such a meeting was finally held in 1967, it was too late: Economic development and political democracy had already begun to part ways. The political objectives were gradually lost, despite the fact that making Latin America a region of functional, vital democracies was of the essence. The Alliance did not die with Kennedy, but its mystique, its élan, and the enthusiasm it generated were soon gone, despite many brave bureaucratic efforts.

It is sometimes said that the Alliance was completely a U.S. program imposed by people who knew little about Latin America. This Monday-morning quarterbacking does not correspond to history. The Alliance responded to Latin America's yearning for democracy with social justice. Land reform and integration were not U.S. ideas; expanding educational opportunity was not a notion invented by the State Department. Educational reform, for example, had been proposed by Andres Bello, Domingo Sarmiento, and Eugenio Hostos during the nineteenth century.

There were, no doubt, many new U.S. Alliance missionaries with misguided zeal who pushed too hard, too soon. But in spite of its many shortcomings, the Alliance period saw a U.S. president mobbed by friendly Costa Rican students and hailed by thousands in Venezuela, Colombia, and Mexico. When Kennedy was killed, Latin America went into mourning. Some peasants in Colombia, I was told, heard the news over their transistor radios and hung black crepe on their front door, as if a family member had died.

I don't expect to live long enough to see that happen again to another U.S.

president. But we should keep faith with the future. Maybe that future U.S. president is now learning his ABCs while eating tacos and tortillas somewhere in the Southwest. The future has, indeed, its mysterious ways.

## BEGINNINGS

### Jorge Sol Castellanos

Much reference has been made to the extent of Latin American participation in the formulation of the Alliance for Progress. As one who was both actor in and witness to this process, I would like to address this question.

My first recollection has to do with the task force entrusted by President Kennedy with the preparation of the Alliance program. I remember that Richard Goodwin was appointed to act as the contact person between the task force and a group of Latin Americans who held important positions in Washington. Goodwin contacted them not so much because of their official positions – although they were significant and influential – but rather as Latin American leaders and thinkers committed to the basic ideals of the Alliance.

Goodwin began his contacts with Latin Americans at the Organization of American States, talking to Dr. José Antonio Mora, then Secretary General, and to me, in my capacity as Assistant Secretary for Economic and Social Affairs. He also spoke with Felipe Herrera, president of the Inter-American Development Bank, Raúl Prebisch, Secretary General of the UN Economic Commission for Latin America, and José Antonio Mayobre, Venezuela's ambassador to the U.S. This initial group was gradually enlarged to include Hernan and Alfonso Santa Cruz, from Chile, Cristobal Lara Beautell, from Mexico, and others. The group met frequently at the Venezuelan embassy, under the leadership of Ambassador Mayobre.

After President Kennedy's inauguration, Richard Goodwin asked the group to submit some basic ideas that could be considered by the Kennedy team in the formulation of the Alliance for Progress. The new program was scheduled to be announced March 13, 1961, during an address by Kennedy to Latin American ambassadors in Washington.

Our group worked intensely for three weeks and, as a result, was able to submit to the Kennedy team a memorandum setting forth what we thought should be the basic philosophy of the Alliance, as well as its main objectives and mechanisms. We delivered our memorandum March 8. Five days later, when we listened to President Kennedy's address, we were very pleased to note that of the ten points he proposed as the basis of the Alliance, at least eight incorporated, in one way or another, the ideas that had been put forward by the Latin American group.

I agree with those who have said that the ideas behind the Alliance were not original, but rather represented part of a body of thought on social and economic development that had emerged during the postwar period. What the framers of the Alliance did was to make use of those ideas that seemed, at the time, to be most appropriate to accelerate the development of Latin America and benefit a majority of its people.

I also agree with those, such as Ambassador Lincoln Gordon, who believe that the diagnosis of Latin America's development problems made by the Alliance planners was essentially correct. In essence, the obstacle to development is the existence of dual societies in which 10 to 15 percent of the society enjoys a relatively high standard of living, while the great majority lives in various stages of ignorance, poverty, and misery that do not allow them to participate in a modern economy or enjoy its benefits.

I also agree that the failings of the Alliance were due to the fact that it never was able to generate a political base powerful enough to overcome the resistance of the privileged sectors who opposed reform. I would add that it was a mistake and a contradiction on the part of the United States to try to create a political base favorable to reform and, at the same time, entrust the proposed reforms to Latin governments and elites that did not believe in them.

Finally, I believe that from the very beginning the Alliance failed to promote appropriate arrangements for a genuine partnership between the people of the United States and Latin America. This conclusion is demonstrated by the fact that most relationships under the Alliance were handled almost exclusively by governments, without any real involvement of grassroots, people-to-people, nongovernmental organizations.

## OBSERVATIONS ON FAST-DISBURSING LOANS

### Miguel Urrutia

Looking at the experience of the Alliance for Progress from one specific perspective, the effectiveness of fast-disbursing loans, provides insight into one strategic aspect of some of the solutions to Latin America's debt crisis being proposed today, such as that of U.S. Treasury Secretary James Baker.

For this purpose, the Colombian experience is instructive. Colombia, like many of its neighbors, had been following a strategy of import substitution in the 1950s and 1960s. There was pessimism about the elasticity of export demand and supply, so the country's efforts to promote its exports were only sporadic. However, in 1966–67, a major foreign exchange crisis occurred. Disagreements over foreign exchange devaluation led to a break in Colombia's dialogue with the International Monetary Fund, the World Bank, and AID.

Late in 1967, however, a set of reforms were adopted that created a whole package of export promotion measures. All three agencies reinitiated dialogue with Colombia, and the results were very constructive. The IMF signed stand-by loans and AID provided substantial fast-disbursing program and sector loans. These were essentially balance-of-payment support loans. The condition for disbursement was continued competitiveness of the exchange rate and gradual liberalization of imports. The Colombian macroeconomic program was discussed periodically with the three aid agencies, as a condition for further disbursements.

The results of this coordinated aid effort were impressive. Colombia received loans that made economic growth possible, while the 1967 reforms began creating the conditions for export growth. In addition, the foreign resources also made possible a major structural change in the economy.

One negative result was that the local currency generated by the program and sectoral loans encouraged very rapid growth of public expenditure to levels that could not be sustained once public foreign credit began to grow more slowly. This effect should be avoided in the present crisis.

In summary, the AID decision to adopt rapid disbursement procedures with program and sectoral loans during the Alliance for Progress years is an important experience to study now, when, with the Baker proposal, we are embarking on a new phase that requires similar policies on a global and sectoral basis.

## CURRENCY, INTERVENTION, AND CARIÑO

### Victor Urquidi

Twenty-five years ago, there was a strong tendency in the United States to generalize about Latin America. That tendency does not seem to have lessened today, but there are differences.

In 1961, when the Alliance for Progress got under way, different countries in Latin America had differing capacities to change, to develop. Two anecdotes about Mexico are revealing. Mexico never accepted the Peace Corps—for political reasons, different attitudes, idiosyncrasies if you wish. Among other things, Mexico has had a common border with the United States for a long time (and still has) and this has played a significant role in the development of its perceptions and sensitivities. A second point is that Mexico was one of the last countries to be evaluated by the Committee of Nine in 1963, because we had no planning mechanism in those days. Miguel Wionczek once wrote an article about Mexico entitled "Incomplete Formal Planning." I usually called it "completely informal planning," since we approached the idea of planning differently. The first draft of the report on Mexico by the Committee of Nine was rejected on my advice by Mr. Ortiz Mena, who was then finance minister of Mexico, because it interfered too much in Mexico's internal affairs—particularly concerning land reform and tax reform. It was politically uncomfortable to have that draft circulating, even as a confidential document. It was later redrafted, with these points softened.

The point is that every country has different attitudes and different problems; Brazil is not Bolivia, and Peru is not Guatemala. This must be taken into account if we are to create effective policies.

Another point I wish to make about the Alliance is perhaps a rather blunt statement. I consider the United States to be an "interventionist" country. I remember having this argument with Joe Grunwald, who was then at the Brookings Institution, many years ago. I said the Alliance for Progress meant intervention in the affairs of Latin America. We may argue that it was well-meaning, that it was "good" intervention (despite some things that have been said about the Alliance's ulterior motives). However, how do we distinguish between good and bad intervention? Intervention in this context means that the United States is always telling other countries what they should do and trying to get leverage to push them to do it. I agree that the Alliance was, on balance, good intervention. But it did not work out. It did not arouse sufficient counterpart interest from many of the Latin American countries. This is an important lesson to bear in mind.

The Alliance for Progress began with the notion that the task of development in Latin America is a task for Latin Americans, as Walt Rostow has emphasized. At Punta del Este, it was calculated that the vast majority (80 percent was the projection) of the investment for development in the region would have to come from Latin America itself. This was correct. Today, however, it is no longer possible. For the most part, our countries have lost their capacity to generate additional savings.

The real lessons of the Alliance must be applied in seeking a solution to Latin America's debt problem. Yet I know of no one who is studying the long-term implications of this problem: what it will mean to us over the next ten to fifteen years in terms of trade possibilities, integration, South-South relations, and so on, not to mention the impact of five years of austerity on real wages.

Very simply, most Latin American countries are on the brink of being unable to make interest payments on their foreign debt. To avert a crisis, I propose that we pay part of the interest in local currency, by opening accounts that could be named "Counterpart Funds for Development." Thus we would pay the interest, but not all in foreign currency, thereby saving foreign exchange. The amount paid in local currency could be put into the local banking system to be channeled into investment. These funds should be used to promote growth, that is, they should be invested in or loaned to projects capable of generating or saving foreign exchange, or to meet other key objectives such as technological development or environmental improvement. Thus we could stop the transfer of our meager savings into the vaults of the foreign commercial banks.

Interest in the 19th century was supposed to be a payment for a service. Today, because of the high rates at which loans were contracted, such payments are really capital transfers from the debtor countries and must be seen as such.

My proposal, of course, requires elaboration and a great deal more thought. It takes a leaf from the experience of the Marshall Plan and the U.S. PL480 program. The transfer of real resources to Latin America has already taken place, in the form of imports of investment and consumption goods, as well as military equipment. Unfortunately, it has been partially neutralized by capital flight. The question now is how to repay that transfer. With another transfer, as was the case with Lend-Lease? We cannot do that; we cannot generate the export surplus to pay for the real capital received, or even the interest. The creditor countries would not be able to accept our goods in the form of a net import surplus to them, even if we could generate such a surplus. So a solution along the lines I am suggesting will sooner or later have to be found. We will not need new organizations for this. It can be accomplished gradually through existing mechanisms and the banking system.

To conclude, I would like to refer to a film I saw recently on the Mexican earthquake of September 1985, in which many poor families lost their homes. It ends with an 11-year-old girl being asked: "What kind of aid would you want most right now?" She answered without hesitation: "*Cariño!*" Compassion! When we were discussing the Alliance for Progress years ago we used to say, only half-jokingly, "In many ways, it's not so much the money that we need; it's the *cariño,* the understanding."

I believe that is still what is needed, but it is totally lacking today. I do not see how Latin America and the United States are going to gain anything from a continuation of this lack of understanding—and it runs in both directions.

*IV*
*The Lessons*

*18*

# The Road to Integral Development

*Joao Clemente Baena Soares*

The Alliance for Progress was a novel program, bold in conception, in the solutions it proposed, and in the vast resources it was intended to mobilize. Its underlying premise was that the purpose of development was to benefit the individual, not to build monuments. It refused to accept the thesis that for the benefits to reach the population, there must first be economic growth: Its basic argument was that economic and social development should be simultaneous. It was a long-range plan, since much time would be needed to alter productive and social structures. Intensive and relentless effort would be required. A large amount of foreign resources would have to be available to complement those of the countries of the region.

In this way, the program addressed the problems posed by the gradual weakening of the region's ability to meet its foreign debts, problems exacerbated by the fact that the region had little diversified export capability. This forced it to dip into its international reserves and to incur short-term debts. At the same time, the Alliance sought to reverse the slowdown that was occurring in the region's growth. The system of inter-American cooperation was the institutional framework in which the Alliance was to unfold and the development of the region was planned.

The Alliance for Progress was the outcome of a realistic dream for channeling the energy, political will, and determination of the inter-American system. Imagination and boldness were the weapons to be used in trying to eliminate the despair brought on by years of slow progress and social misery.

An evaluation made by the General Secretariat of the OAS around 1973 showed that growth was higher than it had been in the previous decade and that seven countries had even outpaced the target growth rate proposed by the Alliance. Important strides had been made in education, health, and housing. Public sector savings and investment were vigorous. Significant progress was made in the area of public management, especially in taxation and budget.

However, that study indicated that no significant progress had been made regarding the distribution of growth; instead, growth had become even more narrowly focused. It also found that the problems that many of the countries had with unemployment and underemployment still persisted.

Brilliant and farsighted though it was, the Alliance for Progress did not include measures to develop export capability or to build the bases of trade policy. Nonetheless, a number of countries managed to diversify, freeing up resources to promote exports and investment in new areas. Because of the Alliance, the structure and cost of foreign indebtedness improved considerably. It stimulated discussion, analysis, and inter-American multilateral negotiation to make external financial support more readily available and to agree upon a workable debt that would not sacrifice development goals.

The Alliance for Progress gave new life to inter-American cooperation. It proved that the countries of the hemisphere can combine their efforts in meaningful and ambitious ventures to improve the lot of Latin America and the Caribbean. It was also irrefutable testimony to the fact that the benefits can accrue to all the members of the system.

But the Alliance was unable to complete the job it had cut out for itself. The redemption and hope it promised have been lost in economic crisis and threaten to remain so for years to come. The levels of economic growth and social progress have fallen. Two and a half decades after this vast inter-American enterprise was launched, the region is worse off, on the whole, than it was then.

The crisis in Latin America and the Caribbean is a clear reflection of the weakness of their economic structures. Many countries still rely heavily on exports of a handful of basic commodities whose prices are declining or, at best, unstable. Both these and the new industrial products face restrictions in the global marketplace. Public administration, which the Alliance regarded as needing complete transformation, has lost the energy it was drawing upon to bring about that transformation.

The capacity to invest is hampered by the fact that any resources generated or attracted must go to cover the enormous payments on the debt. New flows of real external resources have turned negative, precisely at the time that they should be increasing, so that the region can deal with the changes that the world economy is now experiencing.

The Alliance for Progress cannot be recreated, but we can build a new enterprise in inter-American cooperation even bolder than the Alliance. It is imperative that together we undertake a process to put Latin America and the Caribbean firmly on the road to development and to take advantage of the opportunities offered by a world economic structure in transformation.

Becoming part of such a structure will mean expanding and consolidating existing technological capacities, promoting innovation in various sectors, mounting a solid and ever-increasing capability not merely to use to advantage the technology now available, but also to modify it as necessary. The political will of the countries of the hemisphere must be mobilized in a new and sweeping endeavor to develop and modernize Latin America and the Caribbean — to enable the region to shape its own destiny.

This new enterprise in inter-American cooperation must start by changing some key characteristics of the adjustments now under way in the region. Let me go over them very briefly.

First, the multilateral arrangements that have so far been used in seeking solutions to the crisis have involved only financial institutions. The extremely important political and regional security issues associated with the crisis have been ignored.

Second, trade has been considered mainly from the standpoint of solving external financial problems; that is, the objective of trade surpluses has been substituted for that of trade expansion as an instrument of growth.

Third, too little has been done to try to control the impact of external events on the economies of the region. Fluctuations in interest rates, commodity prices, and access to markets frequently cancel out the results expected from internal economic adjustments. The political will for internal economic efforts and for the strengthening of democracy is thus further debilitated, precisely when it is most needed to produce the changes required to start an integral development process.

Fourth, long-range integral development objectives have been subordinated to the priorities of short-sighted creditors. All over the hemisphere, purely financial approaches are overtaking the search for stable, self-sustained real growth.

Fifth, the need for productive and social investments to modernize the region and adapt its productive structure to rapidly changing technological and trade trends in the world market has not been adequately addressed. The region's future competitiveness has been forgotten. Thus, even if the debt problem were suddenly to disappear, another problem would be looming just ahead.

Finally, the specified needs and priorities of smaller countries have received only cursory attention, because smaller countries have smaller total debts. Integral development problems that threaten our collective well-being and our collective security have thus been put off indefinitely.

These points clearly suggest the kind of objectives that should be pursued simultaneously under a new inter-American approach to trade, to technology, to investment, and to development financing.

Essential to this proposal is that we revitalize the multilateral arrangements we have had in place for so many years within the OAS framework. This is the right place for the governments jointly to define the political program now required to face new challenges, the right forum for exploring solutions and coordinating a common approach. Only then can we address all at once the debt, growth, and integral development issues now confronting us.

In this new arrangement, the countries should agree on the most likely course of external events that affect their development strategies and on the range within which adverse changes can be tolerated. Compensatory financing should be made easily available in case these conditions change unexpectedly for the worse. This would generate a much-needed financial peace of mind for policymakers in the region. Under this financial umbrella, new agreements should be reached on trade, investment, and development financing.

A combination of approaches to the debt problem should also be agreed upon, with the objective of stopping the present flow of real resources from the region to developed countries and restoring trade relations more in line with the real interests of all OAS members. Mutual trade interests, including cooperative positions for trade negotiations with third parties, could and should then be fully explored.

# 19

# The Alliance for Progress and Today's Development Policy

*Elliott Abrams*

In 1958, Presidents Juscelino Kubitschek of Brazil and Dwight Eisenhower of the United States exchanged letters in which they agreed that regional cooperation should be broadened to stimulate more rapid development. Kubitschek had in mind "Operation Pan-America," which he envisaged as a plan going beyond even the Marshall Plan in promoting economic and social progress.

The foreign ministers of Latin America and the United States established a Committee of Twenty-One to study the Brazilian proposal. One of the results of the committee's work was the launching of the Inter-American Development Bank (IDB). Dr. Milton Eisenhower expressed this growing interest in hemispheric development when he strongly urged his brother to increase the flow of development capital into Latin America.

Then, 25 years ago today, John F. Kennedy called for an Alliance for Progress, which he defined as "a vast cooperative effort, unparalleled in magnitude and nobility of purpose, to satisfy the basic needs of the American people for homes, work and land, health and schools—*techo, trabajo y tierra, salud y escuela.*"

President Kennedy's call marked the beginning of a magnificent undertaking. It took tremendous optimism and political cooperation to attempt to speed up the development of an entire continent and to attack long-standing economic and social inequities. The Alliance earned a unique place in the history of inter-American relations. The celebration of its 25th anniversary is well-deserved.

## THEN AND NOW

Today, our attention is again focused on the nearer parts of this hemisphere. Some of the causes of our earlier concern are still with us, such as inequitable income distribution and the Cuban threat to the peace and stability of the continent.

But Latin America itself has changed much in the last 25 years. And with those changes must come new ways of dealing with the new obstacles to growth and to democracy that we face today.

What are some of the differences between the situation 25 years ago and the situation today?

Thanks in part to the Alliance for Progress, some of the changes are both remarkable and positive.

- Despite recession and crisis in the past several years, over the past 25 years the real economic product of the Latin American region has increased fourfold in aggregate terms and doubled on a per capita basis.
- Latin America's population is now almost two-thirds urban and almost three-fourths literate.
- Life expectancy at birth has gone up from 56 years in 1960 to 65 today; infant mortality rates have fallen by 40 percent.
- Women have moved massively into the labor force and the educational system.
- In the larger countries, almost 90 percent of all households have radios, and almost half have television sets.
- Industry accounts for a share of the gross national product (GNP) similar to agriculture, and electric power generating capacity is doubling every six years.
- Improvements in transportation and communications are bringing the region together and are simultaneously incorporating the region into the world economy.

There are some equally dramatic negative differences. Foreign debt in 1961 came to about $10 billion; today it totals $380 billion. Ten of the 15 largest debtor nations in the developing world are in Latin America. Servicing the debt greatly reduces, where it does not completely consume, the resources needed for development.

As an aside, I might note that perhaps we should not curse the debt problem completely. It has had the salutary effect of underscoring the interdependence of the United States and Latin America. The recognition of this interdependence and of the concomitant imperative of cooperation could remind us of the spirit of common effort that marked the Alliance.

The rate of population growth in Latin America has put strains on the social fabric almost as impressive as those created by debt. Where the region counted 209 million people in 1961, the same land mass must now support more than 412 million people, virtually double the total at the start of the Alliance.

Population growth has coincided with a massive migration from the rural areas to the cities of Latin America. Because cities have traditionally received the lion's share of resources, some migrants may actually have improved their lot. But the migration from rural areas has led governments to devote still more resources to the urban areas, amplifying the distortion against rural areas, harming agriculture at the same time that the new urban concentrations are creating a need for increased food imports. The speed of this urban growth has also contributed to overcrowding and unemployment, as housing infrastructure and job creation have lagged behind the influx of newcomers.

## DEMOCRACY AND ITS CONTRIBUTIONS

These positive and negative changes have often been accompanied by social tension or ideological extremism. But one cannot talk about how Latin America differs now from 1961 without referring to the growth of moderating forces, and a gradual strengthening of democratic practices. True, Cuba has become consolidated as a Soviet base and is a critical source of organized violence. But apart from Cuba, only a few isolated countries of the region remain actively anti-democratic. More than 91 percent of the people in Latin America and the Caribbean now live in countries with governments that are democratic or largely so.

This upsurge in democratic practices strengthens our ability to cooperate with our neighbors. It is infinitely easier to work with governments that truly represent and speak for their people.

The growth of democracy and greater recognition of our economic interdependence have helped build more equal hemispheric relationships. It is far easier to undertake the necessary reforms if they are not the result of pressure from a "big brother."

One criticism made of the Alliance is that it relied too heavily on bilateral aid. It is true that U.S. bilateral aid has declined in per capita terms. But U.S. assistance to Latin America in 1985 reached $1.5 billion, only slightly less than the equivalent amounts during the 1960s. At the same time, World Bank and IDB lending to Latin America has gone from $6.6 billion between 1961 and 1970 to $51.2 billion from 1971 to 1984.

Even allowing for the recent concentration of U.S. bilateral assistance to Caribbean Basin countries, the change in the mix of bilateral and multilateral aid means that U.S. support for development in the hemisphere as a whole continues at high levels. In fact, when the U.S. contributions of between 20 and 40 percent of the capital of the World Bank and the IDB are considered, overall U.S. aid to Latin America today is significantly larger than it was during the Alliance.

## LESSONS

In the past 25 years, it is not only Latin America that has changed. So has the state of our knowledge about the process of development. What are the lessons that we have learned over the past quarter century? Let's look at some of them.

The President's Council of Economic Advisors and individual scholars like Professor Jeffrey Sachs at Harvard have recently provided important insights into the lessons to be drawn from the economic experience of both the developed and developing countries. I commend their research to you. But let me just mention a few key points:

*Exchange rates.* When market exchange rates are not maintained, domestic inflation transforms initially appropriate nominal exchange rates into substantially overvalued exchange rates. When this happened in a number of Latin American countries in the late 1970s and early 1980s, exports became less competitive, imports were overly stimulated, and foreign debt often increased.

*General price inflation.* Except in the short term, a rapid rate of inflation is generally associated with relatively poor growth performance. In the industrial countries, high inflation generally brought less growth in the 1970s and 1980s than in the lower inflation of the 1950s and 1960s. In the developing countries, there has been high growth even with inflation rates in the range of 20–50 percent, but inflation rates higher than this have inevitably led to economic disruptions.

*International trade policy.* An outward-looking, open policy that promotes exports and international trade is conducive to rapid economic growth. Relatively inward-looking policies concentrated on import substitution have resulted in the costly inefficiencies.

This is one of the key conclusions of Jeffrey Sachs in comparing East Asia with Latin America. Although both regions received comparable external economic shocks in the late 1970s and early 1980s, and both had relatively similar ratios of debt to gross domestic product (GDP), East Asia generally promoted exports and maintained competitive exchange rates – and achieved significantly higher growth rates than did Latin America.

*Incentives through relative prices.* This is crucial in all countries, developed and developing. Where individuals have freedom of choice, they will respond to relative price incentives in deciding on consumption, saving, and in offering their services. This has often been overlooked in countries with a wide disparity in per capita incomes and always with lamentable results.

*Fiscal discipline.* Experience does not prescribe an exact size for the public sector or a specific limit on the fiscal deficit. But nations that run large and persistent deficits at unsustainable levels (for example, 8–10 percent of more of GDP) inevitably suffer great difficulties when they stop living beyond their means. It is important to recognize that the hangover is the result of the binge and not of going on the wagon.

I have listed these lessons separately, but much of the research on the experience of economic development speaks of them as parts of a whole. Turned into a general approach, they generate confidence among both domestic and foreign investors. When this approach is lacking, and when there is too much regulation or state planning, the result has often been capital flight. Conservative estimates suggest that more than $100 billion of Latin American capital has fled since the late 1970s. A recent study concluded that in the ten major Latin American debtor nations, of the $44.2 billion in new net borrowing that was arranged during the period 1983–85, $30.8 billion, or nearly 70 percent, was negated by capital flight. In some countries this hemorrhaging continues. It is difficult to expect significant new foreign capital flows under such conditions.

## ACTION

The challenge we now face is analogous to that faced by the founders of the Alliance: how to apply ourselves to the problems the hemisphere faces today. We must do so with the full realization that both developed and developing countries have obligations.

### Trade

One of our major responsibilities in the United States is to continue to provide access to the U.S. market—the largest single market in the world and the most dynamic in recent years. We have done that for Latin America. From a trade surplus of $1.4 billion with Latin America in 1981, the United States has gone to deficits of $6 billion, then $18, $21, and $19 billion. This is typically forgotten when commentators criticize U.S. trade practices while ignoring those of Europe, whose imports from Latin America are a fraction of ours.

U.S. support for free and fair trade and President Reagan's steps to back up his commitment to it have not always been popular here at home. Our domestic shoe industry clamored to keep out rapidly growing imports that would have cost Brazil alone up to some $300 million annually in current export sales. The President ruled against the recommended quotas.

Another example is copper, where America's mines have fallen on hard times. The copper mining industry has pressed for barriers against foreign competitors and claimed, contrary to the evidence at hand, that Chilean copper benefits from government subsidies. In 1984, the President rejected protectionist restrictions.

The Textile and Apparel Trade Enforcement Act of 1985 came encumbered with barriers to trade in copper and shoes. The Administration fought hard against the severe restrictions the bill would have imposed on all textile trade. At the same time, we pledged that we would try to hold the line on imports from well-developed and low-cost textile industries but would consider import growth from developing nations. The battle on the Hill was fierce. The bill passed both houses of the U.S. Congress. On December 17, 1985, President Reagan vetoed it.

### The Caribbean Basin Initiative

The five principles I mentioned above also underlie the Caribbean Basin Initiative (CBI). The CBI is primarily a program of trade preferences, complemented by aid and investment promotion.

The trade provisions of the CBI (one-way free trade for most products from the region for 12 years) began to be implemented in January 1984. Although our traditional imports from the Caribbean have fallen, nontraditional items have been growing. Thus, our major specific objective for the CBI—broadening and diversifying the production and export base of the region—is being fulfilled.

But that is only a beginning. The rewards of the CBI—increased exports, expanded and diversified production, job creation—will go to those countries that have economic policies that encourage investment, efficiency, and innovation. For the CBI to be fully successful, the region must compete effectively in the international marketplace.

### The Central America Initiative

The recommendations of the National Bipartisan Commission on Central America called for greatly increased aid levels but explicitly recognized that aid alone cannot produce development. The assistance we are providing is, therefore, conditioned on concrete steps toward market exchange rates, liberalized trade, encouraging domestic and foreign investment, removing policies that distort relative prices, and reducing fiscal deficits.

We do not expect overnight results, especially given the security situation in the region, but our policies are reinforcing democratic trends and, we believe, laying the foundations for sustained growth in Central America.

### The Program for Sustained Growth

In October 1985, in Seoul Secretary Baker outlined a proposal for sustained growth which is often associated with his name. The *sine qua non* of this proposal is a more focused and determined effort at market-oriented structural reform aimed at greater efficiency, more domestic saving, and a more attractive climate for domestic and foreign investment.

If, and that is a big if, the debtor countries adopt measures consonant with economic growth, the World Bank, other international financial institutions, and the commercial banks will be able to support their reforms with significant new financing. A key element would be wider use of sectoral and structural adjustment loans of the World Bank. We also believe that under certain conditions the IDB could do more along these lines.

There is reason to expect a number of debtors to follow the outlines of this process to deal with the crucial symptoms of the debt problem: capital flight and slow growth.

These approaches to trade and debt are in harmony with the lessons from the Alliance for Progress. They will work only if both the Latin American countries and the industrialized nations respond to the challenges and opportunities they face and if they avoid overreliance on aid and statist solutions.

## CONCLUSION

Earlier I noted the differences between the Latin America of 1961 and the Latin America of today. I also noted some of the similarities. One common characteristic of that period and this one is the fact that now, as then, the United States must have sustained, consistent, and attentive bipartisan policy toward the region. Both the Alliance and our current policy recognize that a consistent and sustained effort by the United States and by the nations of Latin America—in partnership—is a necessary condition for success.

The greatest contribution of the Alliance is the confidence that if we work together to solve our problems, we can overcome them. Those of you who formed the Alliance taught us this. From you we have learned to cope with the problems we face in the hemisphere. With your model of enthusiasm and spirit, we can move forward with the assurance that we will achieve our shared goals.

# 20

# Kennedy's Vision Revisited

*Abraham F. Lowenthal*

Most of the commentators in this volume were involved in the Alliance for Progress. Some were among its key designers.

I was not. I was too young to vote for President John F. Kennedy. I was still a college student when the Alliance was announced. I cannot offer interesting reminiscences, therefore.

What I can do, as one whose interest in public affairs and in U.S.-Latin American relations was sparked in the 1960s by President Kennedy, is to reflect briefly on some lessons for today of the Alliance experience. I would like to do so by considering what President Kennedy might say if he could return to life.

President Kennedy would surely be pleased to hear about Latin America's economic and social progress since 1961.

He would be impressed by Latin America's economic and social progress since the 1960s: the major improvements in education, public health, and housing; the transformation of Latin America from a largely rural continent to a region of dynamic cities; and the emergence of Latin American nations as self-confident and assertive actors in the world, seeking their own way in international affairs. He would be staggered by the rapidity and enormity of some of Latin America's changes. Brazil in 1960, for instance, obtained more than half of its export earnings from coffee; now Brazil earns more from the export of automobiles and auto parts than from the coffee trade. The Dominican Republic, to cite another example, had fewer than five citizens with post-high school professional education in agriculture in 1961; now hundreds of Dominican agricultural engineers and scientists have substantially diversified and improved their country's economy. He would be staggered by the extent of economic growth all over Latin America— growth that has been rapid even if uneven. He would be stunned by the explosion of education and by the modernization of a continent.

If President Kennedy could return now, I believe he would also agree with many of the searching critiques that have been offered of the original premises and assumptions of the Alliance. He would understand, in retrospect, that the Alliance encountered problems because it pushed reforms and stability at the same time, because it reinforced both the agents of change and those opposed to the redistribution of power.

But if President Kennedy could be with us today, I doubt that he would dwell long on Latin America's progress, impressive though it has been, or on the Alliance's failures, though they were real. Rather, he would focus on Latin America's crisis of the 1980s—on the prolonged depression, the enervating debt trap, and the despair of many in the hemisphere whose hopes were first aroused and then dashed. And he would apply today the personal qualities that produced the Alliance for Progress—the capacity to listen to Latin Americans, a sense of compassion and of urgency, and the ability both to learn from history and to help move events in a different direction.

First, because he had great skill in listening to Latin Americans and did not simply offer homilies about how they should behave, President Kennedy would hear what today's Latin American leaders are telling us. He would understand that Latin Americans believe that the most overwhelming threats in the hemisphere are debt, poverty, and unemployment—not guerrillas, Soviet influence, terrorists, or drugs. He would comprehend that Latin Americans want Washington really to be and to remain an ally for progress on a sustained basis, year in and year out. He would perceive that today's democratic leaders in Latin America are exactly the kind of partners he sought in the 1960s: humane, moderate, pragmatic, reformist, and disposed toward real cooperation with the United States. He would counsel going a long way toward meeting their concerns. He would be urging us to design a policy today as bold and comprehensive as was the Alliance for Progress.

In 1961, John Kennedy said of Latin America:

Millions of men and women suffer the daily degradations of hunger and poverty. They lack decent shelter or protection from disease. Their children are deprived of the education or the jobs which are the gateway to a better life.

If President Kennedy were here today, he would surely be struck by how those comments have increasingly come to apply to the United States. It is painful for us to face, but the United States has seen the steady deterioration at home of many of the dimensions of concern that led to the Alliance. More of our citizens are unemployed now than 25 years ago. More have inadequate housing, or no housing at all. More than ever are illiterate, and more have been driven from the land. President Kennedy would no doubt tell us that if the United States is to remain a world power, it must first make its own society work.

Finally, President Kennedy might well reflect on something that I have learned from my students at the University of Southern California. I teach a course at

USC on U.S. responses to revolutionary change in the Americas. Each fall, I have asked the students on the first day of class to identify ten key phrases in the twentieth century history of inter-American relations.

The results are sobering.

Consistently, only one student out of ten can identify the Alliance for Progress. But more than half the students know about the Bay of Pigs—an event that occurred within a month or so of the launching of the Alliance. What a sad and poignant epitaph on the Alliance and Kennedy's policies!

My student poll points up another lesson. When positive economic development programs are linked to counterrevolutionary interventions, what will eventually be remembered is not the aid but the interference. That is a thought worth pondering today, as we think about the vexing problem of Nicaragua.

I believe President Kennedy would be struck by the fact that the United States in the 1980s is debating policy toward Nicaragua in almost exactly the same terms that dominated the discussion of Cuba in the 1960s. An intense national controversy is taking place today, just as in the 1960s, about how the United States should respond to the challenge of revolutionary change within our Caribbean Basin border region.

The debate rages, as it did a generation ago, about how to respond to the "national security" threat posed by a Marxist movement in one of the small countries of the Caribbean Basin. But it is time to understand that part of our problem today in dealing with Nicaragua, as with Cuba before, derives from national *in*security. It is not that we cannot defend our interests in the region, but that we fear losing control of something we are used to controlling, that is, the internal politics of the small countries near our shores.

Almost 25 years have passed since President Kennedy faced and resolved the national security threat from Cuba during the Missile Crisis of October 1962. No direct challenge to our security has emerged from Cuba since, nor is one likely to emerge from Nicaragua. But we seem curiously stuck: caught in old habits of thought, driven by traditional axioms that were more cogent in the days of coaling stations than they are in the thermonuclear age.

This is not the place for an extensive comment on contemporary foreign policy. But I cannot help but reflect what the Alliance should teach us about the current issues in Central America. It is high time to learn that the way to build social reform, economic development, and democracy is positively, persistently, and cooperatively—not negatively, intermittently, and unilaterally.

# 21

# The Alliance and Hemispheric Economic Cooperation

*Nicolás Ardito-Barletta*

The Alliance for Progress, as a program of hemispheric actions for development, was made up of many things and was meant to influence all aspects of life in Latin American countries. The original ideas were developed by Latin Americans in the form of very concrete action programs for development, about which a wide hemispheric consensus had evolved. They were genuinely embraced and enthusiastically supported by cooperation programs launched by the United States government under President John F. Kennedy. Strong political support and leadership were provided by the United States government.

The national aspects of development, the bulk of the effort, were carried out by each country; the international part of the Alliance concentrated on financial cooperation, a variety of technical assistance programs, and some trade-related issues, in particular traditional commodity prices and markets and the integration of the Latin American economies. At a later stage, other trade aspects were added within the context of the world-wide trade negotiations and the work of the United Nations Conference on Trade and Development (UNCTAD). The hemispheric efforts—whether in dialogue and negotiations or in action programs—concentrated on economic growth, social development, and institution-building issues, in both the public and private domains.

Today, 25 years later, Latin American countries are facing very difficult and complex economic problems with very strong hemispheric and world-wide overtones. How much of what we learned from the experience of the Alliance for Progress could be helpful today?

We are easily tempted to see the similarities between the Latin America of the period immediately preceding the launching of the Alliance for Progress and the Latin America of today. The two periods reveal for most Latin American countries slow economic growth rates, difficult balance-of-payments situations, adverse terms of trade, a need for rapid generation of employment, scarcity of foreign financial resources, a new wave of democratic governments facing the development challenge of the moment, and a growing effort to seek new solutions to the development challenge of the region. Some would even add that there was then the beginning of a different system of government in Nicaragua.

But we also know that there are as many important differences as there are similarities: Some give cause for hope, while others are more negative. The Latin America of today presents a considerably higher level of development. There is far more human well-being; the economies of the region are far more diversified; there is a larger export capacity; population growth rates, although still high, are slowing down instead of accelerating as was the case in 1960; all countries have a far larger urbanized population; there is relatively more trade among Latin American countries; and there is a demonstrated human capacity to deal with very difficult and complex development problems. For better or for worse, there has been greater access to international private capital markets. In almost all areas related to the level of regional and national development, the situation seems to be much better in both relative and absolute terms.

On the other hand, focusing on the short-run situation, the intensity of the economic recession is far worse than it was in 1960; unemployment levels are higher; we are all too familiar with the huge external debt problem; the deterioration in the terms of trade is greater; in the case of some key raw materials, the deterioration of markets and prices seems to be more lasting; moreover, peoples' expectations for a better life have risen appreciably.

In the international setting, the U.S. economy played a far more dominant role in 1960 than it does today. At that time, the world was in the midst of one of its longest, most stable growth cycles; in recent years the world has lived through wide economic fluctuations and even the more developed countries have had severe difficulties. The economic interdependence of the world has grown considerably since 1960, and the need for coordination of international and domestic economic policies is more evident today. Latin America has become a more important market for the U.S. and the other developed countries than it was then.

Throughout the hemisphere there is again widespread support for human rights, for democratic government, for open and free debate on the critical issues of our time. And there is growing concern for the poor and marginal people — values that North and South America have shared for a long time. But there is also a concern that with existing economic difficulties, specifically with the impact of the huge external debt and unstable trade conditions, the prospects for renewed economic growth for the majority of Latin American countries over the next three years look dim — and, as a result, democratic governments could be once again the biggest casualty. Social unrest, and even some changes in economic and political systems, could, for some countries, result in prolonged economic stagnation and deterioration in living standards. The challenge of today appears to be larger than it was in 1960, but there is a much better basis from which to work, in levels of development, in experience, in knowledge, and in the existing basis of international cooperation.

Over the years of the Alliance, many significant institutions were developed, both at the national and hemispheric levels; some of them have disappeared, but the work of others has continued to grow and diversify. Outstanding among them, of course, are the Inter-American Development Bank, the CIAP country review system, and others such as the Central American Integration Bank and some of the subregional integration schemes. Project and program lending in different sectors, spearheaded in Latin America and supported by contemporary theoretical and practical developments, were incorporated in other institutions such as the World Bank and other regional banks: Loans for education, agriculture and rural development, urban development, sanitation, and water systems have become standard practice over the last 15 years.

Even structural adjustment and sector loans have a genesis in the Alliance program loans of the 1960s. The drive to increase and diversify exports began in the latter half of the 1960s, and for some Latin American countries it began to blossom in the difficult decade of the 1970s. The capacity of Latin American countries to design and implement development strategies, plans, and sophisticated economic policies has also grown. But the long-term challenge of a rapidly growing population and the extraordinary oscillations in world economic performance have increased the challenge governments must meet.

The trial and error process of intensified hemispheric cooperation efforts that took place during the Alliance decade brought the understanding of the development process and the use of policy tools to a higher level of achievement by the early 1970s, and they have continued to be used and to evolve since then.

By the time the Alliance for Progress ended as a special program, Latin American countries were enjoying their highest ever rates of economic growth per capita and had favorable levels of trade both in volume and price. It was the tail end of the long and stable period of postwar economic expansion. On the other hand, the United States, overextended both in its domestic social programs and its international military ventures, was beginning to export inflationary pressures through the Eurodollar market. A policy of orderly withdrawal to a less exposed position was introduced in the United States, which included detente with the Soviet Union, greater participation by Japan and Europe in world affairs, an opening to China, and a reduced commitment to development cooperation programs with the less developed world. Soon there was the first postwar devaluation of the dollar and the move away from the Bretton Woods agreements and toward a system of international, flexible exchange rates.

At the time the Alliance ended, hemispheric relationships were strained. As in earlier years, U.S. pressure on Latin American countries to introduce changes considered important by the United States came to be resented. By 1972, Latin American pressure on the United States to increase financial aid and trade cooperation was seen as a no-win situation by the latter, which proceeded to disengage from the so-called "special relationship" through a low-profile policy. I note here that expectations on both sides, inflated beyond the point of realism regarding both change of cultural patterns in Latin America and redefining national priorities in the U.S., led to a reduction of commitment for cooperation and a move away from multilateralism and into bilateralism. Many of us felt then that an excellent opportunity to consolidate very significant efforts begun years earlier had been lost.

The original hemispheric commitment was based on an aura of shared values but also on hard mutual advantage. The experience of the Marshall Plan had awakened hopes that a similar effort, carried over a longer period of time, could create in Latin America a development pattern capable of keeping pace with the population challenge and thereby transforming societies through a peaceful revolution within a Western social, political, and economic tradition. It was also expected that the potential for hemispheric trade would be enhanced by a growing Latin America.

## LASTING CONTRIBUTIONS

The most important of the Alliance's significant and lasting contributions was the least subject to mathematical measurement. Development issues—economic, social, and institutional—became one of the key items on the political agenda of all countries. All groups within the countries of the hemisphere began to deal more profoundly with development policies, growth, distribution, trade, urban development, and human participation. New professions gained greater respectability and access to decision-making; economists, public health experts, agricultural scientists, social workers, and urban developers began to have policy input. Younger generations of technocrats began to play a more significant role, alongside the professional politicians, in the national scenarios.

Economic, social, and political transformation in a democratic setting received, at least for some years, the full support of the United States, giving great legitimacy and impetus to the forces in the region that wanted to lead the increasingly more educated and urbanized population through a peaceful revolution for greater equality.

The approach to policymaking and to development has become more pragmatic and professional throughout the region. This has yielded positive results in times of international economic stability, but it has often floundered during the last ten years with the wide fluctuations of the world economy.

The degree of communication, exchange of information, and cooperation among Latin American countries have increased through a variety of mechanisms and frequent contacts that, in effect, have brought the region closer together and have made it more aware of its diversity.

The region was brought up to a higher plateau of organization, coordination, development, and cooperation that surely would not have been as significant without the Alliance—that joint effort of Latin American countries and the United States. That new plateau proved that the countries could develop faster than during previous stable international periods and had more resilience during periods of great fluctuation.

Above all, political commitment by countries was the key to action. Excessive interference in each other's affairs was a source of major friction. The definition of boundaries for cooperation was one of the biggest gains.

Even though performance has varied greatly among countries, the region as a whole has been made very aware of the long-term development challenge posed by the wave of population growth that has only begun to taper off in the last decade. Indeed, we all know that it is a challenge of dramatic historical proportions, considered on a world-wide basis, especially when its migration, urbanization and age-profile dimensions are fully taken into consideration, together with their impact on the cultural fabric of the nations.

We have even learned a good deal from the failures. For example, as attention has remained focused on the nature of integral development within the particular cultural setting of each country, the early simplified hope of many people was replaced by a long-term commitment to the solution of a far more complex, long-term challenge. Some of the more cherished goals had only begun to be realized when the Alliance ended, but a more important achievement, the more realistic commitment of Latin Americans to their development, was in place and working.

Today many of the same domestic problems remain, but there is another problem in the area of international operation that overshadows the rest: the external debt and its implication for growth and for the well-being of the people.

We know that the debt issue is global in nature because many countries and institutions are involved besides Latin American countries and because it resulted also from the interaction of all economic forces in the world scene—not just financial forces.

The acceptance of that perception led to the solution that has been applied over the last few years: Latin American countries would adjust their economies through new policies for stability and growth; the international financial community would cooperate by restructuring the debt and providing additional funds; the developed countries would grow again, maintaining the debt, providing additional funds, and keeping trade as open as possible. Each one of the parties would do its part, given its opportunities and limitations. The conviction was that through such actions Latin American countries could regain respectable growth, maintain human welfare programs, and service the debt. There is widespread agreement that growth is necessary, given the great population challenge still with us. The fact that most Latin American countries are again working within democratic institutions makes the success of the policy even more critical.

Few years of experience have produced some satisfactory results. But the prospects for growth in Latin America during the next five years are not much better than they were during the last three. Recovery in the developed world faltered in 1985 and so, therefore, did Latin American exports. The net transfer of resources through financing continues to be negative to the region. Trade has improved, but not sufficiently to compensate for the heavy interest payments. This affects growth in the short run and beyond, because it is clearer now that Latin American domestic savings are being used to pay interest abroad instead of being applied to capital formation at home. Under such circumstances, the future of the new democratic governments committed to the welfare of their people does not look very bright.

Growth is needed again to generate employment, improve consumption levels, and incorporate the poor into the development process. The negative balance of payments, including debt service, is the main constraint. This would be relaxed by increased financial flows, both as credit or equity investment; by reductions in interest rates and capital flight; by improvements in export prices and volumes; or by a combination of all these measures. The Baker initiative addresses one of these issues; it is a good first step, but it is not enough and critical time is passing away.

Solutions to the growth dilemma are complicated and have a political price, but they are feasible. The stakes are high, the moment is more difficult than 1960, but the opportunity is a brighter one.

The time has come to build another step of effective hemispheric cooperation on top of previous achievements. Latin Americans are once again searching as a group, ready to sustain their national adjustment efforts, and they are asking for more creative cooperation to ease the process and to make it politically feasible. We can start once more from the lofty plane of preserving shared values, represented in the political arena by new democracies, and the practical ground of achieving larger mutual benefits over the long run in trade and peace.

Understanding that the United States does not enjoy the same preeminence in the international economy that it did 25 years ago, the collaboration sought should be realistic and effective and should bring other OECD countries into the solutions. Accepting that Latin American countries can continue their development in the widest sense, there is no need to overload the new cooperation effort with overambitious goals that can be more effectively handled by each country itself. If need be, a mature commitment on all sides, including the private banks, could be handled through an exercise similar to the CIAP country review process.

Four years ago, the case of Mexico was the trigger that launched the policy applied to handle the debt issue since then. Today, Mexico is facing, in spite of a great national effort, a very severe problem because of the drop in oil prices. Mexico will be hurt while others benefit. Cooperation to complement the Mexican national effort could be the spearhead to new, more lasting solutions to the debt management problem for all the countries in the region.

An international debt management formula and trade policy that would permit Latin America as a region to grow at 5 percent per year when the OECD countries grow at 3 percent per year would contribute toward saving democracy and peace for the rest of the century. Such growth performance was experienced during the early half of the 1970s. Obviously the international cooperation called for requires, as a start, the strong national efforts of each Latin American country.

Many technical formulae have been proposed by the United States and Latin

American experts to meet the requirements of debtor countries, creditor banks, and developed countries. A group of experts guided by the highest policymakers in the key countries of the hemisphere could iron out a realistic proposal. Properly announced, such a policy would awaken again the expectations of thousands of entrepreneurs and investors, millions of professionals and workers, who could once again increase the energies for growth that now lie dormant in the midst of uncertainty. It could even achieve capital repatriation, once the right policies and the new process begin, creating a snowball effect that would facilitate the solution to what now appears to be an insurmountable problem. The peoples of Latin America would then more fully support a process of adjustment with growth and employment generation, just as they now tend to oppose or be uncertain about adjustment through stagnation.

A renewed spirit of cooperation, political commitment, respect for the identity and the limits of each party—in short, a mature partnership—could help us consolidate a regional development process started long ago, which gained greatly during the years of the Alliance and which could measure up to the visionary ideals of our forefathers. Once again, the enthusiasm of the heart tempered by hardheaded realistic solutions is called for. I am sure the answers can be found.

*22*

# The View from Latin America in the Mid-1980s

*Pedro-Pablo Kuczynski*

I was asked to give a Latin American point of view. To distinguish between the Latin American point of view and the U.S. point of view is a little like the difference between the husband's point of view and the wife's point of view in a divorce court. Therefore, let us just say that mine is one point of view.

## GROWTH FROM 1960 TO THE MID-1980s

Let us start with the record of the last 25 years. From 1960 to 1980, Latin America had 6 percent real growth in GNP, the second fastest in the world after a very small group of East Asian countries. The per capita income more than doubled during that period. However, much of that growth was concentrated in Brazil. Even though Brazil has one-third of the population of the region, it accounted for nearly two-thirds of the economic growth.

Second, exports grew at about the same rate as GNP but at a slower rate than world trade, so that Latin America fell behind in its share of world trade. However, within these aggregate numbers it is interesting to note that manufactured exports of virtually all Latin American countries—including my own country, Peru—grew rapidly from 1970 to 1980. The East Asian newly industrialized countries had a 27 percent annual growth, in dollar terms, of their manufactured exports, while the figure for Latin America as a whole was 20 to 25 percent, even though the starting point was quite low, as was the case in East Asia as well.

Third, this economic growth took place in economies that were faced by serious problems of income distribution. These stemmed partly from the relative neglect of agriculture; this, in turn, was the result of exchange rate and pricing policies that, paradoxically, limited the domestic market for manufactures. It is probable, but not certain, that this skewed pattern of income distribution improved somewhat, at least until 1982, as public services in Latin America expanded somewhat faster than was the case in the East Asian countries. This is shown by improvements in longevity and by the improved availability of education, water, electricity, and other public services, according to the annual World Bank Development Report. Clearly, much of the improvement would not have happened without the Alliance for Progress.

Since 1982, however, growth has petered out. GNP has not kept up with population growth. Income, which takes into account the terms of trade effect, has declined to about 10 percent; if Brazil is excluded, the decline was 14 percent. GNP numbers are not an accurate indicator of income changes in this era of falling commodity prices. Much of the income decline has been concentrated in the lower half of urban income groups, including some of the so-called middle class. The income decline has been dramatic.

From 1983 on, in order to service the bloated external debt, Latin America has had to maintain a trade surplus equivalent to about 4–5 percent of GNP, even higher than Japan until 1985. This has clearly had a big impact on U.S. exports to the region. Of the U.S. trade deficit of about $150 billion in 1985, one-sixth is with Latin America. The overall Latin American trade surplus of $30 to $35 billion is about equal to the sum that goes to pay the interest to the commercial banks. It will be difficult for the United States to create a dent in its trade deficit unless former Third World markets revive—especially the biggest and closest such market, Latin America.

Because of commodity price depression, the value of Latin American exports is today, in 1986, below its level five years ago, despite a sharp increase of about one-quarter in the volume of exports. At the same time, because of depressed domestic economies, imports fell sharply in 1982–83 and have barely risen since. Foreign trade in the 1980s has thus been associated with depression in most countries, while in the 1960s and 1970s it was one of the main engines of growth.

Finally, one more major point about the last 25 years: The role of government has clearly increased dramatically, although not in every country. As a percentage of GNP, public sector spending rose from about 25 percent in 1960 to 42 percent in 1984, a huge increase indeed. While the trend has been paralleled around the world, the increase in Latin America was far larger than in other areas and was also far more than seemed reasonable in the light of income trends.

## CHANGE AND TRADITION

Can we learn any lessons from the last 25 years?

First, change is today a permanent feature of the world economy. In contrast, the early 1960s was a period of fairly rapid and stable economic growth combined with low inflation. An example of dramatic change can be seen in Central America: 20 years ago the Central American Common Market was the darling of development economists. It was a great success story. Today one reads little positive about the area, which is mired in a deep political and economic crisis that began even before the oil shock of 1973–74.

A second major change is the skepticism about development aid that exists today, in contrast to the strong support for public sector-sponsored funds, whether multilateral (through the World Bank and the Inter-American Bank) or bilateral. "Aid" has become a bad word, and is attacked both from the left and the right. Development lending has to rebuild its small and fragile political constituency.

A third and most unexpected change is the speed with which Latin America has shifted from being a large importer of capital (until 1981) into a huge exporter of capital, largely in order to service the debt. The shift, from a positive inflow of about 4 percent of the GNP in the late 1970s to the reverse today, a total movement equivalent to 8 percent of GNP, would have been unimaginable a few years ago. The shift is both cause and reflection of the economic depression in most of Latin America.

A final point is the neglect today of the structural reforms that were a very major part of the philosophy of the Alliance. Land reform, the need to improve income distribution, and the social dimension of development are topics that have largely been dropped in favor of the economic debate over enterprise reform, price and anti-inflation policies, and exchange rate and interest rate policies. Because of the debt problem, we have moved primarily into a financial discussion rather than one about many of the basic underlying problems that still remain.

Despite change, some things stay the same. One feature still present, although it is changing under the impetus of the new entrepreneurs that Walt Rostow refers to in Chapter 24, is the concessionaire style of private enterprise in Latin America. After all, much established private enterprise in Latin America really goes back in its philosophy to the inheritance of the colonial period, when a limited number of people received concessions in order to go into businesses. There is hardly any business of importance in Latin America today in which the president of the company does not have to spend much of his time sitting in the Ministry of Economy to get price increases approved or prices decontrolled, depending on what his position is. The enemies of economic liberalization are very often the private sector itself. If we look carefully at most economies in the region, we will find that there are only one or two producers of any given product. Monopoly or oligopoly is partly the result of history, but for the majority of countries it is also the result of relatively small markets.

Another point of continuity, although much less so than a quarter century ago, is the tendency to look to the United States for solutions. This is to some extent inevitable, given the economic and mass media links of Latin America to the United States, which parallel those of East Asia.

## ATTITUDES TOWARD THE PUBLIC SECTOR

The excesses of the 1970s have led to a world-wide change in public attitudes toward the role of government. The trend is also clear in much of Latin America. The 1970s provide an interesting contrast to the 1960s in this regard. During the 1960s, despite the fact that the Alliance was a government-sponsored initiative, the role of government in Latin America increased only moderately. If one looks at the numbers I cited earlier, it becomes apparent that state commercial enterprises did not expand that much, in relative terms, in the 1960s. Rather, the expansion was in public investment for infrastructure and social programs. It is paradoxical that when the international commercial banks got into the act, starting about 1971 and mushrooming after 1972, they provided the resources that enabled many governments to launch a major expansion of their commercial and industrial activity. The private banks wanted government guarantees, but they also liked the idea of lending to enterprises. They therefore channelled a very large part of their lending, somewhat over half of the total, to state enterprises. Much of this went into investment, such as the development by Petroleos Mexicanos of Mexican oil production, but much was also used, in effect, for government subsidies to consumption in the urban areas. There is no doubt that the money made a difference to growth, especially until about 1978, after which much of the borrowed money flowed out again as capital flight stimulated by increasingly overvalued exchange rates—which was, in turn, the result of the borrowing itself.

Lending by the banks added maybe a half point or perhaps 1 percent to growth in the area as a whole, with some differences among countries. It also added an enormous state apparatus. In Mexico, the state grew from 25 to 50 percent of the GNP just in the 1970s. In the period 1979–81, Mexican imports increased by two and one-half times, as the external debt to the banks doubled in those two years, which were also the years that the value of Mexican exports doubled. I think that there is a lesson in the contrast between the 1960s and the 1970s: It is that public initiative per se does not necessarily lead to overexpansion by the public sector, but that easy money does. In the 1970s, the private initiative of the international banks turned into a kind of blank check that, regrettably, underwrote many of the whims and policy errors of the period.

## CAPITAL INFLOWS

A crucial lesson to be learned by comparing the 1960s to the 1980s is that capital inflows are absolutely essential to growth. A very strange idea seems to have taken root in the last three or four years; namely, that developing economies can grow without net capital inflows. Once an economy crosses the threshold from developing to developed, it usually—although not always—begins to generate a current account surplus in its balance of payments, and thus begins to export capital. This is happening today in Korea and Taiwan, but until recently both of these East Asian rapid growth success stories were importers of capital. For the debtors in Latin America, it is unrealistic to think that the economies are capable of paying interest equivalent to roughly 4 percent of the GNP, while receiving no net capital transfers at a per capita income level around $1,700, and at the same time grow at 6 percent per year while the terms of trade are deteriorating by 4–5 percent per year. How can all of this be sustained over a prolonged period? There is something mathematically wrong with such a proposition, which is, unfortunately, implicitly endorsed by quite a number of respectable observers in Washington and New York. I think that the lesson of the need for capital inflows has to be relearned. The central question is not whether capital is needed, but what policies are needed to attract it on a continuous and productive basis and how to use capital efficiently.

The United States has been a huge importer of capital during the last four years. If about $70 or $80 billion of foreign capital had not come into this country annually, interest rates would have been much higher and the whole Keynesian expansion underway since the last quarter of 1982 would have been quite different.

How can Latin America attract the capital? Clearly there has to be a shift away from loans. Such a shift is, in any case, being forced by the marketplace because the commercial banks are certainly in no mood to increase their exposure. After touching bottom, foreign investors in 1986 were beginning to stir, stimulated by the debt–equity swap systems put in place in Chile and Mexico. These systems have accelerated investment decisions that otherwise would have been postponed. Some return of flight capital has also taken place in a few countries, although the major stimulus has been the very tight monetary policies made necessary by fiscal and balance-of-payments constraints. Private capital, however, cannot hope to bridge the balance of payments gap faced by most debtors. A major injection of funds from official sources is needed. Unlike the 1960s, bilateral official flows are likely to be very small, so that a heavy responsibility falls on the multilateral development banks, both the World Bank and the IDB.

## INTERDEPENDENCE

The world setting is as fundamental as the policies of the debtor countries. It is very difficult to grow in a setting that is not conducive to growth. In 1985, even the economies in the Far East slowed down as a result of an incipient downturn in the United States, which fortunately did not materialize. Yet growth in the industrialized countries is at its lowest point in the post-World War II period. In addition, the terms of trade are vital. They are not only important conceptually but because more and more manufactures today behave like commodities. This commoditization of world trade is creating huge swings in prices. In the case of Latin America, the deterioration of the terms of trade since 1980 has been on the order of 15–20 percent. Commodity prices in the postwar period have never been lower than today. The lesson is to start shifting to manufacturing, which, incidentally, means developing agriculture in order to create a market that can generate additional economies of scale in domestic industry.

If we look at the world economy since the 1950s, each decade has had slower growth. The 1950s was a decade of rapid growth, promoted in part by the boom of the Korean war. In the 1960s there was still rapid growth, but it was bolstered at a weakening point by the expenditure on the Vietnam war. In the 1970s there was a substantial downward adjustment, and in the 1980s there has been very little growth indeed. If we put the annual percentage growth numbers for each decade in sequence we get roughly 6, 5, 3, and 2 percent. Each decade has had lower economic growth than the preceding one, a clear and worrisome trend.

## CONCLUSION

Should we simply accept the status quo as inevitable? I think not. We need new thinking and new ideas to rekindle growth in Latin America. The debt crisis has probably had the benefit of inducing the debtors to put their financial houses in order; but after five years of halting or nonexistent growth, there is a need for new approaches. International initiatives are as important as domestic ones.

Where is the new initiative to come from? What should it consist of? As a beginning, it seems to me that one should narrow the debate to a number of fairly simple propositions, which are made by Dr. Rostow in Chapter 24.

One clear point is that the relationship should not be that of donor and recipient, since right now the U.S. is not a donor in Latin America. If that relationship is established on a new basis, I think there is potential for establishing some good points for understanding. I think that we must revive the concept of inter-Americanism. The Inter-American Committee for the Alliance for Progress (CIAP) was, with all its weaknesses, an idea worth pursuing. There was a positive spirit that was lost over the past ten years and ought to be reestablished.

The Alliance had some fairly clear objectives. We may disagree with some of them, but at the time they were clearly understood and progress could be measured against those objectives. Therefore, we ought first to agree on what the objectives are for the next five or ten years. If we were able to agree on that, I believe we would be in a better position to establish mutually agreed goals for economic revival in the years ahead.

*23*

# *The Cultural Component*

*Lawrence E. Harrison*

In most discussions of the Alliance for Progress, one fundamental issue is skirted. Two formulations of that issue come to mind: What explains the vast differences in political, economic, and social progress between Latin America on the one hand and the United States and Canada on the other? And why is the Marshall Plan generally viewed as a success while the Alliance for Progress is regarded as a failure?

These questions evoke several others:

1. Why is the average North American 15–20 times better off economically than the average Latin American?

2. Why are income, wealth, and land far more equitably distributed in the United States and Canada than in Latin America? According to World Bank statistics, the bottom 40 percent of the population in nine representative Latin American countries receives on average 10.7 percent of total income, while the top 10 percent receives 39.2 percent. For the United States and Canada, two countries where, by the way, income distribution is almost identical, the figures are 16.1 percent for the bottom 40 percent and 23.5 percent for the top 10 percent.

3. Why are proportionally so many more North Americans literate than Latin Americans?

4. Why are democratic political institutions, due process, and civilian control of the military so deeply rooted in the United States and Canada and so rare in Latin America?

5. And why does the typical Latin American chief of state—and I hasten to acknowledge that there are exceptions—leave office vastly richer than he entered?

In the early years of the Alliance, we in the United States were motivated, in part, by naivete and arrogance: We diagnosed Latin America's ills as a consequence of neglect by the United States, and we prescribed a large dose of Yankee ingenuity and resources. Most Latin Americans endorsed this approach, notwith-standing its strong implication of Latin American impotence, at least partly be-cause it did not force them to look inward for explanations of Latin America's condition.

It was Ted Moscoso who spotlighted these errors in a speech in 1967:

Just as no human can save another who does not have the will to save himself, no country can save others no matter how good its intentions or how hard it tries. The Latin American countries have been too dependent on the United States, while the United States has been too nosy and eager to force down the throats of its southern neighbors its way of doing things.

The search for external causes reached its pinnacle with the dependency theory vogue. It really wasn't neglect by the United States; it was exploitation by the United States, which made itself rich by keeping Latin America poor. The United States allegedly bought Latin America's primary products cheaply while charging high prices for its manufactured exports. Meanwhile, U.S. investors were allegedly reaping unconscionable profits from their investments in Latin America.

Dependency theory is an intellectual construct that doesn't hold water and leads Latin America down a dead-end street. I won't go into the detailed analysis here—you'll find it in my book, *Underdevelopment is a State of Mind: The Latin American Case*[1]—but I will make the following summary points:

• The United States, Canada, and Australia all developed rapidly and democratically during the nineteenth century as exporters of primary products and recipients of large infusions of foreign investment. Today, the United States is the world's largest exporter of primary products.

• Foreign trade and foreign investment represent a small fraction of the U.S. economy, which may be the most self-sufficient in the world, at least among the advanced coun-tries. For example, the total effective demand of the five Central American countries for U.S. products approximates that of Springfield, Massachusetts.

• Trade with and investment in Latin America represent a small fraction of the U.S. total world-wide. The bulk of both is with Western Europe, Canada, and Japan. For example, the United States trades more with and invests more in Canada than with all of Latin America. There is evidence that Latin American countries with relatively more U.S. investment (e.g., Costa Rica) have done better than those with relatively less (e.g., Nicaragua). There is also evidence that Latin American investors have taken substantially more out of their countries than foreign investors, both in higher profit margins and capital flight.

Most people agree that Latin America's natural resource endowment is at least comparable to that of the United States and Canada. If dependency theory is largely a myth, how else can we explain the striking discrepancy in political, economic, and social progress? What really explains why the Alliance for Progress foundered while the Marshall Plan prospered?

After 25 years of working on Latin America's development problems, 13 of them spent directing USAID missions in five Latin American countries, I am convinced that it is the way Latin Americans see the world—their values and attitudes—that are the principal obstacles to progress in Latin America. Those values and attitudes derive from traditional Hispanic culture, which nurtures authoritarianism, an excessive individualism, mistrust, corruption, and a fatalistic world view, all of which work against political pluralism and economic and social progress. That culture also attaches a low value to work, particularly among the elite, and discourages entrepreneurship, thus further braking economic growth.

Culture is not immutable, although it usually changes very slowly. Spain itself may be evolving toward modern western values more rapidly than its former colonies, largely because of its opening to Europe since the mid-1950s. In this hemisphere, it is the United States that has played the principal regional role in promoting democratic development, above all by its example, but also by its recent policies, including the Alliance for Progress, the Carter Administration's emphasis on human rights, and the Reagan Administration's current emphasis on democratic solutions.

Latin America's future progress will depend strongly on its ability to see itself objectively; to work toward the kinds of cultural change that will enhance the prospects of democratic progress; to suppress the tendency to seek foreign scapegoats; and to assume responsibility for its own future. Those kinds of values and attitudes could perpetuate the current wave of democratization that we all hope will take root and endure. In the absence of such changes, Latin America is destined to relive the tragic abuses and frustrations of almost five centuries.

The real obstacles to progress in Latin America are in the minds of Latin Americans.

## NOTE

1. Lawrence E. Harrison, *Underdevelopment is a State of Mind: The Latin American Case* (Cambridge, Mass.: Harvard Center for International Affairs and University Press of America, 1985).

# 24

# Toward a New Hemispheric Partnership

*W. W. Rostow*

If we are to be helpful to the men, women, and children of our hemisphere, we must look forward with realism, not backward with nostalgia or frustration. The concepts that generated the Alliance for Progress crystallized three decades ago, in the 1950s. Now — on the basis of what we think we have learned and what we can discern over the next generation — we must prescribe for the future, through the year 2010, more than a half century hence.

The bulk of my comments will address the future, based on the lessons we have learned from the Alliance experience. But some historical problems are more deeply rooted and slower to yield than others; and there are some principles which, if not eternal, hold for long periods of time. There are, I believe, eight propositions which, with some modification, are just about as valid in 1986 as they were a quarter century ago.

## EIGHT STRANDS OF CONTINUITY

1. The task of development in Latin America is overwhelmingly a task for Latin Americans. At the Punta del Este conference in August 1961, it was roughly calculated that 80 percent of the investment for Latin American development in the 1960s would have to come from Latin America. The proportion turned out to be 90 percent or more. What the United States does or fails to do has been, and is likely to remain, a marginal factor in the equation of Latin American development, although often a significant marginal factor. In any concerted effort at Latin American development, the United States will be a partner, but inevitably a junior partner.

2. Despite some decline in Latin American birth rates and overall rates of population growth, it will be extremely difficult for Latin American governments

to generate an adequate level of economic and social infrastructure for all their citizens—and jobs for all their workforces—until the rate of population increase is radically reduced. Whether we like it or not, the population problem remains high on the economic and social agenda for most Latin American countries. A Latin American graduate student of mine read this chapter in draft. When I asked for his advice, he said, "You must say something about social justice." I could generate some familiar rhetoric. But as a development economist, I conclude that a high proportion of social injustice in Latin America arises from excessive rates of population increase and from perverse agricultural policies.

3. Latin American integration remains as important as we thought it was in the 1950s and 1960s. Progress has been limited, especially at the intergovernmental level, and Latin American nationalism remains mighty resistant. As we shall see, the need to build up and organize critical masses of Latin American scientists and engineers to generate and absorb the technologies of the Fourth Industrial Revolution raises the potential payoff for progress in Latin American integration.

4. There has been considerable progress toward generating and expanding the flow of diversified exports from certain Latin American countries; but, like its counterpart in the United States, Latin American industry, taken as a whole, still lacks the kind of determined orientation toward the world market that the times ahead demand and that now characterizes, for example, the countries of the Western Pacific.

5. Inflation is still an unsolved problem in many Latin American countries, although recent policies launched in Argentina and Brazil inspire hope.

6. Latin America shares a vital security interest with the United States; namely, that no substantial extra-continental military power emplace itself in this hemisphere. This is not a nationalist U.S. reassertion of the Monroe Doctrine. It is the multilateral doctrine of the OAS by which we have, by and large, lived in this hemisphere since 1962—and, indeed, earlier. One result is that Latin America military expenditures in 1980 were just about half the level of those in any other developing region: 1.5 percent of the GNP, as compared to 2.9 percent for Africa, 12.5 percent for the Middle East, 3.6 percent for East Asia, and 2.9 percent for South Asia.[1] Unless we continue to cherish our underlying, rarely acknowledged consensus on hemispheric security, the hemisphere could easily become a strategic bearpit, with profound degenerative consequences for economic and social progress in Latin America, as well as extremely divisive political effects within our community.

7. Despite the great economic and social progress achieved in Latin America over the past quarter century and the region's expanded economic and political ties across both the Atlantic and the Pacific, the areas of authentic common economic interest between the United States and Latin America remain substantial and justify a continued search for an agenda of heightened cooperation. About 35 percent of Latin America's exports flow to the United States. If one also takes into account the intense financial interdependencies that exist in the hemi-

sphere, it is clear that, at this stage of history, we are locked in partnership. The question is: How wisely will we conduct this inescapable partnership?

8. We badly need, in the second half of the 1980s, something we achieved for a time in the 1960s; that is, a hemispheric consensus among economists and political leaders on the nature of our common economic agenda and on what we ought to be doing together. The balance of my remarks constitutes an effort to contribute to the construction of such a new economic agenda for the generation ahead.

## LATIN AMERICA IN THE DRIVE TOWARD TECHNOLOGICAL MATURITY

So much for familiar propositions that still hold. The most basic difference between the present situation and that of 1961 is that, overall, Latin America is far along in what I call the drive toward technological maturity. Most countries are in the "post-take-off" stage, in which a country demonstrates its capacity to develop increasingly diversified industries and applies to them, as well as to agriculture and services, increasingly sophisticated technologies. In most cases, this stage is associated with levels of real output per capita that the World Bank designates as "upper middle-income." That is the case, for example, in Mexico, Brazil, Argentina, Chile, and Venezuela. I believe Colombia also belongs in this group. I shall first address some of the key present and foreseeable problems of these countries and turn later to the problems of the less advanced countries in the hemisphere.

In 1961, the more advanced countries of Latin America were generally suffering from an economic deceleration caused by a convergence of two forces: first, a loss of momentum as a take-off based on substitution for imported consumer goods—a strategy forced on Latin America by the Great Depression of the 1930s—reached its natural limits; second, a markedly unfavorable shift in the terms of trade after 1951, following almost two decades of relatively favorable terms of trade. Looked at in this way, the Alliance for Progress may be seen as a method for helping Latin America bridge the awkward structural transition between the end of take-off and the achievement of high momentum in the drive toward technological maturity. And that happened in the 1960s and for most of the 1970s.

But in the mid-1980s, a set of forces operating within Latin America and on the world scene slowed up or brought to a halt the drive toward technological maturity. One way to define the task ahead—the task of the re-formed partnership now required—is to generate the hemispheric cooperation necessary to permit Latin America to complete the drive toward technological maturity over the next generation.

In my view, that task has four major dimensions, which constitute the five items on my agenda for the future.

- a shift in the balance between the public and private sectors in Latin America—a task only Latin Americans can undertake, but which sensitive and civilized policies of foreign multinational companies can make easier

- the rapid absorption in Latin America of the technologies of the Fourth Industrial Revolution, a new, large area for cooperation both within Latin America and between Latin America and the United States, as well as Japan and Western Europe

- the ensurance of adequate supplies of energy, food, and raw materials, as well as protection of Latin America's physical environment—another major potential area for intense hemispheric cooperation

- correction of the structural distortions in the U.S. economy, including the achievement of high sustained growth rates, reduced interest rates, and liberal trade policies that would not only better serve the interests of the people of the United States, but are also required to permit Latin America's debt burden to be reduced in an environment of rapid economic and social progress

- concerted efforts of the stronger nations to assist the weaker nations in the hemisphere

## SHIFTING THE BALANCE BETWEEN THE PRIVATE AND PUBLIC SECTORS

The existence of excessively powerful "state bourgeoisies"—pursuing interests that may differ from those of a majority of their citizens—is now acknowledged in every developing region, including the world's two most populous countries: China and India.[2] The phenomenon resulted from the convergence in the 1950s and 1960s of technical, economic, and political forces with certain strongly held attitudes.

On the economic side, there was the inability to earn or borrow (at tolerable rates) sufficient foreign exchange to avoid highly protectionist import substitution policies. These policies led directly to insufficient competition in domestic markets, dampening the entrepreneurial quality of both the private and public sectors. Foreign exchange rationing was also a policy that required large, powerful bureaucracies to decide what should be imported. On the political side, there was the fear of explosions in the volatile cities and many governments decided, in effect, to exploit the farmer on behalf of the urban population. This, of course, had the effect of reducing incentives in the agricultural sector and slowing the rate of increase of agricultural production, forcing increased grain imports at the expense of industrial development.

With respect to attitudes, the word "capitalism" was just as unpopular as the word "socialism" was popular in the developing regions of the 1950s. Capitalism was associated with colonial or quasi-colonial status, representing an intrusive external power; and it was systematically represented as such and denigrated by political leaders across a wide spectrum. Socialism had considerable sentimental appeal during the 1950s: Some of the European social democratic governments were doing quite well; Mao's Great Leap Forward and Chinese Communist policy in general generated considerable enthusiasm among those who did not investigate it too deeply; even Krushchev's boast that the USSR would soon outstrip the U.S. in total output had certain credibility in the late 1950s. To all this one can add that many of the world's emerging political leaders were intellectuals or soldiers, both types inherently suspicious of the market process and inclined, for different reasons, to have excessive faith in the powers of government administration.

The convergence of these problems and attitudes has systematically slowed down economic and social development within Latin America and has complicated necessary structural adjustments.

Obviously, the answer is not and should not be a compulsive Friedmanesque reliance on the market process. But the time has come to examine afresh – and with healthy skepticism – the accumulated economic functions of government and to strike new balances between the public and private sectors. These balances should exploit the potential of private enterprise and competitive markets a good deal more than is the case at present.

There is a very particular reason why such a shift in balance is appropriate for Latin America at the present time. As I suggested earlier, most of the population in Latin America now lives in economies undergoing a drive toward technological maturity. Public authorities everywhere have proven peculiarly clumsy and inefficient in their efforts to manage the production of the highly diversified manufactures that characterize the drive toward technological maturity. Moreover, in contrast to the previous generation, private entrepreneurs now exist in Latin America who are capable of producing diversified industrial products that can compete in world markets. Such flexible private entrepreneurship is certain to prove of critical importance in the Fourth Industrial Revolution.

## LATIN AMERICA AND THE FOURTH
## INDUSTRIAL REVOLUTION

At first glance, history appears to have played a dirty trick on Latin America as it was moving through its drive toward technological maturity. I define that stage in terms of the degree to which a society has efficiently absorbed the pool of existing technologies. Latin America in the 1960s and 1970s was in the process of learning to exploit efficiently the Third Industrial Revolution: the internal combustion engine; electricity, the radio, and television; modern chemicals, including pulp and paper, synthetic fibers, plastics, and pharmaceuticals. Latin Americans had every reason to believe that they were rapidly closing the technological gap with the advanced industrial countries. Then, rather suddenly a set of new technologies emerged as commercial innovations: microelectronics, genetic engineering, the laser, robots, new communication methods, and new industrial materials. Although germinating for some time – and by no means uniform in their timing – I believe historians will date the innovational stage of this technological revolution from, roughly, the second half of the 1970s.

Somewhat arbitrarily, I am inclined to regard this rather dramatic batch of innovations as the fourth such major grouping in the past two centuries. The First Industrial Revolution, dated by innovation rather than invention, came on stage in the 1780s and resulted in factory-manufactured cotton textiles, good iron fabricated with coke, and Watt's more efficient steam engine. The second started in the 1830s and became an extremely large-scale enterprise in Britain and the American Northeast in the 1840s; that is, the railroad which, within a generation, induced the invention of cheap mass-produced steel. The third began around the turn of the century and consisted of electricity, the internal combustion engine, and a new batch of chemicals. In their various elaborations, they run down to the second half of the 1960s, when the leading sectors of the Third Industrial Revolution decelerated markedly in the advanced industrial countries.[3]

The Fourth Industrial Revolution has some distinctive characteristics, as compared with its predecessors. It is more intimately linked to areas of basic science, which are themselves undergoing rapid revolutionary changes. This means the scientist has become a critical actor in the drama, and the successful linkage of the scientist, engineer, and entrepreneur has become crucial to the generation and diffusion of new technologies. The new technologies are also proving ubiquitous, progressively suffusing the older basic industries, as well as agriculture, animal husbandry, and forestry, and all manner of services, from education and medicine to banking and communications. These technologies, in different degrees, are immediately relevant to the economies of the developing regions, depending on their stage of growth, absorptive capacity, and resource endowments. I would underline that no concept is more misleading than the one that declares that we are entering a postindustrial age.

The extraordinary range and diversity of the new technologies result, I believe, in another distinctive characteristic. I find it most improbable that any one nation will achieve and sustain across-the-board technological leadership in the Fourth Industrial Revolution or, indeed, leadership in a major area such as microelectronics, genetic engineering, or new industrial materials. Each such area represents, in fact, a group of highly specialized and differentiated activities. Given the reasonably even distribution of scientific, engineering, and entrepreneurial talent among the advanced industrial countries—and the similar educational level and skills of their workforces—with the passage of time, specialized comparative advantage is likely to be distributed within a considerable range of countries. As a result, we are likely to see a great deal of cooperation and trade in the new technologies, as well as competition. Indeed, if one examines the pattern of joint ventures across international boundaries and the expanding trade in high technology sectors, it becomes evident that this process is already under way, despite Western Europe's somewhat slow start in comparison with Japan and the United States.

The diffusion of virtuosity in the new technologies will be accelerated by their indirect impact on the developing regions. Over the next decade we are likely to see the new technologies vigorously applied in the motor vehicle, machine tool, steel, textile, and other traditional industries. One result of this conversion to high tech along a broad front is that the more advanced developing countries will no longer be able to count on generating increased manufactured exports simply by exploiting their lower money wage rates. There is a lively awareness of this change in prospects in the Pacific Basin because of palpable Japanese progress in applying the new technologies to the older industries. Consequently, there is intense interest among the newly industrialized countries in acquiring the emerging technologies. The Republic of Korea, for example, is gearing its current Five-Year Plan to the rapid absorption of the new technologies, including quite radical changes in education policy. It is time for Latin America to move purposefully in this direction.

Each developing country differs, of course, in both the extent to which the new technologies are relevant and in its capacity to absorb them productively. But, in general, potential absorptive capacity is higher than one might guess.[4] To use the World Bank's vocabulary, between 1960 and 1981 the proportion of the relevant age groups enrolled in secondary schools for "lower middle-income" countries rose from 10 to 34 percent; in higher education, from 3 to 9 percent. For "upper middle-income" countries, the increases were, respectively, from 20 to 51 percent and from 4 to 14 percent. These apparently pedestrian figures reflect truly revolutionary change in the productive potential and technological absorptive capacity of the developing regions.

Consider the case of India, a country with an exceedingly low average real income per capita, when measured conventionally. The World Bank calculates 1981 Indian GNP per capita at $260, as compared with $2,250 for Mexico. Nevertheless, the pool of scientists and engineers in India has increased from about 190,000 in 1960 to 2.4 million in 1984. That pool is sustained by the fact that something like 9 percent of the Indian population aged 20 to 24 is now enrolled in higher education—three times the proportion 20 years earlier. Taken along with the large absolute size of India's population, this means that India is quite capable of assembling the critical mass of scientists and R&D engineers required to solve the kinds of problems increasingly posed by the Fourth Industrial Revolution and its efficient absorption.

Consider Mexico, a case closer to home (see Table 24.1). From 1957 to 1973, the annual average increase in Mexican graduates in natural science was about 3 percent; in engineering it was about 5 percent. From 1973 to 1981, the comparable figures were 14 and 24 percent, respectively—an astonishing, almost fivefold, acceleration. Data on graduates in mathematics and computer science begin in 1980, but they rose from 490 to 1033 between that year and 1981, and, I daresay, a high rate of increase continues (see Table 24.1).

I have no doubt that Mexico's—and Latin America's—basic problem with respect to the new technologies will prove to be the effective organization of this human talent rather than an absolute shortage of scientists and engineers.

All this bears directly, I believe, on the appropriate agenda for future cooperation in the hemisphere with respect to technology.

First, Latin America should accelerate the reorganization of its institutions and

Table 24.1
Graduates in Science and Engineering in Mexico, 1957–1981

| Field/Year | Natural Science | Mathematics and Computer Science | Engineering | Architecture and Urban Planning | Medical Sciences |
|---|---|---|---|---|---|
| 1957 | 389 | | 978 | | 1,641 |
| 1960 | 239 | | 818 | | 1,320 |
| 1961 | 422 | | 992 | | 1,912 |
| 1962 | 506 | | 1,087 | | 2,498 |
| 1963 | 586 | | 1,002 | | 2,290 |
| 1965 | 374 | | 1,729 | | 1,791 |
| 1969 | 463 | | 2,619 | | 2,665 |
| 1973 | 665 | | 2,196 | | 3,805 |
| 1980 | 1,395 | 490 | 14,272 | 2,384 | 18,051 |
| 1981 | 1,925 | 1,033 | 15,032 | 2,341 | 20,744 |

Sources: Anuario Estadistico de Mexico, 1960–61; Anuario Estadistico 1981, Asociacion Nacional de Universidades e Institutos de Ensenanza Superior (ANUIES); UNESCO Statistical Yearbook 1964 to 1983.

policies—which is already beginning to happen—to absorb progressively the technologies that emerge during the Fourth Industrial Revolution. This process has implications for a wide range of activities, from education to tax policy. And, I would underline, it should revolutionize the old manufacturing industries as well as agriculture and services. In the course of this effort, the considerable potentialities for intra-Latin American cooperation in science and technology should be exploited.

Second, the heart of the effort must be the linking of Latin America's scientific capacity and its engineering and entrepreneurial capacity. This new kind of partnership is essential not merely to generate contributions to the flow of new technology but also to absorb efficiently new technologies from abroad and to reverse the brain drain.

Finally, it is a profound common interest of the United States and Latin America that Latin nations absorb the new technologies in all relevant sectors as fast as they can be efficiently transferred. It will increase trade within the hemisphere and strengthen the social and political bonds that need to be cultivated over the next few generations. In bilateral terms, this area should be a major dimension of U.S.-Latin American cooperation—involving both the public and private sectors—and should include intensified assistance to Latin America in education and training for the new technologies. Although, I repeat, Latin America should and no doubt will look to Europe and Japan as well as to the United States.

## ENSURING THE RESOURCE BASE
## FOR LATIN AMERICAN DEVELOPMENT

In 1980 I had the privilege of serving with a group of OAS-appointed experts in an attempt to define a hemispheric effort at cooperation for the 1980s.[5] Our chairman was Felipe Herrera. As in CIAP in the 1960s, I was in my favorite role; the only gringo among a group of distinguished Latin Americans. Our deliberations occurred in the midst of the second great surge in oil prices, a time of powerful inflationary pressure. We devoted a good deal of our report to the need for increased investment in energy, food, raw materials, and protection of the environment.

Right now, as we all know, oil prices are falling, as are the prices of most agricultural products and raw materials. An important question is whether that downward trend will continue, as it did from 1951 to the mid-1960s.

One can argue, for example, that the 1979–80 doubling of the oil price was a grossly excessive response to the loss of Iranian oil exports; that the oil cartel is irretrievably shattered; that enormous reserves exist in the Middle East, notably in Saudi Arabia; and that habits of conservation are now deeply ingrained in the oil importing areas. One can also argue that vast stockpiles in the U.S. and Western Europe overhang the agricultural markets; that China and India have moved successfully to increase domestic output and to reduce agricultural imports; and that other developing countries are likely to follow their lead. As for raw materials, a whole range of substitutes is proliferating—optical fibers, plastics, ceramics—that are likely to break the link between industrial output and certain older raw materials, such as copper, steel, and aluminum.

On the other hand, one can argue that the interest of oil producers in preventing a free fall in the price of oil is great, and they may reestablish, sooner or later, the production discipline necessary to raise current oil prices substantially. The fall itself is rendering a good deal of marginal production unprofitable; it is still to be demonstrated whether India and China have achieved a steady, long-term upward trend or a remarkable, short-term rise in the level of agricultural output. Above all, since 1979, real output in the world economy has grown only about half as much as it did during the 1950s and 1960s.

The fact is that, even with the most sophisticated computers and a vast array of equations, we economists are exceedingly poor at predicting. With two exceptions, I would only commend commodity price structure as an area for concerted study in the hemisphere—commodity by commodity. The two exceptions in which more immediate concerted action based on a hemispheric consensus would be useful are with respect to oil and the physical environment.

With respect to oil and oil substitutes, the lead times for investment are so long that an alternative to a fractured (or reestablished) producer's cartel should be explored; that is, the bringing together of producers and consumers to agree on long-term stable, or slowly changing prices, sufficient to generate drilling for the replacement of oil reserves (or increased capacity in oil substitutes). But prices should not be so high as to produce the grotesque and costly oscillations we have experienced since 1978, which have proved damaging to oil exporters and oil importers alike.

With respect to the physical environment, it is time for a concerted effort throughout the hemisphere—North and South—to check and roll back gross environmental degradation. This is primarily, of course, a task for each nation. But the governments would each be strengthened by undertaking national programs of this kind if their action was part of a hemisphere-wide enterprise. Some of the tasks are inherently international, and investment support from the World Bank, the IDB, and U.S. aid programs would be appropriate.

## THE INESCAPABLE RESPONSIBILITY
## OF THE UNITED STATES

In international affairs it is generally unprofitable to spend much time allocating blame for how one has gotten into a mess, if the common objective is to get out of it as soon as possible. In any case, there is usually an ample supply of blame to be shared, as is the case with the current debt problem in the hemisphere.

But it is a critically important fact that the United States has conducted an economic policy since 1979—primarily for domestic reasons—that has gravely complicated the development tasks of Latin America. Specifically, it has kept real interest rates higher than they should have been, slowed down the growth rate in the world economy, generated enormous fiscal and balance-of-payments deficits (the latter resulting from a grossly overvalued dollar), and it has stimulated, despite a continued flow of free trade rhetoric, important protectionist barriers.

There has also been, of course, the unpredicted impact of U.S. domestic economic policy on the dollar, which has constituted a significant countervailing subsidy to exports from certain Latin American countries—for example, Brazil—to the United States.

Right now the U.S., with some cooperation within the OECD, is seeking to correct these costly distortions. Everyone would like what is called a "soft landing;" that is, gradual reductions in the U.S. fiscal deficit, the trade deficit, the overall balance-of-payments deficit, interest rates, and the value of the dollar—all conducted in an environment of low inflation rates, an expanding U.S. economy, and liberalized trade. The result would be an easing of Latin America's debt burdens by lowered interest rates and expanded exports. Such a soft landing is not impossible to envisage. But, if it is to be sound, it must begin with a determination among the people of the United States to pay our way at home, to pay our way abroad, and to meet our responsibilities to the world economy. We have done none of these things since 1979. And no future hemispheric partnership will be worth a damn unless the American political system faces up to these basic tasks.

## OUR COMMON RESPONSIBILITIES TO THE WEAKER ECONOMIES IN THE HEMISPHERE

I turn now to the fifth item on my proposed hemispheric agenda: concerted, patient, long-run assistance to the weaker economies in the hemisphere. It is one thing to create a partnership that will accelerate the movement of Latin American countries through the drive toward technological maturity; it is quite a different kind of task to see what can be done to assist a country such as Haiti in its frustrated efforts at modernization, or to design long-term policies that would permit the Caribbean islands or the small countries of Central America to establish viable roles in the regional and world economies. These are difficult problems. If they were easy, they would have long since been solved. Moreover, each one has unique features that must be taken into account. But the more advanced countries of Latin America, with their hard-won experience, can contribute a great deal toward solving these problems. As more and more developing countries move through take-off and beyond, they should join in the effort to bring forward those who face special difficulties of one kind or another. In that reaching back, the more advanced Latin American countries have an opportunity to show the way.

## THE HEMISPHERIC TASK IN A LARGER PERSPECTIVE

Let me conclude by switching from the role of a former public servant, recommending an operational five-point policy for the future, to the perspective of the academic historian and economist I am pleased, in fact, to be.

If one pulls back the camera and tries to put in perspective the extraordinary story of our hemisphere since the Napoleonic Wars broke the back of colonialism in Latin America, what do we see? In Latin America, we see almost two centuries of effort by the countries that emerged from colonialism to modernize their societies in ways consistent with their complex cultural inheritances. Along the way, we see an array of social and political problems that had to be solved—different in each country but usually difficult and slow to resolve. The existence of these overriding, noneconomic problems postponed the coming of modern industrialization. For most of Latin America, in fact, the take-off began only 50 years ago, in the 1930s—about a century after the take-off of the United States. We were all aware of the urgency of the debt situation and other current problems, which have slowed the momentum of Latin American progress. But, looking back to the 1930s, Latin American economic and social progress has been extraordinary; and looking ahead, I, at least, do not doubt that in both technological virtuosity and income per capita Latin America, taken as a whole, will continue to narrow the gap with the advanced industrial regions of the world economy.

I believe that within our hemisphere, as well as in the Pacific Basin, it will gradually become clear that our great common task over the next half century will be to make the mutual adjustments required to permit latecomers to modern economic growth to move toward economic and technological parity with the early-comers.

Oddly enough, the man who addressed himself most directly to that process of adjustment was that great Scotsman David Hume, who is certainly among those who can legitimately lay claim to being the first modern economist. Writing in 1758, he posed this question: What would happen to the more advanced countries of his day as their example set in motion a "fermentation" (as he called it) in the less advanced, and they too acquired the advantages of trade and skills in the "mechanical arts?"

Speaking in Japan about a year ago, I proposed that the correct doctrine for the Pacific Basin in the next century was incorporated in Hume's response to that question:

Where an open communication is preserved among nations, it is impossible but the domestic industry of every one must receive an increase from the improvements of others. . . . Nor needs any state entertain apprehensions, that their neighbours will improve to such a degree in every art and manufacture, as to have no demand from them. Nature, by giving a diversity of geniuses, climates, and soils, to different nations, has secured their mutual intercourse and commerce, as long as they all remain industrious and civilized.[6]

I would suggest that we, too, in this hemisphere should work to preserve a system of "open communication" in a community of "industrious and civilized" nations. That, in the end, was the spirit John Kennedy brought to the Alliance for Progress in 1961; and it should suffuse the new phase of partnership our inescapable interdependence and abiding common interests now require.

## NOTES

1. *World Military Expenditures and Arms Transfers, 1971–1980* Washington, D.C.: U.S. Arms Control and Disarmament Agency, March 1983), pp. 33–36.

2. The phrase is quoted in William P. Glade, *Economic Policymaking and the Structures of Corporatism in Latin America* (Austin, Tex.: Offprint Series no. 208, Institute of Latin American Studies, University of Texas Press, 1981).

3. For further discussion, see W. W. Rostow, *The Barbaric Counter-Revolution: Cause and Cure* (Austin, Tex.: University of Texas Press, 1983), especially pp. 54–60 and 88–94.

4. I should like to call the reader's attention to a series of articles by Simon Teitel bearing on the extremely important but little-studied question of technical changes in what he calls "semi-industrialized countries" and what I would call countries in the drive toward technological maturity. Teitel's papers, originally published in various economic journals, are helpfully reprinted in the Inter-American Development Bank Reprint Series. They include: "Towards an Understanding of Technical Change in Semi-Industrialized Countries," Reprint Series no. 118 (1981); "Creation of Technology Within Latin America," no. 120 (1981); "Tecnologia, Industrializacion y Dependencia," no. 125 (1981); "Indicadores Cientifico-Tecnologicos: la America Latina, paises industrializados y otros paises en via desarrollo," no. 139 (1985); "Technology Creation in Semi-Industrial Economies," no. 150 (1984).

5. Our report was entitled "Hemispheric Cooperation and Integral Development," presented to the Secretary General of the Organization for American States, July 14, 1980.

6. David Hume, "Of the Jealousy of Trade," in *David Hume: Writings on Economics*, ed. Eugene Rotwein (Madison, Wis.: University of Wisconsin Press, 1955), pp. 78–79. This passage was incorporated in a talk given at EXPO '85, Tsukuba, Japan, on 22 May 1985, and published in *The Asian Development Bank Quarterly Review* (July 1985), pp. 4–9.

# Selected Bibliography

Agudelo Villa, Hernando. *La Alianza para el Progreso: Esperanza y Frustracion*. Bogota: Ediciones Tercer Mundo, 1966.

_____. *La Revolucion del Desarrollo: Origen y Evolucion en la Alianza para el Progreso*. Mexico: Editorial Roble, 1966.

Aguilar, Alonso. *Latin America and the Alliance for Progress*. Ursula Wasserman, trans. New York: Monthly Review Press, 1963.

Alba, Victor. *Alliance Without Allies*. New York: Praeger, 1965.

Berle, Adolf A. *Latin America: Diplomacy and Reality*. New York: Harper & Row for the Council on Foreign Relations, 1962.

Chenery, Hollis B. *Toward a More Effective Alliance for Progress*. Washington, D.C.: Agency for International Development, 1967.

Comite Ad Hoc de Cooperacion OEA-BID-CEPAL. Memorandum de Instalacion y Informes, OEA/Ser.L./VIII.w, Doc. 1 (eng) Rev. 12 July 1961 and Doc. 2 (eng) Rev. 3, 24 March 1961.

de Oliveira Campos, Roberto. *Reflections on Latin America*. Austin, Tex.: University of Texas Press, 1967.

Domench, Enrique. *The Alliance for Progress and the Inter-American Committee of the Alliance for Progress*. Washington, D.C.: Organization of American States, 1971.

Dreier, John C., ed. *The Alliance for Progress: Problems and Perspectives*. Baltimore: Johns Hopkins University Press, 1962.

Eisenhower, Milton S. *The Wine Is Bitter: The United States and Latin America*. New York: Doubleday, 1963.

Flores, Edmundo. *Land Reform and the Alliance for Progress*. Princeton, N.J.: Woodrow Wilson School of Public and International Affairs, 1963.

Frei Montalva, Eduardo. "The Alliance that Lost Its Way." *Foreign Affairs* 45 (April 1967): 437–48.

Gordon, A. Lincoln. *A New Deal for Latin America: The Alliance for Progress*. Cambridge, Mass.: Harvard University Press, 1963.

Grunwald, Joseph. *The Alliance for Progress: Invisible Hands in Inflation and Growth*. Washington, D.C.: Brookings Institution, 1965.

Gutierrez Olivos, Sergio. *Subdesarrollo, Integracion, y Alianza*. Buenos Aires: Emeci Editores, 1963.

Herrera, Felipe. *El Banco Interamericano y el Desarrollo de America Latina*. Washington, D.C.: Inter-American Development Bank, 1962.

Hirschman, Albert O. *Latin American Issues: Essays and Comments*. New York: 20th Century Fund, 1961.

———. *Journeys toward Progress*. New York: 20th Century Fund, 1963.

———. *The Principle of the Hiding Hand*. Washington, D.C.: Brookings Institution, 1967.

———. *Development Projects Observed*. Washington, D.C.: Brookings Institute, 1967.

Holt, Pat M. *Survey of the Alliance for Progress: The Political Aspects*. Washington, D.C.: Government Printing Office, 1967.

Inter-American Development Bank. *Socio-Economic Progress in Latin America*. Annual Reports 1969, 1970.

———. *Economic and Social Progress in Latin America*. Annual Reports 1971–86.

Kennedy, Robert F. *To Seek A Newer World*. Garden City, N.J.: Doubleday, 1967.

———. *The Alliance for Progress: Symbols and Substance*. Washington, D.C.: The Congressional Record, 1967.

Levinson, Jerome and Juan de Onis. *The Alliance That Lost Its Way: A Critical Report on the Alliance for Progress*. Chicago: Quadrangle Books for the 20th Century Fund, 1970.

Lleras Comargo, Alberto. "The Alliance for Progress: Aims, Distortions, Obstacles." *Foreign Affairs* 42 (October 1963): 25–37.

Manger, William, ed. *The Alliance for Progress: A Critical Appraisal*. Washington, D.C.: Public Affairs Press, 1963.

May, Herbert K. *Problems and Prospects of the Alliance for Progress*. New York: Praeger, 1965.

Mora Otero, Jose A. "Función de la Empresa Privada en la Alianza para el Progreso." Speech for the 417th meeting of the National Industrial Conference in Detroit, Michigan, November 16, 1961.

Morales Benitez, Otto. *Alianza para el Progreso y Reforma Agraria*. Bogota: Aedita Editores, 1964.

Moscoso, Teodoro. *The Alliance for Progress: Its Program and Goals*. Washington, D.C.: Agency for International Development, Department of State, 1962.

Nehemkis, Peter. *Latin America: Myth and Reality*. 1st ed. New York: Knopf, 1964.

Nixon, Richard. *United States Foreign Policy for the 1970s: Building for Peace*. Report to Congress, February 25, 1971. Washington, D.C.: The White House, 1971.

Organization of American States, Inter-American Economic and Social Council (CIES). *Latin America's Development and the Alliance for Progress*. OAS/Ser.H/X.19, CIES/Doc. 1636 Rev. 2, Corr., January 1973. Washington, D.C.: Organization of American States, 1973.

———. Special Meeting of the Inter American Economic and Social Council on the Ministerial Level, Punta del Este, Uruguay, 1961. OEA Ser.H/X.1, vols. 1–3; OEA Ser.H/X1.1. Washington, D.C.: Pan American Union, 1961.

Ortega Aranda, Elena Luisa. *La Carta de Punta del Este y la Alianza para el Progreso*. Santiago: Editorial Juridica de Chile, University of Chile, 1967.

Perloff, Harvey. *Alliance for Progress: a Social Invention in the Making*. Baltimore, Md.: Johns Hopkins Press for Resources for the Future, 1969.

Prebisch, Raúl. "Economic Aspects of the Alliance." In *The Alliance for Progress: Problems and Perspectives*, edited by John C. Dreier. Baltimore, Md.: Johns Hopkins Press, 1962.

_____. *Change and Development: Latin America's Great Task*. Washington, D.C.: Inter-American Development Bank, 1970.

Rogers, William D. *The Twilight Struggle: The Alliance for Progress and the Politics of Development in Latin America*. New York: Random House, 1967.

Saez, S., Raúl. "The Nine Wise Men and the Alliance for Progress." In *The Global Partnership*, edited by Richard N. Gardner and Max F. Millikan. New York: Praeger, 1968.

Scheyven, Raymond. *De Punta del Este a la Habana: America Latina y el Mundo*. Preface to the Spanish edition by Edward Frei. Santiago: Editores del Pacifico, 1962.

Schlesinger, Arthur F., Jr. *A Thousand Days: John F. Kennedy in the White House*. Boston: Houghton Mifflin, 1965.

Shriver, Sargent. *The Point of the Lance*. New York: Harper & Row, 1971.

Silvert, Kalman H. *The Conflict Society: A Reaction and Revolution in Latin America*. Rev. ed. New York: American Universities Field Staff, 1966.

Szulc, Tad. *The Winds of Revolution*. New York: Praeger, 1963.

United Nations Economic Commission for Latin America. *Economic Survey of Latin America, 1970*. Santiago: ECLA, 1971.

United States Senate. Committee on Foreign Relations. *Survey of the Alliance for Progress*. Washington: Government Printing Office, 1969.

Waterson, Albert O. *Development Planning: Lessons of Experience*. Baltimore, Md.: Johns Hopkins Press, 1965.

Wionczek, Miguel S. "El Nacimiento de la Alianza para el Progreso." *La Gaceta del Fondo de Cultura Economica* 8 (8), Mexico, August 1961.

Declaration to the Peoples of America, 180
Defense. *See* Armed forces; National security
De Gaul, Charles, 126
Democracy: Alliance naming and, 196;
  Charter of Punta del Este and, 180;
  ·dictatorships and, 107–8; erosion of, 92;
  growth of, 211; labor unions and, 191;
  liberal Lockean principles of, 110–11;
  middle class and, 106, 180; military and,
  8; multilateralism and, 125; socioeconomic
  modernization and, 97; U.S. model for,
  110–12
Democracy Agenda, 96
Democratic Action party, 75
Dependency theory, 83–84, 112, 236
*Desarrollo*, 185
Development. *See* Economic development;
  Social development
Dewey, John, 111
Dictatorship, 107–8
Dillon, C. Douglas, xix, 63–67, 139, 147
Diplomacy: country reviews and, 155;
  hispanic culture and, 140; IDB origins and,
  139–47
Dollar, overvaluation of, 249
Dominican Republic: agricultural education,
  217; Cuban threat to, 102; 1965 crisis,
  160; U.S. influence in, 109
Draper, William, 97
Dreier, John, xxiv, 97

Earthquakes, 202
ECLA. *See* United Nations, Economic
  Commission for Latin America
Economic development, 13–15, 162–63,
  210, 229; Alliance economic infrastructure,
  29–50; assessment of, 151; bottlenecks
  and, 134–35, 167–68; capital inflows and,
  232–33; CIAP country reviews, 52–53;
  culture and, 83, 237; *desenvolvimientismo*,
  75; dependency theory and, 83–84;
  determinist assumptions of, 102–4;
  domestic reforms and, 171–81; economic
  integration and, 41; external control and,
  136; external debt service ratios, 178;
  foreign exchange and, 242; global strategy
  for, 188–89; global stagnation and, 59;
  government size and, 150; human

development and, xx; industrialization and,
  15–18, 169; inflation and, 170, 212; Latin
  American experience and, 166; long-term
  planning for, 7, 169–71; Marshall Plan
  analogy, 75–76, 106, 178–79; middle class
  in, 105–6; motivation for, 81–88; national
  economic structures, 17; North America
  vs. Latin America, 235; OECD and, 226;
  peripheral capitalism, 61; population
  growth and, 172; price structures and,
  123, 212; reformist developmentalism, 5;
  Santiago model, 166–67; savings rates and,
  176; social reform and, 97, 231; technological maturity and, 241–42; traditional
  institutions and, 105; U.S. assumptions,
  100–15, 131–36, 149; U.S. education
  and, 97; U.S. strategic interests and, 99;
  world interdependences and, 233
Economic integration, 240; Alliance plans
  for, 41, 47; erroneous assumptions on,
  106–7; financial institution promotion of,
  92; Group of Four report and, 55;
  Kennedy's goals for, 13; 1967 Punta del
  Este meeting and, 91; political integration
  and, 106. *See also* Common markets
Education: absorption of technology and,
  245; agricultural sector and, 20, 21, 217;
  Alliance targets for, 24–25; central
  government expenditures on, 38–40;
  communist influence on, 8; Marxist
  doctrine and, 5; Mexican progress in, 245–
  46; 19th Century reform of, 197; progress
  in, 34–36, 124, 130, 245; U.S. model for,
  111; U.S. universities and, 97; of women,
  210
Eisenhower, Dwight, administration: IDB
  creation and, xix, 59, 139; International
  Coffee Agreement and, 50; Kubitschek
  and, 89, 209; 1960 Bogota conference
  and, 67–68; OAS Constituitive Agreement
  and, 89; right-wing dictators and, 99;
  social justice grants and, 64–65
Eisenhower, Milton, xix, 5, 65, 96, 209
Electricity generation, 130
El Salvador, 107
Employment, 17, 18, 25
Entrepreneurship, 6, 231. *See also* Capitalism
Environmental protection, 248

Colombia and, 199; creation of, 139; domestic savings and, 176; housing loans from, 124; IDB charter and, 141; Latin American allocations from, 9; multilateral review procedures, 178; structural adjustment loans, 214
International Coffee Agreement (1962), 5, 50, 60, 64, 123, 162, 165
International Labor Organization (ILO), 14, 52
International law, 121
International Monetary Fund (IMF), 52, 54, 199
International Petroleum Company, 71, 187
Investment: Alliance goals for, 8–9; Baker Plan and, 214; debt payments and, 206; domestic sources of, 9, 176, 201; global competition and, 188–89; Latin American domestic, 239; Mexican oil production and, 232; official external financing, 8–11; OPEC cartel and, 57; private sector and, 60, 70–71; U.S. business and, 70–71
Irrigation, 81
Israel, 52
Italy, 52

Japan, 52, 101
Jimenez, Perez, 191
Johnson, Lyndon B., administration: Alliance demise and, 3; Meeting of the Presidents and, 55; 1967 Punta del Este conference, 91, 160; Peru and, 71

Kennan, George F., 165, 182
Kennedy, Edward M., xv–xvii
Kennedy, John F., administration: agrarian reform and, 20; Alliance announcement speech, 68, 90, 160–62; Alliance goals and, 12, 69, 130; Alliance naming and, 67, 195–96; assassination of, 3, 197; authoritarian regimes and, 108; Betancourt and, 186; Bogota Conference and, 65–66; Cuba and, 219; Hickenlooper Amendment and, 70; inaugural address of, 74; on Latin America, 218; Marshall Plan and, 75–76; multilateral policy of, 122; Muñoz Marin and, 197; private sector role and, 187; State Department bureaucracy and, 98

Kennedy, Robert, 71
Kissinger, Henry, 78, 104
Kissinger Commission, 96, 104, 113–14, 193
Khruschev, Nikita, 243
Kubitschek, Juscelino, xix, 5, 7, 59, 64, 67, 96, 121, 165; CIES committee and, 51; developmentalism, philosophy of, 75; Eisenhower and, 89, 209; Mexico City conference and, 127

Labor unions, 191–93; anti-communism and, 112; Charter of Punta del Este and, 13; Latin American tradition of, 111
LAFTA. *See* Latin American Free Trade Association
Land reform. *See* Agrarian reform
Land tenure systems, 4, 20
Language, economic integration and, 107
Lara Beautell, Cristobal, 198
Latin America: central government expenditures, 38–40; changes in, 221–22; constitutional law in, 132; dependence on U.S., 83–84, 112, 236; historic prejudices against, 104; nationalism in, 8, 61, 72; post-WWII policy on, 63; security interests of, 240; Spanish culture in, 81, 85; Third world and, 85; traditional institutions of, 105; U.S. assumptions regarding, 100–15; U.S.-European ties and, 179–80; will to economic development of, 81–88. *See also specific nations, organizations*
*Latin American Development and the Alliance for Progress* (CIES), 151
Latin American Economic System (SELA), xiv, 56, 92
Latin American Free Trade Association (LAFTA), 41, 47–49, 106
Latin American Institute for Economic and Social Planning (ILPES), 54
Latin American Integration Association (ALADI), xiii, 92
Lending: annual loan commitments, 177; capital flight and, 212; fast-disbursing loans, 199–200; Fulbright Amendment and, 156; institutional skepticism of, 231; local currency payments and, 201;

expenditures, 38–40; changing economic role of, 222, 226; Charter of Punta del Este and, 176; CIAP country review of, 52, 122, 154; congressional actions, xx, 133, 137, 139–47, 156, 180; debt crisis role, 248–49; development assistance strategies, 135; economic development of, 236; economic structural distortions, 242; European ties of, 179; foreigners trained in, xx; Hickenlooper Amendment, 102; historic prejudices of, 104; International Coffee Agreement and, 64; as interventionist country, 200; labor vs. foreign policy, 192; Latin American dependence on, 236; Latin American markets and, 222; markets of, 213, 240; mistrust of, 7; national security interests, 240; post-WWII Latin American policy, 63; protectionism of, 213; State Department, 70–71, 98, 103; strategic interest of, 98–99, 240; sugar prices and, 123; trade deficit and, 230; Treasury Department, 140. *See also specific administrations*
Upton, T. Grady, 64
Urban areas: agriculture and, 242; low-cost housing projects, 124, 173; migration to,

4, 172, 210; socio-economic progress and, 76. *See also specific cities*
Urquidi, Victor, 200–2
Urrutia, Miguel, 199–200
Uruguay, 14

Vaughn, Jack, 186
Veliz, 184
Venezuela: debt service program, 163; democratization of, 75; dictatorship in, 191; distrust of Colombia, 107; economic diversification in, 57; land reform in, 174; 1950s growth, 14; pre-Alliance reforms in, 5
Vietnam war, 233
Villa Kennedy, 124

Water supply, 22, 30–31, 128, 130, 173
Waterston, Albert, 170–71
Wiarda, Howard, 8
Wionczek, Miguel, 200
Women, progress for, 210
World Bank. *See* International Bank for Reconstruction and Development

Youth, jobs for, 18

# About the Editor and Contributors

L. RONALD SCHEMAN is a lawyer in Washington. He was executive director of the Center for Advanced Studies of the Americas (1984–87), Assistant Secretary for Management of the Organization of American States (1975–83) and founder and past president (1977–83) of the Pan American Development Foundation.

ELLIOTT ABRAMS is Assistant Secretary of State for Inter-American Affairs.

NICOLAS ARDITO-BARLETTA is former President of Panama (1984–85). He was Vice-President for Latin America and the Caribbean at the World Bank (1978–1984); Minister of Planning for Panama (1973–78); founder and first president of BLADEX (Banco Latinoamericano de Exportaciones).

JOAO CLEMENTE BAENA SOARES is the Secretary General of the Organization of American States.

ERNESTO BETANCOURT is director of Radio Marti. He was director of foreign exchange of the central bank of Cuba during the first years of the Castro regime and subsequently an officer in the Department of Economic Affairs of the Organization of American States.

RODRIGO BOTERO is a former Minister of Finance of Colombia, and worked at the Inter-American Development Bank during the Alliance years.

C. DOUGLAS DILLON served as Secretary of the Treasury from 1961 to 1965 and as Under Secretary of State from 1959 to 1961. He was the chief U.S. representative to the 1959 Bogota meeting.

WILLIAM C. DOHERTY, JR., has been executive director of the American Institute for Free Labor Development since 1965.

DANTE FASCELL has been a member of the U.S. House of Representatives, representing the Nineteenth District of Florida since 1955. He is currently chairman of the House Committee on Foreign Affairs.

LINCOLN GORDON is former U.S. ambassador to Brazil (1961–66), Assistant Secretary of State for Inter-American Affairs (1966–67), and president of Johns Hopkins University. He consulted the Department of State in the development of the Alliance.

LAWRENCE E. HARRISON is vice-president for International Development of the Cooperative League of the USA. He has directed USAID programs in the Dominican Republic, Costa Rica, Guatemala, Haiti and Nicaragua.

JACK HELLER is a partner in the Washington, D.C. law firm of Kuder, Temple, Smollar and Heller. He was tax advisor to the Alliance for Progress and director of Programs and Planning for the Latin American Bureau of the Agency for International Development in the Alliance years.

FELIPE HERRERA of Chile was the first president of the Inter-American Development Bank, serving from 1960–71. He was also executive director of the International Monetary Fund (1958–60).

EDWARD M. KENNEDY is a U.S. senator from Massachusetts. He is currently chairman of the Senate Labor and Human Resources Committee.

PEDRO-PABLO KUCZYNSKI is chairman of First Boston International. He was Minister of Mines and Energy of Peru (1980–82). During the Alliance years he was an officer of the World Bank.

ENRIQUE LERDAU is senior economist for the Western Hemisphere Department of the World Bank. Formerly he was assistant director of Economic Affairs for the Organization of American States.

ABRAHAM LOWENTHAL is a professor of International Relations at the University of Southern California and Director of the Inter-American Dialogue. He was associated with the Ford Foundation in Latin America (1964–72) and founded the Latin American Program at the Wilson International Center for Scholars in Washington.

ARTURO MORALES CARRION, a historian, was president of the University of Puerto Rico. He currently heads the Fundacion Puertorriquena de las Humanidades. He served as Deputy Assistant Secretary for Inter-American Affairs under President Kennedy (1961–64), and advisor to OAS Secretary General Jose Mora (1964–69).

TEODORO MOSCOSO was first director of the Alliance for Progress in the U.S. Department of State. He is presently a businessman and public servant in Puerto Rico.

ANTONIO ORTIZ MENA has been president of the Inter-American Development Bank since 1971. He was Mexico's Secretary of Finance and Public Credit (1958–70).

JOSE LUIS RESTREPO was Chief of Staff to the Secretary General of the Organization of American States. He has been an economist with the OAS since 1962. He served on the Committee of Nine during the Alliance years. He also served as Director of the National Budget in Colombia.

W. W. ROSTOW is the Rex G. Baker, Jr. Professor of Political Economy at the University of Texas at Austin. He was counselor to the U.S. Department of State and ambassador to the Inter-American Committee on the Alliance for Progress. He has served as advisor on security affairs to Presidents Kennedy and Johnson.

CARLOS SANZ DE SANTAMARIA was chairman of the Inter-American Committee on the Alliance for Progress. He was Minister of Finance of Colombia and ambassador of Colombia to the United States.

ARTHUR SCHLESINGER, JR., is the Albert Schweitzer Professor of the Humanities at the City University of New York. He served with President Kennedy during the Alliance years.

DANIEL SHARP is director of International and Public Affairs of the Xerox Corporation and deputy to the vice-president for Public Affairs. In the early 1960s, he was director of Peace Corps programs in Peru and Bolivia and subsequently directed the Latin American program at the Adlai Stevenson Institute of International Affairs at the University of Chicago.

JORGE SOL CASTELLANOS was assistant secretary for Economic and Social Affairs of the Organization of American States at the beginning of the Alliance. He was subsequently Minister of Finance of El Salvador.

T. GRAYDON UPTON was the first executive vice-president of the Inter-American Development Bank, serving from 1960 to 1971. Prior to that he was Assistant Secretary of the Treasury and led the team negotiating the IDB Charter.

VICTOR I. URQUIDI is a Mexican economist at El Colegio de Mexico where he was president from 1966 to 1985. He served on the United Nations Economic Commission for Latin America (ECLA), 1951–58, and with the Mexican government, 1958–65.

MIGUEL URRUTIA is manager of the Economic and Social Development Department of the Inter-American Development Bank. He was Minister of Mines and Energy of Colombia (1977) and director of Fedesarrollo, an organization in Colombia devoted to economic research.

HOWARD WIARDA is Resident Scholar and Director of Hemispheric Studies at the American Enterprise Institute. He was professor of Political Science, University of Massachusetts, and research associate of the Center for International Affairs at Harvard University.

MIGUEL S. WIONCZEK is director of the Energy Research Program at El Colegio de Mexico. He was director of Information and Advisor at the Center of Latin American Monetary Studies (1954–72).